THE OLD BOYS'
NETWORK

THE OLD BOYS'
NETWORK
A Headmaster's Diaries
1972–1986

JOHN RAE

First published in 2009 by

Short Books
3A Exmouth House
Pine Street
EC1R 0JH

This paperback edition published 2010

10 9 8 7 6 5 4 3 2 1

A CIP catalogue record for this book is available from the British Library.

ISBN 978-1-906021-93-1

Printed in Great Britain by CPI Bookmarque Ltd, Croydon, Surrey

Cover design: Emily Fox

To all my grandchildren:
James, Hannah, Francesca, Naomi,
Michael, Sam, Bronwyn, Lucy, Katie,
Brodie, Cameron, Jude and Jimmy.

INTRODUCTION

For 14 of the 16 years I was headmaster of Westminster School, I kept a journal. I wanted to record what a headmaster's life was really like and especially how he dealt with the problems that arose in trying to educate and be responsible for 600 adolescents in the heart of a great city with all its possibilities and temptations. I thought it was the most wonderful job in the world, but to say that I enjoyed every minute of it would be dishonest. There is a political side to a headmaster's life, times when he is not dealing with adolescents but with awkward and even hostile adults on the school's governing body (his employers), in the staff common room and among the parents of his pupils. But while politics in this sense takes up a lot of the headmaster's time, his overwhelming interest is in his pupils and that aspect of the job I found continuously absorbing. Westminster's boys and girls were no angels but they were almost always good company.

When I arrived at Westminster in 1970, there were 479 boys in the school. When I left in 1986, there were 644 pupils, 566 boys and 78 girls. The increase in the number of pupils by nearly 200 in those 16 years put enormous pressure on the space available and the school did not have the money to buy property in this expensive part of London. It was not until the headmastership of Tristram Jones-Parry between 1998 and 2005 that the school had the money – when it received a large bequest from A.A. Milne – to buy the space it needed to accommodate 600 pupils. When I arrived in September 1970, providing accommodation for that many pupils was a dream, but we never gave up hope that one day this would become a reality.

My predecessor, John Carleton, was a bachelor who had spent nearly all his adult life at the school. Indeed, when term started in September 1970, he had still not vacated his study. An urbane, sophisticated man, he preferred the social side of a headmaster's life to the burden of administration and it was no surprise therefore that the school I inherited had a reputation for being both civilised and permissive. A good example of Westminster's permissive approach to discipline was that illegal drugs, such as cannabis, which were widely used by the affluent young of London, were not even mentioned in the school's regulations. When I was interviewed by the governing body, no one asked about my attitude to illegal drugs. Yet it was illegal drugs that would present me with my most difficult challenge when I became headmaster.

In December 1970, at the end of my first term as headmaster, I expelled three senior boys for possessing cannabis. That was the end of my honeymoon period, if you believe in such things. Early in the term, I had re-written the school regulations to make it clear that any involvement with illegal drugs was a very serious offence that was likely to result in expulsion. Nevertheless, when the three boys were expelled, there was, if not an outcry, then at least an unmistakeable feeling of resentment among the expellees' contemporaries and friends. Some members of the common room, too, thought I had gone too far.

I did not realise at the time that this would be the start of a long struggle to keep illegal drugs out of the school and out of the lives of my pupils. Despite the public assurances of headmasters and headmistresses – 'there are no drugs in this school' – no independent school has yet succeeded in keeping them at bay.

The only other information that might be helpful for the reader to have is the situation of the headmaster's house and my family. No. 17 Dean's Yard was a nine-bedroom Regency house on the east side of Dean's Yard, much admired by architectural historians and much coveted by Abbey canons with large families. It would have suited our family of six children well if it had not been for the fact that true privacy was almost impossible to achieve. The main drawing room, for example, doubled as the entertaining and waiting room for parents or a lecture room for the boys and visiting speakers, and my study was my classroom and the room I used for interviewing parents and boys and for the many masters' meetings. The headmaster's house was also the hub of the school's administration and, with the staff common room occupying the ground floor, every member of staff had a key to our front door. It was not until some years after I left that the governors at last decided to move the headmaster's house to Great College Street outside the precincts.

I hope this brief introduction helps you to understand the context in which the journal was written. At the end of one term, I wrote: 'What a curious life I lead but if reincarnation turned out to be the norm I would not choose a different one.' Twenty years on I feel just the same.

John Rae
2006

A NOTE ON THE AUTHOR,
by Jim Cogan

When John Rae arrived at Westminster in 1970, there was little to suggest that within ten years he would become the pre-eminent Public School head of his day – an educational celebrity and a household name among the intelligentsia. Like Richard Busby of Westminster, in the 17th century, and Thomas Arnold of Rugby in the 19th, John Rae came to combine exceptional headmastering skills with the capacity to influence public life.

He had a rare combination of qualities. In addition to his intelligence he was exceptionally articulate, energetic beyond belief, and striking-looking. Over the years his contribution to the national discourse, on educational and on social matters, cannot be understated. He wrote regularly for the broadsheet press – including a long stint contributing to the *Times Educational Supplement* – he made many television appearances, and was a familiar voice on the radio. He was prepared to articulate uncomfortable truths about the independent sector. In this way, he broadened the area of debate, but not everybody welcomed his interventions or his advice particularly during his time as Chairman of HMC. When Margaret Thatcher introduced The Assisted Places Scheme in 1980, John Rae would have none of it at Westminster. As John said: "You do not deal with a famine by sending a few lucky children to lunch at The Ritz." Politicians of many parties, though, were drawn to him; the Prime Minister, Harold Wilson, sought his advice, came to dinner and attended school events; the "Gang of Four" courted him as their future educational spokesman.

Of course, his constant public exposure led many outsiders to think that he must be neglecting the school. But that was far from the truth. His energy and work-rate were quite prodigious. He was a constant presence about the school and had a detailed knowledge of every pupil. Not only did he know each boy or girl by name, but he could recall details of their background, their prep school and their parents.

The seventies was a period of social and cultural upheaval – traditional authority systems were collapsing, and permissiveness in the form of drugs and sexual freedom was transforming lifestyles, particularly among the London young. Yet John Rae was able to keep a strong grip on the school. Serious wrongdoing was rigorously dealt with and standards of behaviour were valued above length of hair or polished turn-out.

He took pride in the school's achievements. Academic standards rose steadily during his time. By knowing the right people to charm, John Rae managed to raise millions of pounds to enable the school to buy an office building in Smith Square and transform it into state of the art science classrooms way ahead of their time. Westminster also became more competitive at sport and its extra-curricular life was enriched by first-rate drama and music.

When John Rae left Westminster in 1996 after 16 years in charge, he left behind a transformed and flourishing school.

A BRIEF HISTORY OF THE SCHOOL

King Henry VIII founded Westminster School in 1540 when he dissolved the Benedictine monastery and handed the monastic buildings to the new collegiate body of a dean and chapter to run the Protestant Abbey, and a headmaster and under master to run the Protestant school. But the school's foundation was not confirmed until 1560 when his daughter Queen Elizabeth I granted the school a charter.

This constitution governed the school until the mid-19th century when reforming zeal encouraged parliament to look more closely at the way in which these so-called 'old public schools' were run. For one thing, none of the schools was true to the spirit of its foundation, which envisaged the free education of poor scholars, not the expensive education of the sons of aristocratic and middle-class families. The result was the Public Schools Act of 1868 that forced the schools to make provision for the free education of genuinely poor scholars and at the same time to accept a new constitution that placed the government of the school in the hands of a board of governors, the membership of which was laid down by the Act.

Before the Act, Westminster School was governed by the dean and chapter of the Abbey. The Act did not remove the Abbey's influence altogether. The dean remained as chairman ex officio and two other members of the chapter had the right to sit on the governing body. But these three members of the Abbey chapter could always be outvoted by the 15 other members of the governing body, some of whom were identified by the Act, others co-opted by the existing members. So the heads of the two colleges to which Henry VIII had linked the school – Christ Church, Oxford and Trinity, Cambridge – were, like the dean of Westminster, members of the governing body ex officio. Just how close that link had been is suggested by the fact that I was only the third headmaster in 400 years who had not been educated at Christ Church or Trinity.

Under the Public Schools Act, the governing body had the power to hire and fire the headmaster and the headmaster had the power to hire and fire the teaching staff. Much later, provision had to be made for the appointment of a bursar to oversee the school's finances. The trouble was that, as in almost every school, it was not clear how the bursar would fit into the school's chain of command. Was he responsible to the headmaster or did he report directly to the governing body? Because this was not clear, friction between the headmaster and the bursar was inevitable.

1972-73
Play Term[1] 1972

Tuesday 12 September

The day and the new term start with an assembly up school[2]. No amount of experience will entirely dispel the mixture of nervousness and excitement with which I approach an occasion when the whole school is assembled. There appears to be enough of the actor and the dictator in me to make my performance seem confident and relaxed to others, but the truth is I am keyed up, skilful enough to deal with most eventualities but vulnerable nevertheless.

As I walk in the back of the hall, the boys stand and I pass

---

[1] So-called because the annual Latin play was performed in College Hall as part of the Christmas festivities at the end of this term. In 1941, the interior of College was destroyed by incendiary bombs so in the post-war period the Latin Play was performed in the summer in Little Dean's Yard. But the Play Term kept its name.

[2] Most Westminster slang has faded away but the uniquely Westminster use of the word 'up' has survived. 'Up school' means 'in the school hall'. The word 'school' refers to the former monks' dormitory that became at first a school room for the whole school and then an assembly hall and theatre. 'Up' is also used in connection with other parts of the school. So a boy at Vincent Square, the school playing field, is said to be 'up fields' and a boy in his boarding house is said to be 'up house'.

between them to the shallow dais where Dr Busby's[3] table is a reminder of sterner, more despotic days. I ask the school to sit down. One or two familiar faces meet mine. I make announcements, give welcomes, congratulate and comment and then read the form lists. It is a long business and as I near the end I am dismayed to see the paper shaking slightly in my hand. When I have finished, the school stands once again and I walk down the aisle not knowing what expression to adopt.

At 9.25am, I climb the stone steps to the doors of the Jericho parlour in red cassock[4] and black gown. The dean, Eric Abbott[5], awaits me with the under master and the chaplain, and the archdeacon, Edward Carpenter, my one close friend in the Abbey community. We process down the nave, under the screen and into the choir. The boys sing rather better than a year or two ago but the great height of the Abbey seems to draw all sounds up and away. Some boys contribute little or nothing to the service but there is no overt hostility. The disenchanted prefer ironic detachment to aggressive non-participation. The Christian faith and its attendant rituals may inspire in a Westminster boy amusement, historical interest, sincere devotion or intellectual criticism, but seldom resentment.

After the service, I wait to hear how others will comment on

---

[3] Headmaster 1638 to 1695, Westminster's greatest headmaster whose reputation for flogging should not disguise the fact that he was one of the great educators of his time.

[4] A member of the collegiate body of St Peter's, Westminster, the headmaster wears a red cassock at services in the Abbey.

[5] Dean of Westminster, 1959 to 1974.

my sermon, even though I know that thanks will be automatic and praise more often inspired by Christian charity than genuine admiration. How weak I am! My heart leaps when I face 500 boys and my ego yearns for praise as though my whole career depended on the reception of a 12-minute sermon that the boys have had the sense to regard as only slightly more original than the reading of the form lists.

James Robbins[6], the new captain of the school, comes to lunch. He is quietly self-assured and a shade avuncular. I know him to be an efficient organiser and a confident public figure and now I ask myself how well he and I will hit it off. Over lunch, I get the impression that he will operate like a senior civil servant, not hiding the truth but filtering it through his considerable knowledge of how the school works and how much it is good for the headmaster to know. I tell him that frankness between us is one of the keys to the success of both our roles. He agrees and looks away over my shoulder.

At 5.45pm, I have an appointment with the dean. We discuss the problems that I face in the new term: the exact definition of the bursar's responsibilities, the choice of new housemasters for Ashburnham and Liddell's and the need for a senior master to be responsible for routine organisation. We also discuss my salary. The dean, who is ex-officio chairman of the school governors, agrees that a review every three years is unrealistic in times of inflation and promises to speak to the chairman of the finance committee.

---

[6] Now political correspondent, BBC TV News.

Friday 22 September

After school, I see the editors of the *Elizabethan*, the school magazine. They are keen for an article to be written on how the school is governed and they mention the name of a boy who will be willing to write it. Knowing this boy's anti-establishment views, I say that he will be too busy with Oxford entrance and suggest a younger, less committed boy in the first year 6th. It is agreed that this boy should come to me for a briefing.

Monday 25 September

The monitors' meeting[7] drags on at length, as we discuss their proposal that there should be some sort of advisory committee set up to improve communication between the headmaster and the boys. I do not handle the discussion well and instead of saying I do not like the idea, I ask them to make a specific proposal at a later meeting.

After the monitors have gone, I receive a note from the head of mathematics confirming that, despite indications to the contrary a few days ago, he intends to leave at the end of term. This both annoys and depresses me. It annoys because I believe he is putting his own wishes before any feeling of responsibility to the school and it depresses because I know there is little chance of getting an adequate replacement in time for January.

So it is in a somewhat gloomy frame of mind that I set off, with Daphne, for Farm Street in Mayfair. Our Jesuit friend, Father Tom Corbishley, has invited us to dinner. When we arrive

---

[7] Westminster's prefects are known as monitors. The headmaster holds regular meetings with the monitors about the running of the school.

at the Jesuit house, my gloomy mood is brightened almost at once because Tom and Father David Hay, the superior, are so welcoming. As this was the first time that any women had been invited to dine with the Jesuits, Tom had asked Daphne to act as their hostess with 'the ladies'. Our fellow guests turn out to be the Archbishop of Canterbury[8] and the Lord Chancellor[9] and their wives. Resident members of the Society of Jesus, including an African bishop, make up the party. The Jesuits are excellent hosts. Daphne sits between the Archbishop and the Lord Chancellor and in her best uninhibited manner draws from them minor indiscretions. I sit next to the African bishop from Cameroon who speaks little English, but beyond him is Father Edwards with whom I share an interest in the Gunpowder Plot. I attempt conversation with the bishop but it is difficult, and I am soon talking across him with Father Edwards about Guy Fawkes and Robert Catesby. I do not know what the bishop makes of it all; probably very little. When it is time to go, my spirits have lifted. This is one of the joys of being at Westminster – it is impossible to brood on problems for long.

Monday 2 October
In the evening, two senior boys come to see me. They have clashed with their housemaster on the question of hair. He is the only housemaster to have trouble on this score because he insists on interpreting my general guidance as a precise ruling and demands immediate action from boys whose hair touches

---

[8] Archbishop Michael Ramsey.
[9] Lord Hailsham, Lord Chancellor 1972 to 1974.

the collar. He drives them into a corner by setting a deadline by which the hair must be cut. The result is that he wastes endless time and energy and provokes unnecessary hostility. All the other housemasters know how to handle this problem and this makes matters worse, as boys are quick to see the difference of approaches. Listening to the two senior boys, I find it difficult to be loyal to their housemaster.

Wednesday 11 October
In the evening, I take James Robbins to see William Rees-Mogg, the editor of *The Times*, who lives round the corner in Smith Square. James wants to be a political journalist; his mind is quite made up. After a while, I leave them together and return home.

Tuesday 24 October
Dr M comes to talk about one of the candidates for our entrance exam next week. The boy apparently has spelling difficulties associated with depression caused by a series of medical 'incidents': a very difficult birth, meningitis at the age of six and his sister's death of leukaemia last year (he was not warned of this possibility until 36 hours before the event). From what the doctor tells me, I doubt whether Westminster is the right place for this boy but we shall see how he fares in the exam[10].

Friday 3 November
I see one of the editors of the *Elizabethan* and tell him why I am not prepared to let an article be published. The article attacks

---

[10] He failed the exam so the question of whether to admit him did not arise.

a number of masters including the headmaster, their identities only thinly disguised. The thinly disguised headmaster is said to be preparing a radio talk on the Role of the Mature Hypocrite in Society. Headmasters are always said to be hypocrites or two-faced. I tell the editor that criticism of school policy is fair comment but attacks on personalities are not. I am surprised to discover who wrote the article.

Wednesday 22 November

The governing body meets in Jerusalem[11] at noon. For three-quarters of an hour, we discuss the qualifications for entry to College[12] as a Queen's Scholar[13]. The present notice says that candidates for the Challenge – the scholarship exam – must fulfil three conditions: British nationality, 'profess the Christian faith' and be prepared to attend Abbey services as required by statute. I want to see the second condition removed because its effect is to exclude candidates, including Jewish boys, who are honest enough to say they are not Christians.

The discussion opens with Sir Reginald Sharpe, who heads the governing body's statutes committee, stating that the first and second conditions have no basis in law and should never have

---

[11] Part of the medieval abbot's lodgings, now part of the dean of Westminster's house. Rich in history – Henry IV died here while Prince Hal waited in College Hall next door. The school's governing body holds its routine meetings here as well as those special meetings to appoint a new headmaster.

[12] Queen Elizabeth I's foundation was for a headmaster, an under master and 40 Queen's Scholars.

[13] Queen's Scholars are elected each year on the strength of their performance in the Challenge, which is the school's scholarship exam. They must be boarders and live together in College. Eton and Winchester have a similar arrangement for scholars.

been inserted, though it is open to the governing body to put the conditions in if they wish to do so. The question of British nationality is aired. Sir Henry Chisholm makes his expected statement about Queen Elizabeth's intentions and expresses himself strongly in favour of restricting College to bona fide British nationals.

In the discussion that follows, he appears to be supported but when a vote is taken on his resolution to make British nationality a requirement, it is lost. Sir Henry is visibly shaken and says something about considering his position on the governing body. An awkward silence fills the Jerusalem chamber. When the dean tries to ease the tension by moving the discussion on to the question of the second condition, I imagine I will have no difficulty persuading governors to vote against this too. But I am wrong. There is considerable support for retaining the phrase 'profess the Christian faith' and I only just manage to persuade the dean not to take a vote but refer the matter to the statutes committee.

After lunch of cold grouse and claret, the governors discuss whether the proposed new salary scale for masters is or is not caught by the government's pay freeze introduced on 6 November. At one point, I have to intervene to say that some governors are giving a wrong impression that the masters are a money-grabbing, militant lot.

Thursday 23 November

Two days doing business in Oxford. This evening to Keble. I do not know the college and hardly ever send boys here. I stay at the warden's lodge and dine in hall. The warden is kind but the dons who are dining are positively dull and the hall is like a brick aircraft hanger. No wonder Westminster boys do not want to come here.

Friday 24 November

To the dean's lodgings at Christ Church this evening. What a contrast to Keble! Henry Chadwick[14] is very welcoming but rather austere. I dine in hall with two Westminster colleagues who have come up by train. It is Henry Chadwick's idea that each year I should bring two colleagues to meet tutors and discuss the Westminster/Christ Church connection. Both school and college like the connection, for which Henry VIII[15] was responsible, but recognise the difficulty of operating it in the modern climate. The college wants boys of open-award standard to try for closed awards; the school knows that boys of that calibre want to try for open awards. The compromise we operate is that we ensure that candidates for Christ Church are good enough for entry and that one or two are capable of an open award at another college. In return, Christ Church takes the odd borderline case. The evening is civilised and useful.

Friday 22 December

The term is ending at last, a week after boys and masters have departed. News of Oxbridge candidates continues to give pleasure and cause surprise. James Robbins has a place at Christ

---

[14] Dean of Christchurch, 1969 to 1979.

[15] Henry VIII linked Westminster to 'his' Oxbridge colleges, Christ Church at Oxford and Trinity at Cambridge, by endowing scholarships that were open to competition among Westminster boys only – that is to say, they were in effect closed awards.

Church; some boys' careers fly like arrows straight towards their goal. G, whose A level grades in pure and applied maths, physics and chemistry are A1, A1, A, A, has been refused a place at St. John's, Cambridge while P, whose grades in the same subjects are C, A, C, B, has been awarded an open exhibition at the same college. On the whole, Westminster boys do well and the final results will show that we have had a successful year. How important is this? One very able scholar has missed an award and is quite content with a place; he has little respect for the scholarship stakes. His attitude is more mature than that of his peers and of those of us who watch the mounting total of awards on the list in the common room like party managers on election night.

Lent Term 1973

Monday 22 January

I teach three periods this morning and then go to Jerusalem for the governing body meeting. Only a few governors are there as the Oxbridge terms have just begun and the five university members are absent. Despite this, the discussions go well. Governors take their lead from Sir Burke Trend[16], who persuades them to set up a working party to review our procedure for dealing with masters' salaries and conditions of service. After that, it is easy

---

[16] A governor of the school 1970 to 1987, secretary to the cabinet and head of the Civil Service. Subsequently rector of Lincoln College, Oxford.

to persuade them, with Burke's help, to abolish the requirement that Queen's Scholars should profess the Christian faith and to agree that masters' sons should be educated free at the school.

Thursday 25 January
School communion service in Henry VII Chapel[17]. On the way out a master tells me that a boy he is teaching is smelling of cannabis. He is a man whose opinion I respect so I ask him to find out more. This afternoon, to Dolphin Square to train with the swimming team. At the housemasters' meeting this evening, we discuss our policy on the admission of girls to the sixth form. There are 10 girls from other schools who attend A level classes at Westminster. Are we going to admit girls as full members of the school and if so, how many? In a characteristic way, the discussion swings between seriousness and mirth. One housemaster suggests that being so outnumbered is bad for the girls because it prevents them making a realistic assessment of their attractiveness. Another recalls that a girl who was a boarder for a short while inspired poetic activity among the boys, who crept out at night to push sonnets under her door. The sooner we admit more girls and as full members of the school the better.

After that meeting has ended, this term's new boys come for light refreshment prior to a tour of the Abbey. We do this every term. On the way to the Abbey, I overhear this exchange.

'That coffee was rather foul.'

'Yes, but one drinks it all the same.'

---

[17] The Lady Chapel of Westminster Abbey and the chapel of the Order of the Bath.

Algy Greaves, the dean's verger, shows us round the Abbey. The building is empty and in darkness. When the boys are standing in the nave, Algy gradually illuminates the superb interior. It is a breathtaking experience: the size, the grandeur and the beauty of the Abbey are thrillingly exposed. Algy then leads the new boys on their tour. It is amusing to watch him and them. They crowd round him, laughing politely at his splendidly laborious jokes: 'They used to keep relics in the Abbey – they still do but they call them vergers now'. The tour ends with us all standing round the tomb of Queen Elizabeth, the school's foundress, where I say thank you to Algy and goodnight to the boys.

Friday 26 January

I receive a letter from one of last term's leavers who won an open scholarship in classics at Oxford. He writes to thank me for my card of congratulations and goes on to say, 'Westminster has instilled in me a love of learning, which is an asset for life, and accordingly I owe the school a very large debt of gratitude.'

Thursday 8 March

A gloriously mild and fine spring day. It has been a marvellous Lent Term, quite free from the 'rain and ruins' of winter. At noon, a Lutheran pastor from East Germany comes to speak to modern linguists and I take her into lunch in College Hall[18]. She joins in the conversation with senior boys but is surprised and a little shocked, I think, to hear that they have a wine society and are so knowledgeable on the subject. The chaplain has

---

[18] The former dining hall of the abbot's house; now the school's dining hall.

complained that the Wine Society held a meeting yesterday, Ash Wednesday.

After lunch, I stroll round in the sunshine to watch fencing, judo and fives. A column of black smoke rises over Whitehall and we hear that a bomb has exploded[19]. Another bomb outside Scotland Yard has been dismantled and there are rumours of other bombs in central London. The boys go about their exercise with little concern, though one or two run excitedly to the entrance to Dean's Yard. They want to collect bits of debris as we collected pieces of shrapnel as children during the war. Later, a housemaster tells me that a boarder returned to his house carrying a piece of exploded car and was sent round to Scotland Yard to hand it in.

Election Term[20] 1973

Friday 27 April

Today a small publication called *Counterblast* appears. It has been published by boys in the newly formed Catholick Society. Its editorial declares that its purpose is 'to counteract the insidious

---

[19] The IRA's bombing campaign on the mainland was bound to put the school at risk because the Abbey, school and government buildings are so close to one another but apart from a few broken windows, the IRA caused the school no damages.

[20] So-called because until modern times, 'electors' from Christ Church and Trinity came to the school at the end of this term to elect those scholars they judged worthy of a scholarship at their college.

form of Christianity which is sweeping the school like one of the nine Egyptian plagues' and 'to emphasise the importance of orthodox belief and practice'. Elsewhere ,it complains of those scholars who remain on the Christian foundation yet openly declare their atheism. An interesting development.

Wednesday 23 May

After Abbey, I see the parents of a 15-year-old who is having difficulty deciding on a sixth-form course. Unfortunately, I have been incorrectly advised and say that he will be able to do a subject which in fact he cannot. His parents are such nice, intelligent people and I am annoyed at being in a position of appearing to be muddled.

In break, Jim Cogan[21], the scholars' housemaster, tells me that Anthony Murphy[22] was found at 3 o'clock in the morning sleeping in the open in Sloane Square when he should have been in bed in College. I see Anthony and tell him that he must report to Mr Hutchins[23], the night watchman, at 6.30 every morning for a week. Winning an Emmy Award for his role in *Tom Brown's Schooldays* has been difficult for him to handle.

Thursday 24 May

I receive an extraordinary letter from the headmaster of Cranleigh. He believes I have acted most unethically in persuading

---

[21] Under master and master of the Queen's Scholars, 1971 to 1987.

[22] Anthony Murphy played Tom in the successful television production of *Tom Brown's Schooldays*.

[23] The night watchman was on the Abbey payroll but performed unofficial roles for the school.

his chaplain, Willie Booth[24], to come to Westminster a year hence. He says he is 'shocked' and 'amazed' and adds some curious comments about football scouts and how, if all headmasters acted as I have done, they would not invite one another to dinner. The letter annoys me but I do not take it too seriously.

Monday 28 May

My article on the case for keeping our public schools appears in *The Times*. It will be interesting to see whether this provokes any reaction. This evening, I receive a reaction that is unexpected – an abusive telephone call from an ex-public schoolboy who sounds young and pours forth an attack on the 'sadism and homosexuality' of public schools. He says that by defending the schools I have polluted a decent newspaper. He sounds so distraught it is clearly better for him to get it off his chest. What can have happened, and at which school to make him feel as he does?

Tuesday 5 June

I see three boys who are reported to have been involved in drugs. Two of them asked the third to obtain cannabis, and while the third is surely the more 'professional', all three are equally involved and I rusticate them for three weeks. They are all 14 and must represent the tip of a large problem among the younger boys. Rustication is a bad punishment but I am left with no choice. Further enquiries follow as the rustication has the unexpected effect of encouraging some younger boys to talk to their

---

[24] Chaplain of Westminster School, 1974 to 1991; sub-dean of Her Majesty's Chapel Royal; domestic chaplain to the Queen since 1991.

housemasters; it appears that three or four 15-year-olds are said to be hardened professional pushers. If this is true, I must pin them down because here the real problem lies.

Thursday 7 June

Two boys play Bach in Abbey this morning. I then begin the long and depressing business of questioning the boys under suspicion of selling drugs. In one case, a quantity of cannabis was found, in another a small amount. The questions reveal so much but not enough to be certain that drugs have been sold.

This evening we dine with Westminster parents at their apartment in Mayfair. A fellow guest is an architect from Hamburg. He was a protégé of Albert Speer and worked for Hitler on the chancellery and the plans for a new Berlin. He is charming and smooth. He says, 'I worked for the Nazis and for the Jews at the same time,' and smiles. The 14-year-olds involved with cannabis suddenly seem like angels.

Friday 8 June

I see the boy rusticated on Tuesday and he confirms who has been selling drugs. It is a relief to have the evidence. I see the captain of the school and explain why the two drug sellers will have to be expelled and we discuss what can be done to prevent this sort of 'drug bust' in future.

Sunday 10 June

A long talk with Robin Griffith-Jones[25], a school monitor, about

---

[25] Now ordained and the master of the Temple Church in London.

the drugs case. Monitors are in a difficult position and we talk about striking a balance between spying and the responsible passing on of information.

Monday 11 June

At 4.15pm, I talk to the common room about the drugs case. I say more firmly than I have ever done before that they must not turn a blind eye or give the impression that this is not an important issue. I ask for questions and get none. So many of them are good and conscientious men and women, but getting all members of staff to take responsibility for discipline is one of a headmaster's most difficult tasks.

Tuesday 12 June

At 7.15am, my cram class on Henry V assembles on the roof garden[26]. At 9am, a special assembly up school. The boys know what is afoot and there is an air of expectancy. My theme is that Westminster, more than most schools, depends for its success on a fine balance between freedom and law. It is easily exploited because it is open, loosely organised and trad-itionally averse to regimentation. In that context I talk about the drugs case and why the school cannot turn a blind eye.

At 9.30am, I see the two boys who are to be expelled. It is a sad and difficult business and neither they nor I seek to prolong it. I admitted them both and with both I have failed.

After lunch, I go to Dolphin Square to swim with the team.

---

[26] The headmaster's house had a roof garden with a panoramic view of the Abbey and Parliament.

After racing hard over three lengths, I am leaning against the side in the shallow end when a boy, emerging from the water, asks, 'Has X been expelled or rusticated?' 'Expelled,' I reply. Without comment, he swims away.

This evening, the captain of the school, David Newman, tells me that a boarder is growing cannabis in the window box of his study and that despite or because of my drive on drugs, this is seen by the school as a good joke, which of course it is. But I cannot afford to let the joke run. David Newman and I go round to the house, find the cannabis plants and remove them.

Wednesday 20 June

Another cram class before breakfast. Then I see Christopher Martin[27] about a boy in his house he is worried about. The boy is 14, a day boy, and has joined the local cell of the International Marxist Group. There is no objection to a boy holding such opinions, and Westminster of all places could hardly wish to restrict free political thought, but I am concerned, as is Christopher, about the wisdom of a boy of his age becoming increasingly involved in a group with extreme views and made up of people older than himself. I agree to see the boy if Christopher can persuade him to come.

Thursday 21 June

I see the mother of a boy who was under suspicion of selling drugs but against whom nothing could be proved. She is quiet, not very strong and bewildered that her son has become such a

---

[27] Subsequently headmaster of Bristol Cathedral School and of Millfield School.

stranger. The familiar pattern of adolescence has been exacerbated by a more profound rejection of the school. This is partly, I suggest, because he resented being sent to a boarding house by a father who never even bothered to discuss the idea, and partly because of the influence of an older boy who left last April and preached the gospel of alienation. Mother and I agree that she should approach the local maintained grammar school about her son's entry to their sixth-form next term. I am sure he should not continue here for our sake and hers.

Monday 25 June

At 5pm, I spend an hour with Marcus Alexander who is doing O level English literature on his own;[28] we sit on the roof garden going over possible Chaucer questions. Then to Church House[29] in cassock and gown where the dean receives the Honorary Freedom of Westminster. At the reception afterwards, I meet the daughter of my former headmaster and she tells me that her father is dying of cancer. Twenty-five years ago he should have expelled me for being a persistent rule-breaker but he hung on and eventually made me head of school. After I left, the senior masters in league with old boys forced his resignation. He was ordained and has been working in a quiet parish in Hove. I must write to him but how much better to go and see him.

After school, I spend an hour talking to the 14-year-old who has joined the International Marxist Group. Burke Trend, as

---

[28] Westminster did not offer O level in English literature or history so I occasionally coached a boy on his own.

[29] Church House is the administrative headquarters of the Church of England and fills the south end of Dean's Yard.

cabinet secretary, has been able to show me a confidential note on this organisation. The boy and I discuss the aims of the IMG and also of the National Union of School Students. He asks about my attitude to NUSS activity at Westminster and I tell him that Westminster is not the sort of place to put NUSS ideas into practice. It is a tiring hour but interesting. I do not try to dissuade him from his political ideas. Straight from this meeting to the American embassy with Daphne, where the Annenbergs[30] are giving a large party. We admire their private collection of French Impressionists.

Tuesday 10 July

After lunch, I see the parents of a sixth-former who has received very bad reports. They blame the school because they saw their son pass the entrance exam and start at Westminster with such bright-eyed enthusiasm only to drift away into a non-academic, guitar-playing world. I suspect the truth is rather different. They sent their son to a tutor to get him up to the standard of the entrance exam, and this private intense tuition produced an illusion of ability that soon faded once these special circumstances were withdrawn. Subsequently, the boy has been out of his depth.

Wednesday 11 July

At 8.20am, the father of a boy in Ashburnham comes to see me. His son has appeared in court on the curious charge of stealing letters from offices on the way home. The boy – who was given

---

[30] Walter Annenberg, US ambassador to the Court of St James's 1969 to 1974, took a keen interest in the Abbey and the school.

a conditional discharge for two years – says he and another boy did this for a dare. It so happens that the two boys have been reading in form Cocteau's *Les Enfants Terribles*, in which boys steal worthless items for dares.

Thursday 12 July

It is the last full day of term. See leavers individually during the morning and then various colleagues to tie up loose ends. This afternoon to Dolphin Square to watch the house swimming finals and then on to Vincent Square[31] to watch the 1st XI play Charterhouse. It is a close, sultry afternoon and the cricket lacks zest. At 6pm, I see the dean to discuss tactics for tomorrow's governing body meeting. This evening to the school's production of *Twelfth Night* in Ashburnham Garden. It is produced by David Harding. Whatever his limitations as a chaplain, he is an excellent producer. As the light dies, the spell of Shakespeare's genius and the magnificent setting under the walls of the Abbey combine to create a bewitching atmosphere. How lucky we are that no one wanted to move Westminster to the Home Counties. The last night of term and there are lights burning late around Little Dean's Yard.

---

[31] Named after William Vincent, headmaster of Westminster 1788 to 1802 and dean of Westminster 1802 to 1816. Dr Vincent acquired the 10 acres of grass as a school playing field when London started a rapid expansion to the south.

1973-74
Play Term 1973

Thursday 20 September

I see the chaplain after Abbey and then teach (Julian Grenfell and Ivor Gurney). Lunch with Sir Henry Chisholm at the Athenaeum. At long last I persuade him to drop his insistence that Westminster scholars hold British nationality. I am not interested in a scholar's nationality or in what faith he professes, if any, only in the quality of his mind.

This evening to No.10 with Daphne and the deanwhere the prime minister is giving a dinner party in honour of Burke Trend, who retires as cabinet secretary next week (but remains on Westminster's governing body, thank goodness). There are some 40 guests including four prime ministers – Heath, Macmillan, Home and Wilson. Heath speaks of Burke with wit and warmth. After dinner, Douglas Home comes up to talk and is cheerfully critical of what he calls Macmillan's 'old man act' which, he claims, is put on to inspire sympathy. It is midnight when we walk home and I am awakened at 2am by what sounds like another IRA bomb but is only a crack of thunder.

Monday 24 September

I hear this morning from the BBC that they want me to take part in the Sunday Debate on public schools in October. A housemaster catches me in break to tell me that one of his boys is missing. We are both concerned because the boy, though senior, has been under psychiatric care and is neither happy nor stable. Teach this afternoon and then chair an inconclusive common-room meeting on how we can improve our sporting arrangements. After the meeting, the housemaster follows me upstairs to say that his missing boy has been found dead in his father's flat; he has gassed himself. Both his parents are abroad. I do not have time to reflect on this tragedy because I must go straight into a monitors' meeting and then round to the Home Office to brief the Home Secretary, Robert Carr, who is proposing the toast of 'Floreat' at the Elizabethan dinner[32] next month. When I return, I telephone the housemaster to see if there is any more information. There isn't except for the curious fact that the boy left a completed essay on the table; it was due to be handed in today. Later, I go out into Yard and meet one of the dead boy's friends and we talk in the darkness.

Wednesday 10 October

Alan Sillitoe and his wife come to see the school as prospective parents. Twelve years ago, when he won the John Llewellyn Rhys Prize, my novel *The Custard Boys* was the runner-up. His wife does the talking but he is the interesting one; he is quiet, thoughtful and rather diffident. He does not apologise for

---

[32] The Elizabethan Club is the school's association for former pupils.

thinking of private education (as the protagonists in his novels would have done) but takes it all in his stride. Then I see Simon, a head of house. His housemaster says he is failing to do the job and so should stand down. I talk to Simon and say that I think it would be a mistake to stand down so near to his leaving at Christmas. He agrees and goes off with good intentions to do the job properly.

This evening to *Harold*, a satire on the rock world written by two senior boys that has raised a few eyebrows. There is a large and enthusiastic audience. Afterwards, I go backstage to congratulate the players. They have unopened bottles of champagne which, they say, are for a cast party at a boy's home in Kensington.

Friday 12 October

It is Expeditions Day and boys in the junior school have gone to Hadrian's Wall, Snowdonia, Paris, Jersey and so on. I take Walter Hamilton[33], one of my predecessors, to lunch in College Hall. We sit next to Ted Craven and Walter talks in his characteristically doleful voice about headmasters never finding a way of getting rid of elderly masters who aren't pulling their weight. As I have recently eased Ted Craven out of his house because he was not pulling his weight, I do not comment but concentrate on my veal, ham and egg pie.

Monday 15 October

I teach three periods and deal with routine business. This

---

[33] Headmaster of Westminster 1950 to 1957.

afternoon, a senior police officer and a man from Special Branch come to talk with the senior master, Denny Brock and myself about the royal wedding[34] on 14 November. A very extensive security operation is to be mounted and it would be easier if the boys were sent home for the day. We shall probably have to agree but only for the morning. I am blowed if I am going to give the school the day off, which is apparently what the royal bride has suggested. This evening I go to the Elizabethan dinner in the Army and Navy Club. It is a good occasion. The Home Secretary, Robert Carr, proposes 'Floreat' and I reply. Westminster is blessed with urbane, intelligent old boys so that the annual dinner is not the tedious back-slapping affair it is in many schools.

Tuesday 16 October

I have asked Gerald Ellison, the new bishop of London who was at Westminster in the twenties, to come to Latin prayers and beg a play[35]. I do not introduce him well, failing to hit the right balance between humour and information, but he is unperturbed and the school give him a warm reception. This begging a play dates from heaven knows when but there is a letter in the school archives from Warren Hastings[36] in April 1795 asking the headmaster whether he could come across from Westminster Hall to beg a play to celebrate his acquittal on charges of corruption in his administration of Indian affairs.

This afternoon, two people from the BBC responsible for

---

[34] The marriage of Princess Anne to Captain Mark Phillips.

[35] To 'beg a play' is to ask for a half-holiday for the school.

[36] Captain of the school and later governor of Bengal. His trial for corruption and cruelty lasted 145 days and he bore the cost of his acquittal himself.

the Sunday Debate come to see me. They want to avoid any party political wrangling but later in the day, when we meet with Robin Day, who will chair the debate, and Norman St.John Stevas, who is speaking with me in defence of public schools, it is clear that St.John Stevas wants to be party political and I can see that this is going to be a problem.

At 6.30pm, a meeting in my study for housemasters, house tutors and matrons at which a consultant psychologist who specialises in problematic drug-taking talks and answers questions.

Friday 19 October

I see again the 14-year-old day boy who is a member of the International Marxist Group. He now says he wants to leave and go to Hampstead Comprehensive School. He may be right but as we talk I discover that there are family pressures as well as political convictions behind his wish. He tells me that father is not well off and that sister suffers from so much money being spent on a Westminster education. I advise him to see out his secondary education here. He says he will think it over but I expect he will leave.

Tuesday 23 October

After Latin prayers, I welcome a Japanese professor of ethics who is visiting English schools and universities. He is particularly interested in Jeremy Bentham and is delighted to learn that Bentham was educated at Westminster. He sits in on one of my lessons in which for his benefit we discuss ethics and utilitarianism. It is odd to go straight from this to a very difficult session with the bursar. The masters have proposed that they should have an advisory role in deciding priorities for building and maintenance. The bursar is seized with a fit of rage; he thumps the chair and quite loses control. He will produce a paper, he shouts, that will reduce the masters' proposal 'to mincemeat'. It takes half an hour to make him calm down but his relationship with the common room is impossible and the school is suffering as a result.

Thursday 25 October

The Dalai Lama comes to talk to the John Locke Society[37]. He is in England for the first time and the archdeacon, Edward Carpenter, has persuaded him to visit the school. He is quietly on the ball and speaks good English in a slow, deep, guttural voice. The captain of the school chairs the meeting which is a question and answer session. His Holiness talks freely about his faith and about his training in self-discipline, but will not discuss relations between China and Tibet. When I take him into lunch in College Hall, he piles his plate high and obviously enjoys a square meal. After lunch, he sits in an armchair in our drawing room with 30 boys and girls sitting on the floor, and in this more informal session his warmth and good humour come across strongly. His entourage lurks outside the door. According to Edward Carpenter, the government has allowed the bodyguards to carry guns under their robes.

Friday 26 October

The parents of the young Marxist come to see me. They say they have good communication with their son but it is clear that

---

[37] I started the John Locke Society soon after I arrived at Westminster. It was a forum for visiting speakers. John Locke was at Westminster under Dr Busby.

in trying to be understanding and reasonable they have allowed him to be influenced by older dissidents. Mother wants him to stay at Westminster and is keen on academic success; father is more anxious to accommodate their son's political convictions. We agree that the next step should be for him to see the head of Hampstead Comprehensive.

Sunday 28 October

To the BBC Television Studios at Lime Grove on a dull autumnal evening for the Sunday Debate on public schools. The programme is to take the form of a debate between the opponents of the schools – Roy Hattersley, the shadow education spokesman, and Patrick Miller, an old friend of mine who teaches in a state sixth-form college, and the schools' defenders – Norman St.John Stevas, the Tory education minister, and myself. Both sides have brought witnesses. The BBC rather coyly does not let us communicate before the programme so we have tea in separate rooms. I am not impressed by the witness St.John Stevas has brought; she is a typical right-wing woman who describes Hattersley as a 'bully'. Not for the first time on the question of public schools, I regret my allies. The debate will be shown over three Sundays and the first two programmes are recorded this evening. In the five minute break between the two, Hattersley, Miller and I agree to try and stop St.John Stevas making party political points. The result is that in the second programme, Hattersley and Miller concentrate their fire on me, which doesn't worry me at all, but Robin Day, the chairman, urges them to address some questions to 'the minister'. The latter is clearly annoyed at not being the centre of attention and disappears abruptly when the programme is over.

Monday 29 October

The first day of our entrance exam; candidates gather in Dean's Yard, some with and some without parents. A busy day teaching Oxbridge historians, seeing masters who in some cases don't seem to know why they have come to see me and chairing a heads of department meeting that rambles on because I do not close down discussions that have run out of steam quickly enough. In the evening, I spend two hours in Busby's talking to boys in their studies and come to the conclusion that Geoffrey Shepherd, the housemaster, runs a very good house.

Tuesday 29 October

To the state opening of Parliament: the captain of the school and I sit in the Strangers' Gallery of the House of Lords. The boys in the junior forms stand outside to cheer the Queen as she arrives. Later in the day, an officer from Cannon Row Police Station telephones to say that some of the boys in the junior forms booed the Queen. I check with the master who was in charge of them and he says he heard nothing but hearty cheers. I have a pretty good idea which version is correct but it is not worth enquiring further as it would be difficult to establish the truth without a disproportionate fuss.

For three hours this afternoon, I interview candidates for the entrance exam. For some reason they seem less impressive than usual. I ask each of them about their hobbies and one answers that he breeds rats; he buys his rats from Harrods.

Wednesday 14 November

Letters about the television debate on public schools continue to come. Most are complimentary but one magazine article criticises the programme and describes me as 'a perfect Jesuit inquisitor, full of silky menace'. No school this morning because of the royal wedding in the Abbey. A journalist from the *Daily Express* telephones trying to make a story out of the fact that unlike other schools, Westminster is going back to work this afternoon, but I see him off.

Tuesday 20 November

I am very concerned by reports from housemasters that the head of art, who is also the longest serving member of staff, has been swearing at junior forms, calling the boys 'bastards' and so on. I knew his relations with the younger boys were bad but he is due to retire in two years' time and I was hoping to 'see him out'. Now these reports make it clear that my dilatory approach to the problem will not do. Parents and prep schools will be complaining and rightly so.

Thursday 22 November

The head of art has an appointment to see me at 2pm. Walter Hamilton's moan about headmasters never finding a way of getting rid of elderly masters who are not pulling their weight is much on my mind, but my meeting with the head of art turns out to be more straightforward than I expected. He admits swearing at boys and says he can no longer control himself with the younger age groups. Then he says, 'Do you want me to offer my resignation for the end of the summer term?' And I reply, 'Yes, I am sure that would be right.'

At 5pm, the landlord of a local pub appears with a strange story. He was drinking in the bar at 3.45pm with two police-men when three Westminster boys walked in with empty beer flagons that they wanted filled. The policemen challenged the boys on where the flagons had come from; the boys countered by asking the policemen why they were drinking in the middle of the afternoon. Eventually, the boys left with a police 'talking to'. Shortly afterwards, the pub was raided by police from Cannon Row. The station had received an anonymous call to say that two bogus policemen were drinking illegally in the pub. I pacify the landlord and reflect on how unwise it is to underestimate Westminster boys.

Tuesday 27 November

I receive a letter from David Emms who has been forced to resign as headmaster of Sherborne after only three and a half years. In response to my letter of sympathy, he writes: 'It is a sad story for so much has gone well, but the "antis" found unexpected and powerful allies in elevated circles and I could endure no more.' The moral is that headmasters must prevent at all costs an alliance against them of disaffected senior masters and interfering governors.

Monday 3 December

A former Westminster parent has invited me to lunch to meet Shirley Williams[38] and talk about Labour's attitude to public schools. The success of the Sunday Debate on television has made me the schools' unofficial champion, which does not please some of my headmaster colleagues. Shirley Williams says she is in favour of a state system that educates all children with

---

[38] Opposition minister of state for education and science 1966 to 1969. Secretary of state for education and science 1976 to 1979.

no independent schools outside but she is opposed to abolishing public schools until choice is a reality in the state system. She urges the Headmasters' Conference not to develop a barricade mentality, but what does she expect when even the right wing of the Labour Party would like to see the schools disappear?

Tuesday 4 December
After teaching, this morning I lunch with Clement Freud at the Clermont Club. He is the Liberal spokesman on education and has a son in the school. He is sad-faced and generous – roast pheasant, wild strawberries and claret – but our conversation does not take fire. He does however assert a number of times that he is not an abolitionist as far as public schools are concerned. Then halfway through the pheasant, he suddenly complains that on a school trip to Paris his son had to share a bed with two other boys. He says this is a scandal. I do not take it seriously but it obviously concerns him as though it was evidence that public school homosexuality still flourishes under the cloak of cultural expeditions.

Wednesday 5 December
At 6pm, I go over to the House of Commons to talk to the Conservative parliamentary education committee. I speak to 12 MPs for half an hour, answer questions and have a drink with them in the Strangers' Bar. They support all that I say about public schools but I am struck by their lack of certainty as to what Conservative policy on education is or should be.

Monday 10 December
After Abbey, I work at routine business until break. Tell the

common room that their failure to fill up the report forms properly has caused housemasters unnecessary extra work. Teach this afternoon, a sluggish end-of-term period and then draft a note to be sent to keep people in the independent school world informed about my discussions with the three political parties. This evening the leavers' dinner is held in College Hall. A small group of leavers had the idea and organised the event. I gave permission regardless of housemasterly misgivings. I go as a guest as do three other masters and there are some 50 leavers. Some boys are in dinner jackets and treat the whole thing as a regimental dinner; others adopt a plebeian approach in dress and manners. I speak and so does the organiser. Some boys drink too much, most manage to control it well. It is harmless but awkward. The leavers are neither here nor there, living at home after Oxbridge exams but still at school, and this ambiguity of status makes the imposition of authority difficult. I shall not allow a dinner in this form next year.

Tuesday 11 December
This evening I walk over to the House of Commons where I am a guest at a dinner of the Coningsby Club[39]. Margaret Thatcher[40], the Conservative secretary of state for education, speaks and answers questions. On independent schools, she says that her reason for defending them 'is more fundamental than Dr Rae's' and explains that citizens should have the right to spend their money as they please as long as the activity is not illegal.

---

[39] A Conservative dining club.
[40] Secretary of state for education and science 1970 to 1974.

I do not think that is more fundamental than the freedom to run a school independent of the state but I say nothing.

Friday 14 December

The last Abbey of term. Edward Carpenter stands in for the dean; if only he could succeed Eric Abbott who retires in the New Year. Afterwards, I see leavers, shake their hands and wish them well. One or two eyes glisten, other faces suggest they are keen to be on their way. The usual end of term scenes: play scenery trundled across Yard; old essays blowing in the keen wind; trunks standing near the archway and leavers standing about not knowing quite what to do. At 5.30pm, the school carol service in St. Margaret's, a packed church and good singing. In the icy wind, Daphne and I stand outside after the service saying goodbye and happy Christmas. Cars loaded with boys and trunks drive away into the December night.

Saturday 15 December

The dean of Christ Church telephones to say that X has not done well enough in his history papers to be offered a place but the college like him and are anxious to do well by him, especially in a year when we have sent them such a good crop of candidates. Would X be willing to read geography instead? On X's behalf I say yes and the dean promises to consult his geographers. Just as well Roy Hattersley does not overhear this conversation.

A senior boy comes to see me. Although housemaster and parents have urged him to come, he says it is his own decision. What he says is this: there are two boys in his house, one in the Remove[41] and one in the Shell[42], who have been supplying cannabis to the school. Neither name comes as a surprise and it is a relief to have the evidence at last. But the extent of their involvement in the drug scene outside school is disturbing if it is true. The older boy is so involved he could be in serious trouble; the younger boy has access to LSD. Both are clearly a danger to other boys and I will summon them to see me next week. I thank my informant and promise to keep his name out of the enquiries I make. He has been very forthright, almost unnaturally so, and I brood on this. We take our children to see the film of *Camelot*.

Tuesday 18 December

The term is dead but won't lie down. Sitting at my desk early, I hear a roar and the study windows rattle. I gather later that a car bomb has exploded in Horseferry Road a few hundred yards away and that people are injured.

I have arranged to see the two drug boys this morning. The older boy comes looking as though he has smoked pot on the way here. He is in a school suit, no doubt at mother's insistence, and denies ever bringing cannabis into the school. That is his story and he refuses to change it. The younger boy comes with his mother. He too denies everything but eventually says that the older boy did on several occasions provide a joint to smoke in a café behind Church House. I shall have to see both boys again to establish the truth, but how discouraging the whole business is.

Wednesday 19 December

At noon, I see the older of the two boys said to be involved

---

[41] Remove is the A level year.

[42] Shell is the O level year.

in drugs again, this time with housemaster and parents. It is a difficult session. The housemaster and I suspect he has brought cannabis into the school. He continues to deny this.

His parents are confused. Mother argues that their son is a typical adolescent, concerned about 'the starving in India' – she actually uses that phrase – and that drugs are part of his rebellion against society. It is pretty corny and old hat. I say I think their son is lying. They say that he may do many things wrong but he never tells them a lie. How blind parents are to believe in the truthfulness of their children. The meeting ends with my urging the parents to talk to their son and to try to establish the truth. When they have gone, I hear that Christ Church are going to give X a place to read geography. I telephone him and he is very excited.

Thursday 20 December
Still finishing off a number of school matters before everything closes down for Christmas. The mother of the older boy involved with drugs telephones; her son admits bringing cannabis into the school and 'sharing it' with the younger boy. I thank her. I then decide that both boys should not be allowed to return to the school next term. Their involvement with illegal drugs is neither passing nor experimental and they must pose a threat to other boys.

Lunch with the Jesuits at Farm Street as Tom Corbishley's guest. Sit next to Father d'Arcy who is ancient but full of life and reminisces about T.S. Eliot and Wyndham Lewis, both of whom he knew well. This afternoon meetings with a housemaster and head of department about a boy who has failed to get a place at Oxford. The police ring; there is a suspected bomb in Parliament

Square and we should close our curtains against flying glass.

This evening, to the Drapers' Hall as the guest of John Hargreaves. An excellent dinner with no speeches. We emerge into a wet, cold December night and, unable to find a taxi, we go down to the underground. In our dinner jackets and no doubt looking rather pleased with ourselves, we wait on the platform. A group of young Asians appear on the opposite platform and seeing us, start chanting 'Tories out, Labour in' to John Hargreaves's acute embarrassment.

Friday 21 December
Oxbridge results confirm that the lottery is getting easier to win. Most boys who in any sense deserve to get in do so, though one or two telephone calls are still necessary to find places for the borderlines. DavidCarey telephones to discuss our approach to Colin Peterson, the prime minister's appointments secretary, about who the school would like to see as the new dean when Eric Abbott retires. David is legalsecretary to the archbishop of Canterbury and a governor of the school. He is devoted to the school but he is an intriguer who likes to be the kingmaker, the man behind the scenes who influences key appointments. I want Edward Carpenter to be the new dean but Carey will have his own candidate.

Lent Term 1974

Friday 11 January
See Reg Pullen, the receiver general, about the timing of school

services in the Abbey. We also talk about the dean's retirement and his possible successor. Reg has already seen Colin Peterson and gives the impression that he has urged Edward Carpenter's candidature but he warns that Edward will be ruled out because the Establishment fears he will let his political and ethical convictions influence his actions as dean; that if Bomber Harris dies and approaches are made for an Abbey burial, Edward would object on pacifist grounds.

This evening, I go round to Little Cloister to see Edward and it is soon clear that he has some hopes of the deanery. He would be so good and the appointment would be a reward for a brave and intelligent man. Of course, I have a selfish reason for wanting Edward to be dean and ex-officio chairman of the governors; it would strengthen my hand vis-à-vis the governing body. But I fear the Establishment will play safe and dull.

Sunday 13 January

A boy in the Remove comes to see me to say that he doesn't want to return to school this term but to work for his A levels at home. The problem seems to be that he is a non-academic boy in an intensely academic environment; his sense of being amid alien corn is exacerbated by being a member of an A level English set with the most sharply intelligent and articulate boys in the school, boys who are known as 'pseuds' to the less able, but that is a defensive rather than an accurate use of the slang.

Monday 14 January

The Lent Term begins today. This afternoon, I see again the boy noted yesterday who wants to leave. He is so cheerful, clear-headed and determined I cannot bring myself to persuade him to stay. I see David Carey about our visit to Colin Peterson on Wednesday. Carey is open about his tactics: he will argue against Edward Carpenter (too Liberal), suggest Bishop Geoffrey Tiarks (who he thinks would not accept), leaving the field open for his real candidate, the bishop of Ely.

Wednesday 16 January

I take the morning Abbey service and then see a woman who is writing a book on drugs and schools. One of her sons, she says, was expelled from Eton for smoking pot and subsequently, at the age of 15, killed himself by jumping out of a window on an LSD trip. At 4pm, David Carey and I walk to No 10 to see Colin Peterson. It is an interesting meeting. Peterson says very little; he listens and makes notes. I tell him what the school wants in a new dean: the ability to lead the governing body and an interest in the school. Then I cannot resist adding a pastoral gift for bringing warmth and Christian love to the whole Abbey community, which has lacked these qualities for so long.

This evening, I dine at the Beefsteak as the guest of a parent. A.J.P. Taylor is dining there and we leave together. He had a son at Westminster and comments that you can always tell a Westminster boy because his handwriting is awful and he does not know how to walk properly.

Saturday 19 January

I see some prospective parents, a sound middle-class couple, intelligent and realistic. Father is an engineer. They live in Surrey and might have been expected to send their son to Charterhouse. I would like to see the boy come here because this type of parent helps to offset the rich sophisticates of Chelsea and Hampstead.

Sunday 20 January

I pay a call on the dean this evening and he talks openly about who he would like to succeed him. He would like Owen Chadwick from Cambridge and failing that, Michael Stancliffe, the dean of Winchester. No mention of Edward Carpenter. I suspect the dean has timed his resignation while there is a Tory prime minister to ensure Edward does not get the job.

Wednesday 23 January

The governing body meets in Jerusalem. It is the dean's last meeting. Lord Butler, the master of Trinity, as senior governor, pays a tribute to the dean, the effect of which is somewhat spoilt by the fact that he refers to 'the government' instead of 'the governors' as the body on whose behalf he is speaking. The matter of the Queen's Scholars is finally settled on the lines I wished. British nationality and professing the Christian faith are no longer required. It has taken a year to achieve this.

Thursday 24 January

There is a school communion in Henry VII. Sir Alan Cottrell, the chief scientific adviser to the cabinet, comes to talk to the John Locke Society. I take him into lunch and ask him what science non-scientists should do in the 6th form. He replies without hesitation 'biology'.

At 3.30pm, to Lambeth Palace to see Archbishop Ramsey about the dean's successor. As it happens, I have 10 minutes first with Bishop Geoffrey Tiarks, the archbishop's senior chaplain, who has been strongly tipped for the job. Our discussion is on two levels. We talk about the school's hopes of the new dean but we both know that we may soon have to get on as headmaster and chairman of the governors. He asks my opinion of Edward Carpenter, presumably to find out how close I am to Edward. He then says that he thinks Edward may be 'a little unstable' and I correct him. Tiarks is a governor of Marlborough, we talk about the relationship between the governors and the headmaster.

At last I see the archbishop and spend a few minutes explaining why the choice of dean is so important to the school. He listens and asks a few questions and then I depart.

Thursday 31 January
Take voluntary Abbey
Welcome David Talbot-Rice who is visiting the school
Dictate letters
Business during break in the common room
Teach Shell English
Chair question and answer session with junior forms
Lunch in College Hall
Drive to Putney
Follow our trial eights from the launch
Back to Westminster
Father of the boy I expelled for drugs, uncomfortable interview
Housemasters' meeting
Discussion with housemaster about boy who says he obtains drugs from parties at the house of an international celebrity
Supper
8pm onwards – attacking the pile of paper on my desk

Thursday 7 February
It is now certain that there will be a general election on 28

February. If the new dean is not chosen by then, a change of prime minister will affect the outcome.

Tuesday 19 February

Two housemasters come to see me about a colleague who, they say, has become emotionally involved with a 14-year-old boy and his family. The boy's father died last year and the family were badly shaken. The master showed sympathy and apparently sees his involvement as being with the whole family, but the housemasters think it is much more boy-orientated than he realises. The master concerned is such a good teacher and gives so much to the community it is essential to prevent his attachment to this boy developing any further. I decide to go over to his rooms this evening. He is marking essays and offers me a whisky. I say, 'I am worried about you' and he replies, 'I am worried about myself.' We talk for three-quarters of an hour. I think he understands what I am saying. He is tense and drawn and clearly unwilling to admit he has done anything wrong; I leave realising the problem is far from being solved.

Friday 1 March

We wake to find that a Labour majority is predicted. To Oxford, where Daphne and I are staying the night with Burke and Patricia Trend. Burke is now rector of Lincoln College. With the exception of Edward Carpenter, Burke is my closest ally on the governing body. We dine in hall. The dons are really rather dull and I wonder what Burke thinks of them after being in one of the most influential positions in the country. I sit next to a fellow guest, a suffragan bishop who is self-satisfied, a little bossy and rather stupid. Where does the

Church of England find these men?

Monday 4 March
A crucial meeting of heads of department in which I argue that we must drop our Westminster entrance exam and use the common entrance exam like other schools. We are losing bright boys because prep schools cannot afford to run a separate Westminster class. But there is clearly a consensus against my proposal and I am going to have to impose common entrance whether they like it or not.

Monday 11 March
At 4.30pm, I chair a common room meeting on the school's finances. Explain why money is tight and the relationship between masters' salaries and fees. In the general discussion, one or two men take the opportunity to make oblique attacks on the bursar. It is extraordinary how some men believe they could do the bursar's job much better than him. They could not, nor do they want the responsibility for the decisions he has to take.

Friday 15 March
To Sidney Sussex College, Cambridge for the Foundation Feast. I sit next to a man who gives me this example of public school snobbery. He was a master at Stowe under Roxburgh, a notoriously snobbish headmaster. Roxburgh appointed him to the staff believing he had been educated at University College, Oxford when in fact he had been at University College, London. When Roxburgh found out, he refused to accept the truth because he only employed Oxbridge men and insisted that the official list of masters continued to put 'University

College, Oxford' beside this man's name.

Tuesday 19 March

Drive to Putney for the Schools' Head of the River Race on a blustery afternoon. Westminster do well, being runners-up to Eton and having the best 2nd VIII. Gerald Ellison, the bishop of London, who rowed for Westminster and Oxford, gives out the prizes. During the long wait for the results, he looks wistfully across from the Westminster boathouse towards Fulham Palace, which he had hoped to occupy but it was denied him by the Church commissioners. In the evening, I attend the first meeting of the Headmasters' Conference political sub-committee, set up to improve the public schools' contacts with the political parties. Over dinner, David Newsome[43] says that at Christ's Hospital seven boys stripped off and streaked across the centre of the school. Asked what he did about this, Newsome replies that he beat them all. How extraordinary that sounds.

Friday 22 March

The last full day of term and on cue Theo Zinn[44] appears to talk about the position of Latin and Greek. He is the doyen of senior classics masters but still needs reassurance. He comes every term about this time and our discussion always follows the same path. After teaching, I see a group of boys who have been caught trespassing above the stage and on the roof. It is the wrong time of term to deal with them and when one enters with both hands in

---

[43] Headmaster of Christ's Hospital 1970 to 1979 and of Wellington College 1980 to 1989.

[44] Head of classics at Westminster 1950 to 1983.

his pockets I tell him off in no uncertain terms.

Election Term 1974

Wednesday 17 April

I am discussing the budget and fees for 1974/5 with the bursar and Vic Shannon, the accountant, when the telephone rings. It is Edward Carpenter who says simply, 'The age of miracles has not passed.' I understand at once what he means and am overjoyed but I replace the receiver and continue with the financial discussion. The news is confidential until next week. Later Daphne and I go round to Little Cloister to see Edward and Lillian to congratulate them and to express our delight that Edward is going to be the next dean. Edward shows me Harold Wilson's[45] letter; it came by hand, an envelope within an envelope, 'My dear archdeacon'. It is marvellous news. I did not give Edward much chance because the Church establishment was against him, but the arrival of Wilson at No.10 made all the difference. For the school, it is an appointment of the greatest significance and it is for my future too; to work with Edward as the chairman of the governors is a pleasure I never thought to enjoy.

Wednesday 1 May

I have set aside today to interview all the boys in the top Shell form as part of a programme of interviewing all boys in their

---

[45] Prime minister 1964 to 1970 and 1974 to 1976.

O level term. I find it useful and rewarding. I want to ensure that I know them and that they know I am interested in them. The interviews last until 2.30pm. The monitors' meeting at 4pm throws up an awkward clash between Theo Zinn and the housemaster of Rigaud's. Theo rehearses his annual Latin play in Yard during prep and the housemaster of Rigaud's is complaining that this distracts his junior boys from their work. Both men are bachelors who think their standing in the eyes of the boys depends on not backing down. So they want the headmaster to give a ruling.

At 5.30pm I meet with the chaplain, the director of music and three senior boys in the choir to discuss how we can improve the singing in our morning Abbey services. The director of music argues that good singing depends on religious fervour. I tell him the school will take a lead from the organ, the choir and the masters in that order, and that it is essential to choose hymns and chants that are familiar.

Tuesday 14 May
The master of the Queen's Scholars, Jim Cogan, and I interview the candidates for the Challenge. All pretty good and one or two outstanding. I am mildly shocked by the attitudes instilled by their prep schools – or is it by their parents? One boy, when asked to say what he means by respect for other people, replies, 'You should treat people as their status requires.'

Tuesday 21 May
Up at 6.30am to attack my desk. After Abbey I see the master whose relationship with a boy and his mother has been a cause for concern. At last he realises that he has become too emotion-

ally involved and agrees that he must withdraw. He is a good man and an inspiring teacher; I don't want his career to go off the rails. At 2pm, start a five-hour session interviewing entrance exam candidates. It has never taken so long but the ever-changing faces make the time pass quickly. At the end, I am too tired to go out to dinner so Daphne goes bearing my apologies and I slip away to the cinema in the Haymarket to see *The Sting*.

Thursday 30 May

I teach two periods and am caught out by a young scholar who knows better than I do what a syllogism is. Lunch in Grants, one of the boarding houses, and then see a woman from Yorkshire Television. I have four school monitors with me because she wants 75 Westminster boys to provide an audience for a panel show in which the panel are teenagers and the topics are teenage topics. The idea is appallingly trite but I do not have to say so. Politely but ruthlessly, the four monitors expose the shallow triviality of the programme. The woman departs, sadder and wiser, I hope, and no doubt surprised than anyone should question the great god of television.

At 5pm, I see the leading boys in the Catholick Society. They want my permission to take a group to a Cowley Fathers retreat house in Oxford next term – and I give it.

Housemasters meet at 6pm and we have an important discussion about how far it is our business to give parents advice about the weekends – parties and so on. Opinion is divided.

Sunday 2 June

It is Whitsun and Edward Carpenter preaches for the first time at Abbey Matins as dean. I have to reprimand one of the

Queen's Scholars – Oliver Tickell – for sleeping through the sermon. This afternoon, I take part in a sponsored walk in aid of Namibia, though what or who in Namibia remains obscure. It has been organised by a master who is the embodiment of enthusiasm and good works. We raise £300. London Broadcasting wish to interview some of the boys who have taken part but I refuse to allow this. I am not convinced that they know what they have been raising money for.

Monday 3 June

I have to lay down the law with the parents of the day boy who is a member of the International Marxist Group. He is leaving in July to go to Hampstead Comprehensive School but he is already cutting lessons when they clash with his political activities. Last Saturday, he failed to appear at all and when challenged by his housemaster, said he had to take part in a 'squat' organised by the party.

Monday 10 June

After school, I have a go at the common room on what I expect of them on the subject of checking breaches of the regulations and lapses of good manners. I insist that all members of the common room are equally responsible and that failure to do something is not an option for them. I hope it sinks in.

Friday 21 June

At 11am, Daphne and I walk round to St. Ermin's Hotel where I am to give the address at the graduation ceremony of the American Community School. It is a curious and rather depressing occasion. The boys and girls graduating seem pretty passive and the boy who is 'President of the class' gives an address in which he twice says that the aim of his classmates and himself is to find 'a comfortable corner' in which to live out their lives in peace. I have already spoken but I am hard pushed not to spring up again and harangue the assembly on not looking for a comfortable corner. We depart as soon as good manners allow and have lunch with the scholars in College Hall. How superior British boys are. They are more intelligent, more genuinely independent, more willing to live instead of seeking comfortable corners.

Wednesday 3 July
A meeting of the Headmasters' Conference public relations sub-committee this evening. The BBC want to make a full-length documentary, provisionally called 'Anatomy of a Public School'. The headmasters on the sub-committee are not sure whether to encourage this or not. We are all ambivalent – not wanting to risk bad publicity but equally not wanting a rival school to have the good publicity if that is how the programme turns out.

Monday 8 July
A housemaster appears to show me cannabis found in a boy's pocket; boy claims it was planted on him at a pop concert – an unlikely tale. When the housemaster has gone, I suddenly feel very tired and sink into a chair.

Tuesday 9 July
An early night has done the trick and I feel better. Boys to see about pre-A level entry to Oxford. The new head of art, Christopher Clarke, comes up from Marlborough to tie up some loose ends about accommodation and improvements to the art school.

This evening, I am working in my study when our cat jumps up to the bookcase and sniffs at the book behind which I have temporarily hidden the cannabis found in the boy's pocket. A cannabis-sniffing cat is a suitably eccentric idea for this stage in the summer term.

Friday 12 July

Election Day. This is how the school year ends. The day starts fair but soon clouds over. At 8.30am, the College Race for young scholars in College Garden[46]. At 9am, prize giving in the library, no parents, no ritual, just the prize-winners and me. Then leavers come individually to my study to say goodbye. At 10.30am, the last assembly. I say goodbye and thank you to the three masters whose departure I have engineered, comment on the term and wish the school a good holiday. To the Abbey for the end of term service at which the bishop of Southwark preaches but loses his audience by saying at the start that he has given the same sermon recently to a congregation of judges. What a curious mistake.

The governing body meets this afternoon in Jerusalem. The lunch is too good and the afternoon too warm for controversy, so the agenda slides smoothly by. This evening, the Election Dinner[47] in College Hall. As usual we congregate in our drawing room. Guests include von Hase, the West German

---

[46] Disputed territory. The school calls it College Garden; the Abbey calls it the Abbey Garden.

[47] The Election Dinner was originally given for the electors of Christ Church and Trinity but by the post-war period it had become a public relations exercise for the school to say thank you to the many figures in public life it had reason to be grateful to.

ambassador whom we have got to know well over the last year, Enoch Powell[48], A.J. Ayer, the Bishop of London[49] and those dons from Oxford and Cambridge whose goodwill we need. Von Hase is excellent company at dinner. An elderly governor said over sherry that I should not have invited a former officer in the Wermacht but von Hase's credentials are impeccable. He tells me about his war experience. He fought in Russia for four years and spent a further five years as a prisoner of the Soviets. Near the end of the war, he married in a radio ceremony which was permitted for men who were defending 'fortress' towns against the advancing Russians. However, in the chaos of the time the marriage was not confirmed and he went into captivity not knowing whether his radio marriage was official or not. In Russian hands, he was not allowed to communicate with his 'wife' for two years, so she remained ignorant of his whereabouts. He often wondered whether they would ever be reunited. He was related to Dietrich Bonhoeffer and was connected to the plot of 20 July 1944 to kill Hitler through his uncle, General von Hase, the Commandant of Berlin, who was executed by the Nazis.

After dinner, scholars and guests contribute epigrams on the published theses in Greek and Latin. Enoch Powell contributes Greek iambics which he jots down on the back of his menu between courses. Then we all go to Ashburnham House for drinks, the senior boys and scholars mixing with our distinguished guests. The last guest leaves at about 1am and I go to bed.

---

[48] Enoch Powell enjoyed coming to Westminster because it meant he could indulge his love of the Latin and Greek languages.

[49] Right Reverend Gerald Ellison, at Westminster 1924 to 1929, loyal supporter of the school but never interfered.

1974-75
Play Term 1974

Monday 9 September

I see Jim Cogan, the under master, about various questions concerning members of the common room in the new school year. Will this man really find a new lease of life after being in the doldrums for some time? Will that man settle at Westminster as we hope? It is a routine but useful alerting of each other's mind to some of the personnel problems we face. At 11am, a long, beginning of term common room meeting which goes smoothly. It is good to see Willie Booth, the new chaplain, and Christopher Clarke, the new head of art, among the more familiar faces. The captain of the school, Stephen Garrett, comes to lunch. He has been captain for two terms but I have been unsuccessful in developing a close relationship with him. Why, I do not know. In sunshine and thundery showers, the boarders return and the buildings come alive again.

Thursday 12 September

See a housemaster who has three boys whose O levels were poor and the housemaster wants to know whether they should really be starting on an A level course. I say they should all be allowed to start on the A level course; we took them in at the age of 13, so we must see them through unless an alternative is clearly preferable. The Catholic Society have invited the secretary of the Theosophical Society to talk. She is disconcertingly like Margaret Rutherford[50] in speech and manner but not uninteresting. This afternoon, some sorting out of Oxbridge colleges. There are some clashes because Westminster boys and girls want the best colleges and would rather have a place at Merton or Magdalen than an open scholarship at Hertford or St. Peter's.

Wednesday 18 September

Daphne and I go to Covent Garden before breakfast to buy fruit for the family. After Abbey, I teach Oxbridge historians and discuss the value of psychoanalysis to historical biography. Bob Tyson[51], whose daughter is in the school, has lent me a copy of a psychoanalytical journal with an article on the psychology of Martin Luther and Woodrow Wilson. Draft a regulation on the use of mopeds by senior boys to come to school – the reduction in underground services is affecting some journeys badly. After break, I see a housemaster about a 17-year-old who is alleged to have exposed himself to a master's eight-year-old daughter. The evidence sounds convincing and the housemaster must now see the boy's father; boy is at home and said to be ill. John Edrich[52] and his wife come to the school; a nice couple who have lunch in a boarding house with Tom Rider, captain of our cricket XI.

---

[50] Character actress famous for playing eccentric women in positions of authority such as headmistresses.

[51] Psychoanalyst and academic.

[52] English cricketer.

This evening, I walk over to Farm Street to get some material from the Jesuit library on historical bias (different views on the Inquisition) and return in time for communion in St. Faith's Chapel. After supper, the captain comes round for a talk about school problems. It is announced that there will be a general election on 10 October.

Thursday 19 September

Voluntary Abbey is well attended – curiosity about the new chaplain or a genuine interest? After teaching – more on historical bias – I welcome Professor Arthur Ellison of City University who is talking to the John Locke Society about 'Extra Sensory Perception – fact or fallacy'? He attracts a large audience and speaks well about the evidence to justify his own belief in this phenomenon. I take him to lunch in College Hall where he tells the scholars why he is convinced there will be survival after death.

Swim with the team at Dolphin Square this afternoon. At teatime, Dominic Grieve[53] looks in. He is trying for Magdalen, Oxford but wants to talk about his father's campaign in Solihull, a safe Tory seat. This evening, Father Ronald Macdonald, the Catholic priest of Dulverton in Devon, comes in for a drink. He is an old friend and was the model for Father Ronald in my first children's book *The Golden Crucifix*.

Friday 20 September

I interview the daughter of a Labour MP who has been an

---

[53] Now Conservative MP for Beaconsfield and an opposition front bench spokesman.

outspoken opponent of private education. He has written asking whether we can take her into the A level year. I have met him once or twice. The daughter is sensible and serious about wanting to come and the other masters who interview her agree that we offer her a place. We might also persuade father to modify his views.

Wednesday 25 September
As we emerge from this evening's school communion in St. Faith's Chapel, we see Mr Hutchins, the night watchman, a pproaching with his Alsatian dog. He tells me that security anxieties after the recent attempt to steal the stone of Scone mean that the dog is let loose in the Abbey between 9.30pm and 10pm, so that our communicants have to leave promptly, if they do not wish to pay a high price for their devotions.

Friday 27 September
At 4.30pm, leave to drive to Eton where Michael McCrum[54] has arranged a meeting of 12 headmasters and 12 headmistresses to discuss the transfer of girls to boys school sixth forms. Fascinating. The headmistresses just refuse to acknowledge that the reason girls want to leave could have anything to do with the quality of their own schools.

Tuesday 1 October
Headmasters' Conference annual meeting in Oxford. George Steiner[55] in excellent form addressing the conference this morn-

---

[54] Headmaster of Eton 1970 to 1980.

[55] Professor of English and comparative literature, University of Geneva.

ing. After lunch, there is a meeting of the public relations sub-committee to discuss the projected BBC documentary on a public school. An intriguing session with 10 of us present. Fear and suspicion of the media, anxiety to be the chosen school or at least to prevent a rival being chosen, are all presented as rational arguments for and against co-operating with the BBC. Envy of Westminster and of my own passing celebrity reveals itself; there are those who would like to prevent Westminster being chosen at all costs. The discussion ends inconclusively with Dennis Silk of Radley and I deputed to take the matter further. Dinner this evening in Keble's bleak hall. Morale is high despite inflation and the probable return of a Labour government. Schools are full, confident and optimistic. There are shadows however: the Houghton Report on teachers' salaries may present difficulties; the girls' schools are hostile to the spread of co-education, and the inflationary wind may yet blow very cold.

Thursday 10 October

Election day, though there is little enthusiasm around. At Covent Garden before breakfast, Daphne and I find that most of the men say they will vote Conservative. I vote after voluntary Abbey and find Harold Wilson on the steps of the library in Great Smith Street being photographed after casting his vote. A tramp beside me shouts 'Good old Harold'. I vote Liberal and return to my desk. Willie Booth looks in to say that rumour has it that senior boys are smoking cannabis in a local café in break. But I have to welcome Dr C who is a spokesman for the Voluntary Euthanasia Society, who is talking to the John Locke. He is so old and doddery he appears pretty near the end himself. He takes a vote which gives a small majority in favour of legalising euthanasia. It is the beginning of Expeditions weekend and the junior boys are off to the wilds. At 6.30pm, I go to the BBC for a discussion on class with John Cousins of the Transport and General Workers Union. We agree on nothing, except on our dislike of the honours system, but we get on well. I warm to his directness and no-nonsense idealism. This evening, Daphne and I watch the first election results and by midnight it is clear that there will be a small overall majority for Labour.

Tuesday 15 October

The BBC telephone. They are interested in making the public school documentary here subject to visits from the producer and director. After Latin Prayers, I teach a new boy form to get to know them; they are lively, intelligent and full of ideas about the implications of the election result. See the captain of the school about the rumour that boys are smoking dope in a local café; I am surprised and pleased when he suggests that monitors should make spot checks. Tour of the Abbey this evening with new boys. When I return, three housemasters are waiting to see me about boys who took a flask of whisky on a junior school expedition. At 13, they need a warning; 'on probation' for the rest of term will probably do the trick. Supper at 10 o'clock.

Friday 18 October

Talk to the whole upper school, warning them that if anyone is caught smoking dope in a local café, he will be at risk of expulsion. Later, I am driven out of my study by a bomb scare in Church House, but it turns out to be an alarm clock ticking in a bishop's briefcase. This afternoon, to two of the school's local community visits, the old people's home in Vauxhall Bridge

Road and the day centre for the handicapped in Warwick Row. In both, Westminster boys and girls seem to be giving practical, unpatronising help and to have formed good relationships. Too good, I wonder, in one case? A young scholar has taken an old man from Bethnal Green under his wing; he brings the old man a bottle of Cyprus sherry every week which the man consumes in large gulps.

Wednesday 23 October
Jeremy Bennett, a BBC producer, spends the day with us. He is inclined to make the public school documentary here, but I doubt whether the Headmasters' Conference will agree to it being made, particularly if Westminster is the chosen school. I am having difficulty choosing the right successor to Geoffrey Shepherd as housemaster of Busby's.

Monday 11 November
Various announcements in the common room in break, then welcome an RAF liaison officer who will not get much business here; the link between Westminster and the armed services is weak, apart from the occasional regular soldier. At 4.30pm, a mother and son come to see me with the boy's housemaster. Boy is 15 and has for this term and last been irregular in his attendance. He is depressed and increasingly isolated from his peers. He is seeing a psychiatrist but not co-operating much. No one seems to know for certain what is wrong. Father is dead. Westminster has hung on but the boy has only attended for 10 days this term. I tell mother and son that unless he is now regular in his attendance, he will have to leave.

Wednesday 20 November

More rain – it is the wettest autumn for many years. This evening, to a house play, 'Zigger-Zagger'. When the curtain goes up, there is our eldest daughter, Siobhan, who is a day girl in the house, sitting on stage in a short skirt and fish-net stockings, smoking a cigarette. The play is energetically performed but drags in the second half.

Thursday 21 November

I see Jeremy Palmer before school to explain why I am making two scholars junior to him school monitors. He is such a good person I wish I could promote him now. Later, I see Marcus Alexander, who is one of the two scholars junior to Jeremy. He is only 16 but I think he has the right qualities to be captain of the school when Stephen Garrett leaves at Christmas. I am impressed by his response to being made a monitor – cool, intelligent but neither priggish nor too well prepared. After supper, the head of Grant's and the boy who will be his successor come to talk about the group of disaffected and difficult senior boys in the house. They say that the housemaster is afraid of these boys, which makes their own job impossible.

Friday 22 November

See David Hepburne-Scott, the housemaster of Grants, and try to steer him onto a sensible but firm course in dealing with the mutinous senior boys. I do not have much confidence that he will get it right. Then Jim Cogan who is housemaster of College. He has picked up a rumour that one of his brightest Oxford candidates has been stealing hundreds of pounds' worth of valuable books from shops in the West End. It is hard to believe but experience suggests that such rumours must be followed up.

Monday 25 November

After Abbey, I see two of the disaffected senior boys in Grants and tell them that one more breach of the regulations and they will be sent home. One of them is the son of the man I am try-ing to persuade to make a large contribution to the school build-ing fund. Teach and then welcome an Austrian physicist I met recently and have invited to lunch with the scholars. His name is Fritjof Capra. I am soon lost as he talks with the scholars about (I think) the connection between higher mathematics and religion. This afternoon, a difficult mission to two leading bookshops. Jim Cogan has discovered expensive books in the room of the senior scholar who is rumoured to have stolen them. The shops are quite unable to say whether these particular books were stolen; they lose many and apparently keep no list. They give the im-pression that they would rather I had not mentioned the subject. At 6pm a bomb explodes in a letterbox down Victoria Street.

Thursday 28 November

The gates into Dean's Yard will be closed early today on Scotland Yard's advice as the anti-IRA bill is going through the House. Sir Geoffrey Jackson, who was British ambassador to Uruguay, talks to the John Locke Society about his experience of being kid-napped and held hostage by terrorists. This afternoon, I see the senior scholar suspected of stealing books. After a long and un-happy interview, he admits to the offence, though insisting that the total value of the books is 'only £50'. I tell him he may no longer be a member of College and must spend the rest of term living at home. It is, of course, no great punishment and he is

74

lucky that the bookshops are not interested in prosecuting. His attitude to the stealing appears to be amoral; it gave him intellectual and emotional satisfaction. He is an only child and highly intelligent. Where shall we look for the origin and nurturing of his crime?

Friday 6 December
Out of the blue, a letter from Lord Blake, head of Queen's College, Oxford. He urges me to send more Westminsters to the college and takes the opportunity to be indiscreet in his criticism of Christ Church.

Monday 9 December
After teaching this morning, I go to the Café Royal for the Lord's Taverners Christmas lunch where I am to reply on behalf of the guests. There are some 600 people there and I have to follow Tommy Trinder[56], who is brilliantly funny. I do not recall a more difficult moment at which to speak. I am flat beer after champagne. I keep it short and hope for the best.

Thursday 12 December
See Marcus Alexander and offer him the post of captain of the school. Though he is young, he is the outstanding candidate and really cares about the school.

Monday 16 December
To Covent Garden early to buy a Christmas tree and holly. The tree is always lit for the first time on December 17, which is our

---

[56] The most famous comedian of his day.

daughter Penelope's birthday. At noon, see the parents of a day boy whose behaviour is a running sore of minor disciplinary offences no one thing serious enough to merit rustication but a disaffected attitude and a string of petty crimes. I warn that this pattern of behaviour must be broken or a minor offence could lead to the boy being sent home. I think housemaster and parents have been too indulgent and too easily persuaded by the boy's promises of reform. Then I see the parents of the scholar who is guilty of stealing books. Father is critical of our handling of the case, mother insists that other boys involved have got away with it. We part on chilly terms. This evening, we dine with the Chains. Their daughter is in the school and their son left two years ago. Father, Ernst Chain, won the Nobel Prize for his work on penicillin, and mother, Anne Chain, is a Beloff and hardly less formidable intellectually. What genes their children have inherited.

Thursday 19 December

Oxbridge results. The amoral scholar who stole books has won an open scholarship while the decent, straightforward boy who has served the community well has been rejected. That is academically correct but so much status and prestige attaches to Oxbridge here,that these decisions appear unjust. Sign letters to the governors about the need to impose a £75 surcharge on fees next term. This will hit some parents hard but all schools face the same problem of inflation. Another bomb this evening, this time in Oxford Street.

Lent Term 1975

Thursday 23 January
Governors meet this afternoon and I feel irritated by them. After a good lunch, their attack on the agenda is blunted, some of their comments are worthless and there is no sense of urgency in this critical situation with escalating fees. No organisation that wishes to survive in these difficult times can afford to be so casually governed. After the meeting, I see the day boy who insists on committing a string of minor offences and whom I gave a last warning in December. He comes with his father. His behaviour is no better this term; he is unwilling or unable to live within the regulations and I have to tell him and his father that he cannot stay at the school any longer.

Sunday 26 January
A fine, clear morning. Attend Abbey matins with the scholars. It is a dismal service that provokes me to anger. What is the point of it all? The choir perform, the congregation cannot join in, the sermon is long and tedious. Why is the Abbey so unaware of this? Play fives afterwards to get the service out of my system. This evening, a housemaster rings to say he has found evidence that a senior boy has been smoking cannabis in his study. Boy is a difficult case and has my sympathy. Father died while living with another woman. Mother has remarried, has attempted suicide and now lives abroad. I shall have to rusticate the boy because if I do not, the gossip in Hampstead and Dulwich will be that Westminster has abandoned its hard line on drugs. But where can he go? His guardian lives in Kent and will no doubt be

none too keen to have him for two weeks.

Tuesday 28 January
See Lord X whose daughter is not happy here and wants to leave. She is the first girl to wish to do this but it comes as no surprise. She came under pressure from mother and mother has recently died. Daughter now feels free to follow the course she wanted in the first place and has the sense to see that Westminster's intellectual intensity is not for her.

Thursday 13 February
A fine spring-like morning. I take Mrs Lloyd into lunch with the scholars. She was instrumental in persuading the Uvedale family to give the Majesty Scutcheon from Oliver Cromwell's coffin to the school and it now hangs on the wall outside of my study. In 1658, as Cromwell's coffin was being carried into the Abbey, a 16-year-old Westminster scholar, Robert Uvedale, snatched the silk banner from the coffin and vanished into the crowd. Soldiers were so fearful of a demonstration against Cromwell that they let him get away with it. There is something typically Westminster about the incident so it is right that the trophy should be on the wall outside the headmaster's study. At 4pm, I see a mother about a modern problem. Her son has been caught smoking for the umpteenth time and I have decided to rusticate him. Mother shows no surprise and admits to being a chain smoker herself. Father is dead. When I see the boy, he says nothing in response to my judgement but looks at me grumpily from under his dark eyebrows.

Tuesday 18 February

Attend a meeting of the examinations committee of the Schools Council representing the independent schools. My vote is needed to stop the National Union of Teachers pushing forward their plans to abolish grades at O level. Just as well I turned up. The NUT proposal is defeated 10-8.

Friday 28 February

See the boy rusticated for smoking on his return to school. He is still beetle-browed and resentful. I warn him that his future now rests in his own hands. The platitude sounds flat but it seems only fair to drive the point home. This afternoon, I walk in St. James's Park for a short while, enjoying the superb weather then back to attend Ernst Sanger's Lower Shell German class. Ernst is Austrian and has all the Continent's respect for hard work and learning by rote. He is close to retiring and deplores what he sees as declining standards. He is contemptuous of complaints that he sets too much prep to the boys in the Lower Shell. When I enter the classroom, Ernst is all smiles and I am reminded of the wolf in 'Red Riding Hood'. The boys, who are usually overawed and possibly frightened of him, are somewhat taken aback by his uncharacteristic affability.

Play fives this evening in the first round of the school competition. My partner – Charles Piggott – is a conscript and he is good enough to carry us both into the second round.

Sunday 2 March

A housemaster rings to say that a member of staff has been rude and offensive to the mother of a boy in his house – just what we do not want with fees rising and surcharge imposed.

Thursday 6 March

A critical meeting of the governing body's finance and general purposes committee. Governors cannot accept the recommendations of the master's salaries advisory body; increases for the most senior men are cut back and will not be backdated. In the present financial climate, these are responsible decisions. Westminster's problem is that it has so many men at the top of the salary scale. The meeting reflects growing concern about the future of independent schools, threatened as they are not so much by hostile politicians as by rising costs.

At 5pm, I tell the members of the master's salaries advisory body about the governors' decision; there are long faces. This evening, the dean, Edward Carpenter, comes round to talk informally about religion and philosophy to a group of senior boys and girls. As it happens, two senior boys who wish to complain about their housemaster arrive at the same time and are swept into the religious discussion with no chance to register their complaint. With good grace they contribute to the discussion.

Saturday 8 March

The company that provides the school with computer time is up in arms because one of our 15-year-olds has discovered and publicised a flaw in the computer's security. One of the company's customers is the Ministry of Defence so their anger is understandable. But shouldn't they also be grateful?

Sunday 23 March

Interviewing girls for sixth-form entry most of the day; the quality is very high – these are not less able girls seeking boys – and we should have no difficulty selecting 15 good candidates.

This evening, I see a father who is being posted overseas and is worried about his son's future when he is so far away. Boy is small for his age and underdeveloped. At his prep school, the Dragon, he was systematically bullied in a particularly unpleasant way; boys urinated on bread and forced it into his mouth on more than one occasion. He is bright but his potential has not been realised, which is hardly surprising in the circumstances. As far as father and I are aware, he has not been bullied here.

Election Term 1975

Thursday 1 May
May Day and on cue the communist Viet Cong take control of Saigon and re-name it Ho Chi Minh City. To Marlborough for another meeting of headmasters and headmistresses on the issues raised by the transfer of girls to boys' sixth forms. It emerges that 70 boys' schools now admit girls and that it is clear that a number do so primarily for economic reasons; they are filling the gaps created by falling boarding numbers.

Saturday 10 May
The economic crisis deepens and seems to cast a gloom over the common room. A father telephones to say that his 17-year-old son refuses to obey him and insists on spending the night with his girlfriend. Father wants me to say that if the boy does this he will be expelled, but I point out that whatever my views on the boy's behaviour, I cannot possibly threaten him with expulsion. At the

weekend, the boy is his parents' responsibility.

Friday 16 May

I spend most of the day interviewing boys in the Upper Shell. My plan is to see all boys individually for 10 minutes in their O level year. At 4pm, a former Westminster scholar comes to ask advice. He works in publishing and earns £6,000 a year but he has five children and wonders whether he will ever be able to send his son here even with a scholarship. He has some invested capital from his father's writing but the capital is depreciating fast. If this sort of cultured, middle-class family cannot afford to send a son to Westminster, the character of the school will change.

Monday 21 May

After Abbey, see Dick Taverne[57] who is interested in his 15-year-old daughter coming to Westminster next year. She is at Pimlico Comprehensive where – according to father – she is bored by the lack of stimulus and intellectual challenge. Then I see the father of a boy who is due to come in September. Father tells me that his son is one of the most promising cricketers Surrey has seen for many a year. I warm to father, who is unpretentious and very proud of his son. I hope the boy passes the entrance exam. Heaven knows we could do with a good cricketer. Monitors meet at 4.30pm. A good discussion on bringing the school regulations up to date. I say little as Marcus Alexander handles the meeting well.

---

[57] The Right Honourable Lord Taverne, QC, Labour Member of Parliament 1962 to 1972. Resigned from the Labour Party 1972. Independent Social Democrat Member of Parliament 1973 to 1974.

Thursday 29 May

I hear from the police that the father of a boy in his first year has been arrested on a burglary charge. I check with the housemaster and find that the boy is at home with 'a heavy cold'. How terrible for the boy.

Wednesday 11 June

An Irish female voice telephones a bomb warning to one of the housemasters, who rushes round to tell me, pale and unnecessarily shaken. We call the police and clear the boys out of buildings on to the green in Dean's Yard. Police dogs go through the classrooms and the houses. They find no bomb but – they report to me – a pipe recently smoked and a smell of cannabis. The hoax has been a bad joke for somebody.

Monday 16 June

A fine morning giving way to rain. After break, a long talk with the assistant director of music. It is clear that I cannot postpone any longer a comprehensive attack on the weakness of music at Westminster. Quite apart from the fact that we are letting our boys and girls down, our reputation as a civilised school is suffering. We have talented individuals – currently three, Alistair Sorley, George Benjamin[58] and Charles Peebles, all in one house – but they cannot disguise the lack of leadership in the music department.

This evening, I am a guest speaker at the National Sporting

---

[58] Composer and conductor; leading exponent of contemporary music; professor of composition at the Royal College of Music 1985 to 2001. His compositions have won many international awards.

Club's dinner in honour of Gary Sobers[59] at the Café Royal. It is a long, enjoyable and good-humoured occasion. I propose the toast of 'cricket', a game I know little about and have not played since childhood. The speech seems to go down well, though in their cheerful mood the audience would have received anything faintly witty with roars of mirth. I sit between Len Hutton[60] and Wavell Wakefield[61] and find both good company. Jo Grimond proposes Sobers' health and Sobers replies with a false modesty that is embarrassing.

Friday 11 July

The end of another Election Term and of our fifth year at Westminster. My love for the place grows and I can see that one day departure is going to be difficult. The familiar pattern of the last day of the school year unfolds. Saying goodbye to leavers one by one in my study, I find I am surprised that some of them have lasted the course – and glad too. In Ashburnham Garden after the Election Dinner, I speak to Tom Howarth who was high master of St Paul's and is now tutor for admission at Magdalene, Cambridge. I suggest the college has a public school horse and hound image and he responds by telling me that this year one of the undergraduates rode in the Grand National. He borrowed books from his tutor to do some revision in that vacation but when the books were returned, the tutor found that one was missing. The undergraduate apologised. The book had been eaten by the horse.

---

[59] Famous cricketer and captain of the West Indies Test team.

[60] Famous cricketer and captain of the England Test team.

[61] Famous rugby player and captain of the England team.

Saturday 12 July

Grey and drizzling. The wind blows paper about in Little Dean's Yard. End of term business to tidy up. I see the top scholar and his parents. Boy is 15 and has had a bad term. After the Election Dinner, four bottles of Pimms found their way from Ashburnham Garden to his room in College. Mother is Russian and puts her son's problems down to 400 years of Cossack intransigence; she speaks of him as though he had left Russia last year and was having difficulty adapting to British society. I warn that his scholarship is at risk if the Cossack behaviour continues.

1975-1976
Play Term 1975

Saturday 13 September

The new school year has started quietly. I see two potential school monitors and offer them the job, which they accept. A third says he does not want to be a school monitor; he finds himself unexpectedly head of his house and doesn't want the wider responsibility. I am not impressed.

Teach, dispose of routine business and then to Vincent Square to watch football practice. This evening, I am disturbed to read a series of articles in the *Times Educational Supplement* arguing that as Britain is now multi-cultural schools should no longer pass on a mono-cultural tradition. What nonsense. If the history and literature of the country are watered down to suit ethnic minorities, the United Kingdom will be little more than a geographical expression. Happily, Westminster does not have to take any notice of this misguided idea. A good argument for keeping independent schools – they can ignore the fads and fashions of educationalists.

Wednesday 17 September

A dinner party at the German embassy as guests of the von

Hases. I talk to Roy Hattersley[62] and he makes no secret of the fact that he is keen to take over from Rees as minister responsible for Northern Ireland. He says he wants to be the man who announces in the House of Commons that the six counties are no longer a part of the United Kingdom, thus assuring for himself a place in history.

Wednesday 24 September

To Manchester for the AGM of the Headmasters' Conference. On the way, I address the Manchester Luncheon Club on 'Can the public schools survive?' Lunch first with the committee, one of whom, Sir Henry Hinchcliffe, is from a family who have sent their sons to Westminster for generations. The first Hinchcliffe was at Westminster in the early 18th century, the son of a livery stable keeper who became headmaster of the school and master of Trinity College, Cambridge. Sir Henry tells me that he was playing cricket at Oxford against the Radnorshire Gentlemen on the day the First World War broke out. As men completed their innings, they hurried away to join their regiments leaving dwindling numbers to finish the match as the summer evening drew in. My talk is in the Free Trade Hall, built on the site of the Peterloo massacre. It is well received but by tradition there are no questions. Then on to the university for the AGM. This evening, the question of who should be next year's chairman is discussed informally. My name is mentioned but I am not much concerned either way and will neither lobby nor play hard to persuade.

---

[62] Right Honourable Roy Hattersley, Labour Party spokesman on education 1972 to 1974.

Thursday 25 September

The *Times* and *Telegraph* carry reports of my speech which will irritate some of my headmaster colleagues. Ian Beer[63] button-holes me on the question of the next chairman. We are old friends and rivals in the headmasters' world and he is clearly dismayed to hear my name mentioned at all. He suggests we both support another candidate, Roger Young, the principal of George Watson's in Edinburgh. I agree. He will be a good chairman. This evening, a service in a nearby Victorian ecclesiastical monstrosity with headmasters singing themselves into a mood of confidence with 'Lift up your hearts'. Followed by the annual dinner which is pleasant enough, though the speeches are of the usual mediocrity.

Tuesday 30 September

I have been invited to visit King Alfred's School, Hampstead, a late 19th-century progressive school, fee paying, all day boys and girls, and patronised by forward-looking north Londoners. I am particularly interested in how the elected school council of pupils and staff operates, as from time to time there are requests that we should have one at Westminster instead of appointed school monitors. I find King Alfred's relaxed but curiously unreal. With what earnest determination staff and pupils call each other by their Christian names. With what serious informality the school council discusses matters of trivial importance. Does it really teach them anything about the workings of democracy? The pupils will criticise authority anyway – much better that

---

[63] Headmaster of Lancing College 1969 to 1981 and of Harrow School 1981 to 1991.

they should criticise the real thing than become disenchanted with democracy at such a young age.

Wednesday 8 October
Enoch Powell comes to talk to the Political and Literary Society. He is billed to talk about the impact of Ulster on Westminster politics, but without warning, he launches into an uncompromisingly erudite talk with quotations from Tacitus on the non-historical nature of the Gospels and the significance of the Last Supper and the Passion in post 70 AD Jewry. The pupils listen attentively, held, I suspect, less by the subject than by the fascination of listening to the logical working of a brilliant classical mind.

Friday 10 October
An important meeting of the governing body's statutes committee. At last the governors agree that we can no longer regard the admission of girls to the sixth form as 'experimental' and must regularise the legal position, if necessary by changing the statutes.

Tuesday 14 October
Michael Oserov of the Soviet news agency Tass visits the school. He wants to write an article on Westminster for the Soviet press. When I explain how academically selective Westminster is, he smiles. The Soviet education system is, he assures me, just as selective and elitist despite appearances. He goes off to talk with Marcus, the captain of the school, and other senior boys and girls.

Thursday 23 October

In break, I see boys whose excellent work has earned them a 'digniora', that is, a piece of Maundy money[64], a supply of which is kept in my study. One boy, Tom Holt[65], tells me he has just finished his first novel and is rewriting the early chapters in the light of his greater maturity. He was 14 last month.

This evening, to the College play. It has been written by a 16-year-old scholar called Adam Boulton[66]. He has skilfully updated Marlowe in the style of Stoppard and called the play 'Dr Fistus'.

Friday 24 October

At 5pm, monitors meet in my study and tell me that a number of boys are planning to demonstrate against school uniform by turning up to school in 'shag' one day after the exeat. This has a pleasantly old-fashioned ring and I do not take it seriously. When some monitors suggest that I say something at Latin prayers tomorrow to 'de-fuse' the situation, I decline. Headmasters cannot be seen to react to the threat of protest or demonstration. I tell the monitors that it is their job to warn the would-be protesters that refusing to wear uniform would be counter-productive. After supper, I take Marcus Alexander and Ben Campbell to the cinema to see Arthur Penn's *Night Moves*. One of the duties of senior monitors is to accompany the headmaster to his favourite pastime.

---

[64] The specially minted money distributed to pensioners by the Queen on Maundy Thursday. By tradition, the headmaster of Westminster receives a number of sets of Maundy money to give as prizes for good work.

[65] Became a successful novelist.

[66] Went on to become political correspondent for Sky News.

Friday 7 November

A long discussion this morning with Oxbridge historians on Ranke and Carlyle. Then to see the mother of a 16-year-old who for two years has failed to attend school regularly. Father is dead (how many dead fathers there are) but housemaster and I think an ultimatum to mother and boy is needed; come regularly or leave. The uniform protest scheduled for today did not take place.

Friday 14 November

To the Cambridge Union to speak against the motion 'Private education is anachronistic and socially divisive'. It is socially divisive, of course, but not anachronistic. We win too easily by 444 votes to 245. Former Westminster boys to meet afterwards over a glass of beer.

Tuesday 25 November

After school communion in Henry VII Chapel, talk to Jim Cogan about a strange case of stealing in College. Money is being stolen mostly from one boy, but why does he keep leaving sizeable sums around? The obvious culprit is a boy of the same age with whom the loser of the money is said to have had a homosexual affair; both boys were the objects of such attentions from an older boy now at Oxford. But what has their emotional life to do with the stealing? To add a further twist, both boys have this term been rivals in a heterosexual interest in one of the girls attached to College. Is the money being stolen by one to spite the other or is the money not stolen at all but the loss claimed by one to put the blame on the other? Jim and I are baffled.

Wednesday 26 November

I am co-opted onto the committee of the Headmasters' Conference for 1976, a necessary step if I am to be considered as a possible chairman for 1977. Returning to Westminster, I encounter some boys rushing out of Dean's Yard, excited at the thought of joining a large demonstration against unemployment in Parliament Square. I turn them back because the demonstration is a Far Left affair at which young public schoolboys would not be welcome.

Thursday 27 November

In the middle of the housemasters' meeting this evening, I receive a telephone call from the landlord of The Two Chairman, a pub nearby. He says several Westminster boys are drinking there illegally. I send two housemasters off at once to check but it turns out to be a hoax. It was a boy who rang and the two or three monitors in the pub are over 18 and not breaking the law or the school regulations. It is typical eleventh week of term stuff.

Wednesday 10 December

The end of term brings its familiar rush of problems to be solved or postponed. Some colleagues look drawn and talk gloomily about the selfishness of the young, a sure sign that the term has gone on long enough. See the parents of a Westminster girl who was left in their flat over the weekend and invited a number of Westminster boys to stay the night. Parents say that it is the first time they have done this and it never occurred to them that she would invite boys. This evening, to a party at A.D. Peters', my literary agent, and talk to an old friend, John Roberts, who is a history don at Merton College, Oxford. He tells me he has just finished writing *History of the World* and that tomorrow he is interviewing Christopher Duggan[67], one of our best historians. I sing Christopher's praises. Those literary parties have their uses.

Monday 15 December
Thick fog reminiscent of the 1950s shrouds London. The term has ended. Oxbridge results trickle in – no injustices but not a vintage year. This evening, to the Dorchester as the guest of Westminster parents at a Greek charity ball. A fellow guest is the Reverend John Kelly, the principal of St. Edmund Hall, Oxford, and a former vice-chancellor of the university. We seldom send boys to St. Edmund Hall, but while other members of the party are noisily Greek dancing, John Kelly leans across the table and offers me a deal. If we will send a Westminster scholar to the college, he will persuade the tutors to admit some of our borderline cases. I promise to think it over.

Monday 22 December
A Cambridge good-luck story. X, a good linguist, has been turned down by Clare. I telephone Tom Howarth at Magdalene, who at that moment is discussing with the director of studies for modern languages whether to take X or another candidate from the pool. I persuade Tom that X is the one to choose and he agrees. But what of the other candidate and what if my call had been half an hour later?

---

[67] Professor of Italian history and director of the Centre for Modern Italian History at the University of Reading.

Lent Term 1976

Thursday 29 January

The *Times* and the *Daily Telegraph* have a story about criticism of Westminster School in the Moscow press. What appears to have happened is that the senior boys and girls who talked to Michael Oserov of the Tass agency last term decided to take the poor man for a ride. They pretended that they knew nothing about Russia and had never heard of the Revolution or the Great Patriotic War, and Oserov took their comments as proof of the ignorance and limited outlook of the privileged young in Britain.

Friday 30 January

This evening a telephone call from John Vaizey who asks whether I can help Harold Wilson's political secretary, Marcia Williams[68], who wants to get her two sons, aged seven and eight, into our Under School. I say she will have to contact me direct.

Friday 6 February

This evening I lead an informal discussion with eight colleagues on how to encourage intellectual liveliness among senior boys and girls. We talk late into the night. The general view is that we should spend more time teaching specialist subjects and that general studies or non-specialist studies are often a waste of time. Such a view runs counter to current opinion and may

---

[68] Later Lady Falkender.

be difficult to put into practice. Did Ben Jonson or John Locke or Edward Gibbon do non-specialist studies when they were at Westminster?

Monday 9 February

Marcia Williams comes to see me with Sir George Weidenfeld[69], who is the godfather of one of her sons. We discuss her wish that the two boys should try for places at the Under School and eventually for Westminster if they are up to standard. She appears rather nervous and is obviously very protective of her sons, particularly on the question of publicity, but I am impressed by her directness and can see no reason why the boys should not go to the Under School. As he leaves, Weidenfeld gives my book-case a searching look as though checking on the number of his own publications.

Saturday 21 February

After morning Abbey, I take a new boy form to get to know them. We read and discuss Julian Grenfell's poem 'Into Battle'. I cannot disguise my sympathy for Grenfell's romantic, idealised view of war, but these 13-year-olds do not agree.

After lunch, I play fives with colleagues and then go up fields to watch football. When I return, I meet Brother Edward, an elderly Anglican Franciscan friar who was a boy at Westminster in the thirties, and take him into tea in College Hall. He says there was so much bullying at Westminster in his day, the young boys in his house formed themselves into a protective union.

---

[69] Lord Weidenfeld, publisher.

Each member contributed two pence and the committee hired the services of two older, stronger boys in another house. These 'heavies' were paid six pence for an act of protection, which apparently meant taking the bully on one side and threatening him. They were called Bengough and Davis. The bullies styled themselves 'The Kings of Under' but the union of younger boys and their protectors broke the bullies' power and, according to Brother Edward, ushered in an era of tolerance in the house.

Brother Edward recalls another union – the Union of Progressive Forces, a leftwing popular front in the school that gave von Ribbentrop a rough ride when he came to talk (von Ribbentrop had a son in the school). In the evening, I look up Bengough and Davis in the Record of Old Westminsters but do not glean much other than that Bengough died young after being invalided out of the army in the Second World War.

Friday 27 February

Talk to all the O level forms about the importance of their A level choices. Then a housemaster comes to complain about my failure to appoint his candidate as a school monitor. He takes the opportunity to moan about the lack of discipline and the failure of the present monitors to do anything about it. It is all characteristic of this emotional man who sees himself as the sole upholder of good discipline in the school. I am impatient with him because a sharp rebuke does him no harm.

Saturday 28 February

Ruffle feathers today. I ask a senior master to stand at the gate of Dean's Yard and take the names of boys and girls who are late for morning Abbey. I have noticed gaps in some houses recently and want to know whether housemasters are doing anything about it. The senior master hands me a list of 19 names and I circulate this to housemasters asking what action they are going to take. Some housemasters are offended, but that is probably because they have been slack in checking on late-comers themselves.

Tuesday 11 March
I have been asked to go round to the old War Office building, room 055, and have no idea why. It turns out that this is a security services suite in the Ministry of Defence. My host is a charming man in his early fifties who appears to be responsible for tracking Soviet espionage in the form of 'disinformation', spreading rumours and so on. He says he thinks Michael Oserov who came to interview me and boys at Westminster and wrote a criticism of England's elite education in the Soviet press, was engaged in spreading 'disinformation' on behalf of the KGB. Over coffee, I answer questions about Oserov's visit and explain that Oserov himself was taken for a ride by the boys and girls at Westminster, so it is not clear who was spreading the disinformation to whom.

Saturday 20 March
The end of term again. A fine, bright morning and my 45th birthday. As I walk into assembly, the school sings 'Happy birthday to you'. How we schoolmasters love this sort of surprise. It persuades us we are regarded with affection.

Sunday 21 March
I attend a very special occasion in the Abbey. Edward Carpenter,

the dean, has invited the new Roman Catholic Archbishop of Westminster, Dom Basil Hume[70] of Ampleforth, and Benedictine monks from all over England to sing vespers in the Abbey. The Abbey is packed for the first time in goodness knows how many years and 150 Benedictine monks sing vespers in what was once their monastic church for the first time since the Reformation. Edward introduces the archbishop and Basil Hume responds, at which the congregation bursts into applause. There is applause again when dean and archbishop walk out together through the choir and down the nave. It is altogether a very remarkable, historic occasion, and I cannot help thinking that no other dean would have allowed such an ecumenical service to be held in the Abbey.

Sunday 28 March

George Weidenfeld telephones to ask if I will be free to see the prime minister at 5.30pm tomorrow. He says Harold Wilson wishes to thank me for my kindness to Marcia Williams.

Monday 29 March

At 5.15pm, Weidenfeld calls for me and we drive off to Downing Street in his car. We are taken upstairs to the prime minister's study where Wilson greets us warmly. 'Hallo Dr Rae, I have heard a great deal about you.' The study is a pleasant room overlooking the garden. Wilson's desk is at one end and in front of this is a low table with the day's newspapers, including the communist *Morning Star*, all of which are so neatly folded I am

---

[70] Abbot of Ampleforth 1963 to 1976, archbishop of Westminster 1976 to 1999. Cardinal 1978.

sure none of them has been read. At the other end of the room, a marble fireplace, a sofa and two easy chairs. Above the fireplace, a Lowry painting.

Wilson looks tired (he has already resigned and is due to leave office shortly), but once his conversation gathers momentum, he becomes animated. He gives me a sherry but does not drink himself. How shall I describe what was, in fact, a monologue that lasted for an hour? Marcia Williams' sons are never mentioned. He talks about his own schooldays and the fact that the headmaster encouraged him to leave early because he had nothing more to achieve and was becoming restless. He was at school when Asquith died and remembers the guest speaker on Prize Day saying, 'Who knows, in this hall may be a future prime minister.' 'And there was I,' Wilson says, 'thinking you silly old fool for saying that.'

He talks, too, about his time at Oxford where he read PPE, though he gives the impression that he wishes he had read history. He says his favourite reading still is military history, the Peninsula War, the English Civil War. He even claims to have won the February 1974 election by using the same tactics that Cromwell used at Marston Moor. Just as one of Cromwell's generals held Prince Rupert's charge successfully, leaving other forces free to attack the Royalists at different points, so Wilson got Callaghan to hold Heath's single-issue campaign – 'Who governs Britain?' – while Wilson and others attacked the Tories on other domestic issues.

His monologue then switches to the fate of Jeremy Thorpe[71].

---

[71] MP for Devon North 1959 to 1979, leader of the Liberal Party 1967 to 1976.

He says the South African secret service was involved in bringing Thorpe down and he is scathing about those Liberals who failed to support Thorpe in his hour of need. He describes Cyril Smith, the Liberal chief whip, as 'that fat slob'. Making a rare contribution to the conversation, I confess that I am lunching at the South African embassy tomorrow, at which Wilson warns me that everything I say at lunch will be recorded.

Wilson now returns to his first love – history. He expounds at length on two of his pet theories: that King Arthur is buried in the Scilly Isles and that the 'W.H.' of Shakespeare's sonnets is William Hawtrey, who built Chequers. I think he must be pulling my leg but no, he gives me detailed evidence, even at one point quoting a passage from Maitland's *Constitutional History of England* word for word. Does he have a photographic memory?

All this time I await some indication as to the purpose of my visit but I am given none. An hour of his time and the rambling but intriguing monologue are presumably his way of saying thank you. Marcia Williams joins us. Champagne is served, a tray diverted from the reception for workers from Transport House that has already started in the room next door. Wilson stands up, holds out his hand and says goodbye. George Weidenfeld drives me back to Dean's Yard. A curious episode.

Tuesday 30 March
Lunch at the South African embassy. The ambassador is a thick-set man who talks about rugby and mutters something about South African boys at Westminster, but the only South African boys I can think of are the sons of Progressive Party supporters such as Randolph Vigne's son who joined the school last term, and I doubt whether the ambassador

has invited me on the strength of that.

Marcia Williams told me that Harold Wilson would like a copy of my book *Conscience and Politics*. I expect it is her idea but I sign a copy and take it round to Downing Street. As it happens, Neville Walton[72], a former Westminster scholar who is also a family friend, is visiting so I persuade him to come with me. Security at Downing Street is casual. Neville and I are shown into Marcia Williams' office, where after a few minutes chat, Harold Wilson appears smoking a cigar. He does not seem at all surprised to see Neville there and launches into one of his monologues about Oxford, how he was once offered a college post by H.A.L. Fisher, the warden of New College, and how, much more recently, the announcement of his resignation prompted two Oxford colleges to ask if he was interested in becoming master of the college. 'But I do not fancy that life,' he concludes. He thanks me for the book and disappears.

Election Term 1976

Thursday 29 April
To Winchester for an unpublicised meeting of eight major public schools: Eton, Winchester, Westminster, Harrow, Rugby, Charterhouse, Shrewsbury and Marlborough. We dine in the warden's lodgings and before and after dinner we talk about the

---

[72] Queen's Scholar and president of the Elizabethan Club. Died in 2006.

threats to the future of our schools at a time of rising fees, falling numbers and political hostility. We agree that whatever happens, we eight will act in concert. The unspoken agenda is that our schools must survive even if other independent schools go to the wall.

Wednesday 12 May

It is the captain's birthday and I join Marcus and his fellow monitors for a champagne breakfast in Yard. This is followed by a badly handled hymn practice up school. Jonathan Katz[73], so admirable a schoolmaster in every other way, seems to lose his head. He starts calling out senior housemasters by name, saying that he cannot hear them singing, and then, to the boys' delight, he tells the housemasters and house tutors to sing the next verse on their own. It is no good stopping him as it would only under-line his error of judgement, but after 20 minutes I walk forward to indicate the practice is over and say a prayer to sober things down.

Monday 17 May

Spend much of the day interviewing Upper Shell boys about their A level choices. At noon, Stuart Hampshire[74] comes to talk to the John Locke Society on 'Freud and Physics'; he is lucid and charming. This afternoon, I see three senior boys who have completed a research project on drug treatment centres in London and I am impressed by the report they have written. Then to evensong in the Abbey at which there is an address to remem-

---

[73] Joined Westminster staff in 1975; master of Queen's Scholars 1987.

[74] Warden of Wadham College, Oxford.

ber our Jesuit friend Tom Corbishley. Tom often walked over from Farm Street and looked in for tea or a drink. In his final illness, he was sent to a home for the dying which he called 'the knacker's yard'. He is still very much alive in my imagination.

Wednesday 19 May
After Abbey, I see the housemaster of Grant's and his two school monitors. A 16-year-old in the house has been causing endless trouble and I shall have to rusticate him for two weeks. The housemaster agrees, the monitors do not. I arrange to see father later today.

Spend the morning interviewing Challenge candidates.

This afternoon, Christopher Martin, the master in charge of our Local Community Unit, has organised a 'mediaeval fayre' to raise money for various social service projects. He has asked me to open the Fayre in the guise of Richard the Lionheart riding a horse. I wear stage armour, the cross of St. George and a tin helmet. I have never sat on a horse before but Christopher assures me that all will be well because this is a police horse and comes with a handler. All does go well until we reach the centre of the green in Dean's Yard, where some coloured streamers suddenly blow in the wind. The horse rears up and I am thrown backwards onto the ground. Bruised but with nothing broken, I mount again with help but the horse is still frightened and rears again. Can this really be a police horse? This time I hang on to the horse's neck, but the handler advises me to dismount. I open the fayre on foot by cutting a ribbon with my sword. The frisky horse is led away by its handler and the fayre begins.

At 5pm, I leave to see the father of the 16-year-old I rusticated this morning. It is an awkward interview with fayre noises in the background and my bruises beginning to hurt. This evening, a not unfamiliar footnote to the fayre. Some boys and girls have won wine on the tombola and have retired to a boarding house annex in Barton Street to drink it. The housemaster reports – with satisfaction? – that among those caught are a school monitor and one of our daughters who is in the school.

Monday 24 May
I am the guest at a dinner party at George Weidenfeld's on Chelsea Embankment. The guests I identified include Harold Wilson, Marcia Williams, the novelist Edna O'Brien, Jimmy Goldsmith, John Vaizey, Lew Grade, Marcus Sieff, the Duke of Devonshire, along with assorted wives and mistresses. I gather from Marcia that Harold Wilson is expected to make a speech congratulating those on his resignation honours list to the accompaniment of champagne, but this never happens. John Vaizey, who is expecting an honour, is on tenter hooks because the list has been altered so often and no one knows whether the honour he has been promised will in fact materialise. It is a bizarre and fascinating evening at which I am an observer from a different world.

Tuesday 25 May
Teach this morning and then to Vincent Square. The sunshine, the boys of all ages in the nets, the masters coaching – all this is a breath of fresh air after last night's party. At 5.30pm, I see a Marlborough boy aged 15 who ran away from school to Paris and now tells me he would like to be a day boy at Westminster. I will get others to interview him but I doubt whether he is up to it academically. This evening, to one of our principal feeder

prep schools to take part in a panel discussion on co-education arranged by the parent teacher association.

Wednesday 26 May

Join governors to interview candidates for the headmastership of our Under School. One candidate, Dicke Dawe[75] from Christ's Hospital, stands out and will surely be chosen. We have known each other from Cambridge days. Another candidate is from Gresham's School and has a reference from his headmaster, Logie Bruce Lockhart. Logie has always been critical of my style of headmastering, and sure enough, in the reference this phrase occurs: 'his modesty makes him less full of that vulgar bounce and salesmanship which distinguishes some of my more successful colleagues.' Well, well, am I that bad?

This evening, a successful school concert. I have made the occasion more formal than in the past – headmaster in red cassock, school monitors with pink carnations in button-holes, the school song to end proceedings. At the end, I say a few words of thank you and farewell to the director of music whose last concert this is.

Tuesday 8 June

Four hours interviewing entrance exam candidates this afternoon. Time for a bath and change before going to Theo Zinn's production of Plautus's *Asinaria* in Yard. I don't understand a word but it is excellently done and those who do understand tell me it is the best Latin play for years. Westminster's Latin play has

---

[75] Appointed headmaster of Westminster Under School 1977.

been produced every year since the 16th century with very few gaps, one of which was during the war, the Civil War that is.

Sunday 13 June

Attend the civic service in the Abbey. Colourful ritual of church and state. Basil Hume, now a cardinal, preaches for eight minutes, a model of how it should be done, and quotes the Rule of St. Benedict on the role of authority: 'the abbot should study rather to profit his brothers than to Lord it over them.' There is a reception up school afterwards. As the procession of clergy and councillors passes through Yard, a Westminster boy who is sitting reading in the sun looks up briefly but not much interested. I notice the book he is reading is *A Short History of the Papacy in the Middle Ages.*

Saturday 19 June

Jeremy Liesner is sent to me by Jim Cogan for fooling around with others late at night in College. It is a typical hot-weather story – 'they poured water over me, so I poured wine over their beds, so they poured floor polish over my head'. 'Go away, Jeremy, and grow up.'

Friday 2 July

A party this evening for the director of music who is leaving. As the light fades and we listen to the music scholars playing, the occasion takes on a romantic flavour, but when the director replies to the toast, he cannot resist referring to 'headmasters playing God.' I can't blame him. I have effectively forced him to resign.

Tuesday 6 July

Gregory Wilsdon, the scholar with Cossack ancestors, comes to question my decision to rusticate a scholar who brought six bottles of champagne into College to celebrate the end of A level. Gregory is clever and tenacious and whatever I say, he will not leave the subject alone, so that eventually I have to push him out as there is other work to be done.

Friday 9 July

Election Day and the end of the school year once again. All goes well until the guests are assembled for the Election Dinner. The archbishops of Canterbury and Westminster, Coggan and Hume, and other VIPs are drinking sherry in our drawing room, when Jim Cogan appears looking solemn. He whispers that the caterer's van bringing all the food for the dinner has broken down en route and there is no chance of the dinner going ahead. I go down to College Hall and find the bursar sitting on a bench with his head in his hands. He doesn't know what to do. Jim suggests taking the VIPs to local restaurants; Denis Moylan[76], a senior master, says we should take them to our clubs for dinner, as if we were all members of clubs in St. James's. Someone else suggests buying 150 Chinese 'takeaways'. I decide to gamble: serve more sherry and hope the caterer's van arrives. It is a nightmare situation but it has a pleasing element of farce.

The gamble pays off. The van arrives and the dinner starts half an hour late. And when it does, it goes really well. Perhaps the extra half-hour's sherry has created a stronger than usual feeling of bonhomie.

---

[76] Classics master 1951 to 1983.

1976-1977
Play Term 1976

Monday 6 September

A week before term starts, Colin Harris, the head of physics, comes in for a talk. He says he is concerned about bad manners, poor discipline and low morale among A level candidates last term and he somehow manages to link this to the disappointing A level results in the physics department. When I put it to him that the physics teaching may also be to blame, he looks surprised.

Tuesday 7 September

A young master asks whether he may be excused the first few days of term. His wife has given birth to a child with Down's and they are shattered. I say of course he may be excused, but I am not sure whether it is right to add that they have my sympathy. Is sympathy the right thing to express in these circumstances?

Tuesday 14 September

The first full day of term is as usual something of a speaking marathon for me and a listening marathon for the boys and girls. Reading school lists, making announcements, preaching in

Abbey. Roger Young, the chairman of the Headmasters' Conference, looks in this afternoon to ask whether I would be prepared to be chairman next year, and I say yes.

Monday 20 September

Cardinal Basil Hume comes to the John Locke Society; he prefers to answer questions than to give a talk. His modesty, sincerity and thoughtfulness make a profound impression on the boys and girls. After lunch, Charles Keeley, an ex-housemaster who is a Roman Catholic and a mediaeval historian, comes to meet the cardinal in our drawing room. He falls onto one knee to kiss the cardinal's ring, his knee hitting the floor with a bang that must have shaken the common room ceiling below. Alas, the cardinal is not wearing his ring and Charles scrambles to his feet with as much dignity as he can manage. But Basil Hume swiftly puts him at his ease.

Michael Duane attends the housemasters' meeting this evening. Michael was the controversial head teacher of Rising Hill School, a state school that attracted hostile publicity for its radical approach. We met a year or two back and I have asked him to teach one day a week and be a sort of visiting commentator on our way of doing things.

Wednesday 29 September

Take Michael Duane into lunch in College Hall. He is in good form and describes a discussion he has just had with sixth formers about the role of the headmaster. The familiar accusation that the headmaster is two-faced was raised, and Michael explained why the head can appear to be saying one thing to pupils and another to staff. The truth is that there are times when you know the boys are right but you compromise and appear to be two-faced because you have to support your staff.

Wednesday 6 October
Roger Young telephones to say that the Headmasters' Conference committee have voted for me as chairman in 1977. This good news is followed by a typical headmaster's problem. I have asked a senior housemaster to chair a small working party on improving Westminster's 'work habits'. It is too vague a brief and I should have foreseen that this particular housemaster would take the opportunity to have a crack at me and others in the senior management team. I now receive the working party's draft report which reads: 'From discussion with a number of members of the common room it is evident that there is a lack of confidence in the general control of the school. Our priorities are not clear because they have been blurred by too many changes and experiments in the timetable which has caused frustration and a lack of conviction and professionalism.'

I rewrite that paragraph and send the draft back to the housemaster but I expect a difficult meeting when it is discussed by housemasters and heads of department next week.

Monday 11 October
Rabbi Hugo Gryn[77] talks to the John Locke Society about anti-Semitism. He is so reasonable, humane and articulate that I cannot imagine anyone not agreeing with him. I note that about half

---

[77] Senior Rabbi, West London Synagogue.

his audience is Jewish. This afternoon, the meeting of house-masters and heads of department to discuss the working party's report is easier than I anticipated. The reason is that the report is so sweeping in its criticism that almost everyone in the room feels threatened by it. It is the mistake that Robespierre made. I have little difficulty harnessing the resentment of the majority in favour of a more positive approach to improving Westminster's work habits.

Tuesday 12 October
School communion in Henry VII Chapel this morning; 35 attend. Then a number of routine meetings: with the captain and prin.opp[78] to talk about the prevailing mood among the 'student body'; with Willie Booth, the chaplain, to talk about any pastoral concerns he wants to share with me. This evening, to a play written and produced by a 16-year-old, Harry Chapman. It is about Scott of the Antarctic and is called 'The Last Expedition.' It is so professional and sophisticated, I feel sure that Harry, who will go to Cambridge next year, will make his mark in the theatre. I write to congratulate him.

Tuesday 19 October
Prime Minister Callaghan's speech in Oxford yesterday seems to open the way for the public schools to take part in what is now being called the great debate on education. For far too long we have been on the defensive, afraid of creating enemies by

---

[78] Abbreviation of 'princeps oppidanorum' or the head of the town boys. In practice, if it was used at all, 'prin opp' referred to the deputy head of school.

expressing an opinion on any educational topic. Eton Group headmasters meet at Westminster this evening and discussion turns to the problem of elderly governors who will not resign. Peter Pilkington of King's Canterbury caps all our horror stories. One of his ancient governors had been a civil servant in what was then the War Office. Peter asked him which of the secretaries of state for war he had known and admired most and the man replied, 'Haldane'. Haldane was secretary of state for war before the First World War.

Thursday 21 October
This evening, I see the school monitor who was caught drinking and tell him he cannot remain a school monitor. It is a sad occasion but this is not the first offence and we have both seen this moment coming. My judgement was wrong, no doubt, in appointing him.

Friday 22 October
Rain again. We have had too many dark, damp mornings which seem to have an effect on the common room's morale. Masters see problems where there are none and discern unwelcome trends without any evidence. Lunch at Drummonds, the school's bankers, and then to Cambridge to dine at Emmanuel and put in a good word for our applicants to the college. Before I go, I drop a note to Richard Woollett, the housemaster of Busby's. He has written me a rather emotional letter about the school monitor in his house that I have just demoted. Richard runs a freer, less hierarchical house than the other housemasters, which makes him feel vulnerable to the sniping of more senior colleagues, and the demotion of a school

monitor will, he fears, be seized on by his critics. I reassure him of my confidence in him but take the opportunity to tell him that 'less hierarchy' must not mean less respect for school regulations.

Wednesday 27 October

At 5.30pm, a stranger comes to ask me to take back into the school a boy whose father owes us a year's fees. The stranger, whose standing in this matter is not revealed, is a smooth, unpleasant man who manages to convey the impression that private schools in general and Westminster in particular come out of this affair with little credit. I am sorry for the boy but we cannot allow him to come back unless father is prepared to pay.

Thursday 11 November

This morning I see the mother of a boy who failed our entrance exam and wants a second chance. Mother says that the boy was badly upset by tensions in the home and that he saw her husband throw her down the stairs, breaking two of her ribs. I agree to let the boy take the exam again in the summer.

Saturday 27 November

Out of the blue, parents have asked to see me and to bring their seven year-old son who is said to have an IQ of 160. They live in the East End and could never afford Westminster's fees. I like the parents and the boy, who is certainly very impressive in that he handles abstract concepts with calm, unprecocious confidence. I promise to see whether our Under School could take him though he would have to live with a family as the journey from east London would be too difficult. But what about fees?

Monday 6 December

I see the editor of a house magazine which has made an attack on falling academic standards at Westminster, implying that my policies are to blame. He is an intelligent, floppy boy who says that some of his teachers are uninspiring. We talk for a long time. I tell him that by any measure such as exam results the academic standards have risen in recent years but I know he is right about one or two of his teachers. This afternoon, parents of a boy coming next term. One of their questions about the school is this: 'On our last visit we saw a notice on a house board with "No Jews" written across it. Is this common?' I say it is not at all common but what harm one piece of graffiti can do.

Tuesday 7 December

John Thorn of Winchester comes for a talk about his role as chairman of the Headmasters' Conference's political and public relations sub-committee. We are agreed that the central aim of independent schools over the next five years must be to shed our defensive, almost apologetic stance and fight our way back into the mainstream of the education debate.

Wednesday 8 December

Fifteen-year-old Francis Fitzgibbon comes to see me. He wants to change house. He says his age group in his present house are philistine, smoking in private study periods and so on. He asks whether he can be a day boy attached to College where all his friends are. I am sympathetic but cautious. If I allow him to change house, who will follow?

Friday 17 December

The last day of term. Snow on the roofs that quickly melts and then it rains all day. Good Oxbridge results continue to come in. We have 28 awards, equal to the best ever and easily the best in my time at Westminster. What a slap in the eye for the pessimists who have been moaning about falling standards. Marcus Alexander has an open scholarship in classics at Christ Church. He has been captain of the school for two years, a feat that is unlikely to be repeated. His contemporaries in College say he only works at night when everyone else has gone to bed. He has been an outstanding captain and I pay tribute to him at assembly and then again when monitors come in for a farewell drink. Gregory Wilsdon, too, has an open scholarship in classics at Oxford, but as he is still only 16, he will stay on until the summer. The carol service in St. Margaret's is better than for many years largely because Stewart Murray has at my request organised it efficiently, to the dismay of the laissez-faire brigade in the common room who think that efficient organisation is 'unWestminster'.

Monday 20 December

As the incoming chairman, I lead a small delegation to the Department of Education to discuss with officials how the Headmasters' Conference can contribute to the Great Debate. An under-secretary chairs the meeting and while he is friendly' he is also sceptical about the Great Debate achieving anything very much. But we have made our point. Lunch with David Carey. As a governor and a former Westminster boy, he cannot forget what it was like in his day. He seems to be obsessed with the idea that the audience should stand up immediately the headmaster appears at the school concert or Latin play. He says that when his headmaster, the Reverend Harold Costley-White, entered the hall for the Latin play, the audience stood and the orchestra played 'Hail the conquering hero comes'.

Lent Term 1977

Tuesday 18 January

Willie Booth, the chaplain, preaches well at the first Abbey service of term and I tell him so. I see the new boys at 10am and talk to them about Westminster. At 12.30, the governing body's statutes committee in my study. It is an intolerable meeting with Sir Reginald Sharpe and Sir Henry Chisholm squabbling like children about footnotes and punctuation. Sir Reginald then questions whether the governing body would approve of my membership of the Cathedral Choir School's governing body because the headmaster of Westminster should not be associated with the Roman Catholic Church. Irritated, I say it would make no difference whether governors approved or not and Gordon Pirie, one of our sane governors, says 'Hear, hear' so forcefully, Sir Reginald is silenced.

Thursday 20 January

I see a group of boys caught in a pub and gate them for a week. One of their mothers comes to see me to say how difficult it is for her; she is a widow and he is her only son. Later, I am told that the girl I propose to appoint as a school monitor, Emily Reid, has been in tears because two boys in her house say they will refuse to talk to her if she accepts the post.

Sunday 23 January
Jim Cogan reports that the scholar I gated for being in a pub, and whose widowed mother came to see me, has now been caught with a girl in his room in College. The girl is from outside the school. I shall have to send the boy home for a spell and I telephone his widowed mother to tell her.

Thursday 27 January
About £40 has been stolen from coats and lockers in one of the day houses. Suspicion points to two 14-year-olds on the ground of conversations overheard. They have been questioned by the housemaster and deny being involved. The housemaster feels every offence committed by a member of his house as a personal blow and is depressed about what has happened. Parents of both boys come to see me and resent their sons being accused on flimsy evidence. I understand their concern but tell them this offence is so serious I am going to ask the police for help

Sunday 30 January
Write an article on the great debate on education for the *Times* and deliver it to William Rees-Mogg's house in Smith Square. Some headmasters do not like me writing so much in the papers but it is one sure way that an independent school's voice can be heard.

Saturday 5 February
A fine, Spring-like day. I take morning Abbey and then see the parents of a 14-year-old who wants to leave Eton and come to

Westminster. Then a possible classics master; he has a double first but is so diffident I fear Westminster boys would eat him alive.

Monday 7 February
At Latin prayers I see two boys giggling rather obviously under my eye. I stop the prayers before the pater noster, send the two boys out, then say 'pater noster' and prayers continue. After prayers, I telephone the secretary of the Independent Schools Joint Council to tell him that boys' schools cannot accept the proposed circular on 'Girls in Boys' Sixth Forms' which is a one-sided document written to pacify angry headmistresses. Ivor Mills, professor of medicine at Cambridge, talks to the John Locke Society about 'coping with sexuality in the modern age'. He is clear, factual and fluent and when he asks for questions, the girls are much keener to ask than the boys.

Thursday 10 February
Oxford has invited our 1st VIII to act as pacemakers for the blue boat. I think it is a good idea; the master in charge of rowing, who was at the London School of Economics, dislikes the idea. I overrule him. After lunch, a session with Denny Brock, the senior master, at his request. It is a pleasant and moving talk about his own future. He says he is thinking of retiring a year or two early to live in his house in Scotland. I say how much I value him and appreciate all that he does. He is such a mature and balanced schoolmaster and for that reason such a good influence in the common room that I do not want to see him go. House-masters meet at 6pm and have a constructive and thoughtful talk about stealing. Despite police involvement, we are no nearer to

solving the theft of money from the day boy house.

Monday 14 February

Isaiah Berlin talks to the John Locke Society about 'The Russian obsession with patterns in history'. It is a wonderful talk lifting the spirit by its humanity, range and sheer intellectual brilliance. He draws a crowded meeting and holds them for 50 minutes non-stop. Over lunch in College Hall, scholars do their best to quiz him and it is good to hear them. To put boys and girls in touch with a great mind and to give them the opportunity to test their fledgling intellect on his is an essential part of learning, but in how many schools, in how many universities, for that matter, is this possible?

Peter Newsam, the chief education officer of the Inner London Education Authority, comes round from County Hall for a talk. We have met once or twice at those discussions about getting more able boys and girls to do engineering. We mull over the possibility of persuading the government to set up an English version of the Massachusetts Institute of Technology.

Tuesday 15 February

After Latin prayers (in which there is a faint odour of a stink bomb, a throw-back to former days of Billy Bunter and *Just William* when boys' protests had no political overtones), I interview candidates for the Adrian Boult Music Scholarship. There is one obviously outstanding musician called Charles Sewart[79], and he interviews well too.

---

[79] We awarded him a music scholarship. Now a concert violinist and a member of York University's resident string quartet.

This afternoon, I walk over to the club to attend the London Division meeting of the HMC and find some members sniping at my article in the *Times*. Should the chairman of the HMC publish views that are not HMC policy and so on? It is the old resentment of my being in the public eye and I do not take it seriously. I do enjoy having articles published and it gives me a position as a commentator on education for which the independent schools should be grateful.

This evening, Michael Duane comes to dinner and then talks to the common room about progressive education. There is a poor turn-out which annoys me. How dull they are at times. They may not like progressive education, but this is too lazy a way of showing it.

Monday 21 February

Spend much of the day interviewing this term's new boys. It is good to start getting to know them but they do seem rather solemn as though worried at the age of 13 about their pension. Perhaps it is a sign of the times. Later this afternoon, I see a mother and son. The story is this: Boy is a loner with no friends, a flautist in a philistine house. He complains of being victimised by a group of his contemporaries and fears it might turn to physical violence. Mother is sensible but rather overpowering. Boy appears neurotic, almost paranoid, just the sort of personality unfortunately that attracts aggression from other boys. I suspect his fears are exaggerated but I will ask the housemaster and the head of house to see that no harm comes to him.

Saturday 26 February

See the parents of the two young boys who have been

interviewed by police about the thefts of money in the day boy house. Parents insisted that a solicitor should be present and this meant that the interviews were more formal and that the police were less friendly. So now parents have come to complain about the police methods. The truth is that for the first time, Westminster boys have been exposed to a full blast of the tough London cop and the parents don't like it. But the problem of who stole the money is still not solved.

Tuesday 1 March
St. David's Day – daffodils in buttonholes at Latin prayers. I see the police sergeant who has been in charge of the enquiries into the thefts of money and he tells me that the police can find no case against the two boys they interviewed; and that means the case will be dropped. Are the boys innocent or just tougher than the adults realise?

This evening, a meeting of the HMC's political and public relations sub-committee. A frank exchange about the tensions under the surface of the independent sector: between boys' schools and girls' schools; between day schools and boarding schools; and between the so-called 'minor public schools'; which are short of pupils, and the so-called 'great schools' such as Eton, Winchester and Westminster, which are doing alright, thank you.

Saturday 5 March/Sunday 6 March
To Uppingham, an old-style public school. The headmaster, Coll Macdonald, meets me at Kettering Station. He was the runner-up when I was appointed headmaster of Westminster but we do not mention this. I do not warm to him (or to me, I guess) but it is a pleasant enough weekend. On Sunday, I preach at the

compulsory morning service. I have two sermons, one in each side pocket of my jacket, and I make a last-minute decision on which to give when I get the feel of the congregation. How strange these country boarding schools seem to me now, and how very different from Westminster in their style and flavour.

Tuesday 22 March
A long and difficult session with a barrister parent who believes his son is being victimised by his housemaster. He comes with a wad of notes and talks to me as though I am the jury, flicking over each page of notes with a flourish that seems to say, 'there is even better evidence to come'. But his case is thin. The boy is rather a shifty character with some proven dishonesties to his name and the housemaster, not unnaturally, does not trust him completely. After an hour of this courtroom procedure, I escape to meet some prospective parents.

This evening, Father Harry Williams gives the second of his Lent talks. He is from the Community of the Resurrection at Mirfield and is spending three days in the school, giving Lent talks, visiting houses, joining classes and so on. This evening, he takes the modern theological line (not quite God is dead but getting on that way) with clarity and sensitivity, and I can see that some of the more traditional Christian boys are unhappy. In discussion, one of these boys, Christopher Loveless[80], argues angrily with Harry and eventually storms out in disgust.

Thursday 31 March
I go with an independent schools deputation to see Shirley

---

[80] Ordained priest 1991 and curate at Willingdon, Sussex.

Williams, the Secretary of State, to ask her to compromise on her proposal to end the department's inspection of independent schools. She agrees that the inspectors should work with independent schools to set up a separate inspectorate, organised by the schools and assessed by her department. That is a satisfactory outcome but the girls' schools will not like it because it will cost them money. Shirley Williams is professional and courteous.

Saturday 9 April
Rise early to catch a train to Eastbourne for the annual conference of the National Union of Teachers. The chairman of the HMC is always asked but seldom goes. I sit on the platform as one of the 'fraternal delegates' and when I am introduced to the audience, the boos are louder than the perfunctory applause. I talk to Ashley Bramall, who is currently leader of the Inner London Education Authority. He was at Westminster between the wars. I have written an article in the *Times Educational Supplement* suggesting the creation of an elite sixth form college in central London, based on Westminster and called – just to be provocative – 'Cromwell College'. Bramall says it has taken so long to get the comprehensive schools going that any further change of direction would be disruptive. Lunch in a pub with Peter Newsam of ILEA and discuss the problems of education in London. He says the priority is to raise the expectations that teachers and parents have of the 11-16 age group and then there will be time to think about an elite sixth-form college. I tell him that in two or three years I might want to move and that I would be interested in working for ILEA.

Election Term 1977

Tuesday 3 May

A housemaster reports that a 15-year-old has brought a bottle of valium tablets to the house and given another boy three on a 'close your eyes and open your mouth' basis. I do not have time to deal with this as I must attend a press conference at which the annual statistics for independent schools are published. Overall numbers in independent schools have risen but the press do not notice that this is because schools have filled empty beds with pupils from the Far East and seem determined to write about a 'public school boom'. Back to Westminster to see the parents of the boy who was playing fast and loose with valium. Father is another of those barristers who addresses me as a jury, inviting me to consider this point and that, but we get nowhere. Neither parents nor I are sure how to respond to this behaviour. I say they should take the boy home for a day or two.

This evening, some members of the cricket XI look in after supper to tell me how they got on in their match against Bradfield, and when they have gone, Gregory Wilsdon arrives at my door. With his Oxford scholarship won and time on his hands, he is producing Oscar Wilde's play *Salome*. He wants to know whether the girl who is to play Salome may end her dance naked. I say no. Being Gregory, he does not take no for an answer. Do I realise that the dance is supposed to be erotic? His intellectual analysis of the importance of nudity to the play sounds strange coming from this rather introvert classical scholar, but I decline to change my mind. I must protect the girl and I know all too well how my critics in the common room would react if I allowed the dance to go ahead as Gregory wishes.

Thursday 5 May

Harold Wilson comes to dinner and to talk afterwards to some 40 boys and girls in our drawing room. It is obvious he loves talking to the young about famous people he has known and they are quick to grasp how to feed him cues. At half past ten and with a brandy and cigar, he is still telling them how Malenkov ordered the murder of Beria, the head of the Soviet secret police.

Thursday 26 May

I see a group of boys accused of bullying. They protest the whole affair has been exaggerated and they were only 'fooling around'. I warn them off. This afternoon, a long meeting to choose 10 Queen's Scholars on the basis of Challenge marks, prep-school headmasters' reports and interviews. After the meeting, Jim Cogan tells me that it is just as well I persuaded the governing body to agree that scholars no longer needed to profess the Christian faith and hold British nationality. If I had not done so, only three of this year's Queen's Scholars could have entered College.

Monday 13 June

Much of the day spent worrying about the budget for the next school year. The registrar, the accountant, the under master and I go over the figures to be presented to the governors later this month, and to our dismay, it appears that if we add to our various heads of expenditure the anticipated percentage for inflation, we shall have a day fee of £1,500 a year. We know that our two principal competitors for day pupils, St. Paul's and Dulwich, are expected to have a day fee next year of about £1,000. We shall be at a great disadvantage in attracting parents. Masters' salaries are the largest single item of expenditure; and we have too many masters at the top of the salary scale and there is nothing we can do about that.

Thursday 23 June

Theo Zinn, the head of classics, comes for his termly agonising about the future of his subject. He wants my help to ensure that enough scholars choose to do Latin and Greek at A level. Will I have a word with this and that young scholar or with the parents? No, I will not. Talk to the common room in break about a 14-year-old who was sent home from Expeditions weekend for foul language and bad behaviour. It now turns out that he has for many weeks been a disruptive influence in one of the new boy forms. What angers me is that no one appears to have dealt firmly with him and yet members of the common room are now saying that he ought to change schools. That is all very well, but how much is his bad behaviour a reflection of the licence he has been given?

Lunch at Brooks's, with a parent whose son is taking A level. He is a QC and his approach to his son's education is that contacts matter as well as qualifications. He tells me that he made a useful contact with the senior tutor of Pembroke College, Oxford when they were both guests of a merchant banker at Newmarket racecourse, and arranged for his son to visit the college. He now wants to make sure that I will be contacting the senior tutor on his son's behalf. So his son's future is planned between races at Newmarket and over lunch at Brooks's.

Monday 27 June

Parents this morning of the foul-mouthed 14-year-old who was sent home from Expeditions. They are an unhappy couple, long divorced but united in their desire to put the blame for their son's behaviour on the school. I say that the boy is now on a final warning. This afternoon, Lady Hailsham comes to give Westminster the 'once-over' on behalf of her daughter who is at Roedean. Girl wants to come to Westminster, mother want her to stay at Roedean. 'What a pity Eton doesn't take girls,' mother says.

Saturday 2 July

Before Abbey, a housemaster greets me with this story. He was rung up in the early hours by Wood Street Police Station in the City. Fourteen Westminster boys, all aged 15, had been arrested for disturbing neighbours at a party to celebrate the end of O levels. Parents – I am delighted to hear – were summoned at 3am to collect their sons. I am happy to leave this one to parents and the police.

Friday 8 July

The end of the Election Term. I have asked Justin Byam Shaw[81] to be captain of the school next term and he has accepted. I say goodbye to leavers one by one in my study. Even the most roguish and disaffected figures appear, and I can sense their ambivalence, keen to leave but a little uncertain of the future. I am moved by the long line who wait patiently on the stairs to bring their schooldays to an end. At the final assembly, I make an

---

[81] Christ Church, Oxford. Founder and managing director of Legion Telecom.

unfortunate mistake. Saying goodbye and thank you to Ted Craven who has been on the staff for 31 years, I forget to mention the high point of his career as housemaster of Ashburnham. As he was a bad housemaster and I eased him out of office, my omission is misinterpreted and I have to move quickly after assembly to apologise to Ted and quash murmurings among his friends in the common room.

An enjoyable Election Dinner in College Hall and drinks after in Ashburnham Garden, where senior boys and girls and scholars mingle with the guests. By 1am, the last guests have gone and Jim Cogan and I sweep the scholars off to bed.

1977-1978
Play Term 1977

Tuesday 6 September

The school is larger than ever – 547 at the last count – so that as I walk into the beginning of term assembly, the aisle is so narrow I brush against elbows as I pass. Justin Byam Shaw looks in to talk about his role as captain, about possible new school monitors and about his own application to Christ Church. His great uncle had a distinguished career at the college as an art historian.

Wednesday 21 September

The annual general meeting of the Headmasters' Conference begins in Oxford today. I have written my chairman's address and it has been circulated to the education correspondents. It is deliberately controversial because I want the independent schools to be seen to be contributing to the Great Debate on education. Two recommendations for educational reform will, I know, not have the support of other headmasters. One is that we should end early specialisation in the sixth form and make all pupils follow a broader curriculum, and the other is that the government which funds education has the right to insist that certain subjects are taught in all schools. For good measure, I have also suggested that by opening their sixth forms to girls, the boys' schools are increasing equal opportunity.

Daphne and I drive to Oxford. The conference is based in St. Edmund Hall, a modest college where Revd. John Kelly[82] is the principal. I give my address to members and guests in the Gulbenkian Theatre at 5pm. The reaction afterwards is as I expected – gratitude that the chairman did not take a bland or conventional line, strong disagreement with some of my arguments, enjoyment at being provoked. I am pleased the address has had the effect I wanted but I know the long-term reaction among headmasters and headmistresses will be more hostile.

Thursday 22 September
Harry Judge, who runs the Education Department in the university, speaks well to the conference this morning. This evening, the annual service is held in New College Chapel. I have asked Cardinal Hume to preach and am once again delighted with the simplicity and sincerity of what he says. Returning to St. Edmund Hall to change for the annual dinner, I am handed a note by the porter. It is a message from my father to say that my mother died this morning. She had had two strokes and was in hospital, unaware of the world most of the time. If she had lived on, her life and my father's would have contained little joy. But she was my mother and she is dead. I feel sad and disorientated. Though I had seen her all too seldom in recent years, that is less important than the knowledge that she brought me into the

---

[82] Principal of St Edmund Hall, Oxford, 1951 to 1979.

world, nursed me and helped me grow. How little did I ever express my gratitude to her; and now it is too late and I express it to my journal. I hope she sleeps in peace.

Henry Chadwick, the dean of Christ Church, and Roger Young[83], last year's chairman, speak at the annual dinner. At the top table, I sit next to John Kelly. Under the table, Kelly keeps putting his hand on my knee. Every time I gently but firmly move it off, after a few minutes it returns. It is a relief to be able to stand up, thank the speakers and declare the evening at an end.

Saturday 24 September

The dean admits the new Queen's Scholars to the foundation at Abbey this morning. Teach the Oxbridge historians and then try to catch up with work I have left undone during the conference in Oxford. Fives with colleagues this afternoon. This morning's *Daily Telegraph* has a leader critical of my suggestion that there should be any central control of the curriculum and the *Times* has a letter from the headmistress of an independent girls' school accusing me of male chauvinism. It is a good letter, claiming correctly that some boys' schools are admitting girls because they are short of boys. But it is also true that some girls want to leave because they are seeking, not boys, but a higher calibre of teaching at A level. With a few exceptions, a weak sixth form is the girls' schools Achilles' heel.

Tuesday 27 September

The fall-out from my address in Oxford continues. The *Daily Mail*

[83] Sir Roger Young, principal of George Watson's College, Edinburgh, 1958 to 1985. Chairman of the Headmasters' Conference 1976.

carries an extraordinary interview with Miss Manners, the head-mistress of Felixstowe College, in which she accuses headmasters of using 'totally unscrupulous means' to entice girls into their sixth forms. Headmasters' motives are certainly not always altruistic but the idea of public school headmasters enticing unwilling girls into their schools would be a suitable subject for Victorian melodrama and bears no relation to the facts.

Thursday 29 September

A housemaster comes to tell me that he has received an unpleasant, anonymous letter. As this is one of the hazards of a school-master's life, the brief letter is worth quoting:

> 'I hate you and I want you to know that I am not alone in that feeling. Learn how to treat people and maybe there won't be so many people around who hate you. I'd like to cause you as much pain as you have caused others, maybe I'll get the chance one day. With all the hatred I possess from someone who hates you.'

The housemaster says suspicion falls on a 16-year-old he has been having trouble with and he wants me to confirm his suspicion by asking a handwriting expert to see the anonymous letter and an example of the boy's handwriting. I agree to do so. The boy in question is the youngest member of a talented family. Father is at the top of his profession; two older brothers sailed into Oxbridge. This boy is not in that class but is a likeable, slightly oafish youth who would probably have done well in a country boarding school.

Monday 3 October

Max Morris, an ex-communist and former president of the

National Union of Teachers, talks to the John Locke Society and puts the case for the abolition of public schools. He has to face some hostile questions and I reflect that five years ago he would have received a more sympathetic hearing. Westminster, so radical a few years ago, has shifted to the right.

Monday 10 October

The handwriting expert from Scotland Yard says that the anonymous letter was definitely written by the boy the housemaster suspects. I must now decide what to do. While I am contemplating this problem, a boarding-house matron comes to see me. She is very worried about a 13-year-old who joined the school this term. He has accumulated a number of detentions in the first weeks of his first term, he is totally scatterbrained and hopelessly disorganised, yet said to be gifted in maths and mature in his approach to adults. Matron thinks he was badly affected by parents' separation.

Wednesday 12 October

See young scatterbrained. He is nervous at first but then relaxes and is surprisingly adult. When I ask what he is going to do about being so disorganised, he says, 'I am addressing myself to the problem.' There is a hint of mockery in that answer.

See the author of the anonymous letter. I am sorry for him; he is in the wrong school. I rusticate him for a week.

This evening, I wander round College talking to scholars, getting to know the new ones.

Thursday 13 October

I have asked Anne O'Donnell, who has joined the staff this

term, to attend the housemasters' meeting and tell us what she thinks of the way Westminster treats the 30 girls in the sixth form. Politely but firmly she accuses us of doing the girls a disservice because we treat them as special cases. We are, she says, failing to prepare them for the adult world where they will have no special privileges. One or two housemasters are provoked and it is interesting to hear one bachelor becoming heated on the subject. He says he wants to treat girls as special but is told that this is sexism and that he only does so because he thinks he is superior to the girls. Anne O'Donnell handles the discussion well. We clearly have much to learn about the way we treat the girls in our sixth form.

Friday 21 October
A housemaster reports that he has caught two boys stealing. Both are 17 and have had chequered careers at Westminster, including cases of smoking. They have been given many chances. Both lack a father's guidance. In one case, father is dead, in the other, parents are separated, so it is the mothers who have to come and see me. I see the boys and they are tearful. I see the mothers and so are they. There is a sad air of inevitability over the whole affair. I decide to expel them because stealing is a serious offence and comes on top of too many other offences. But I feel guilty all the same because I have brought two school careers to an end.

Tuesday 25 October
Spend all afternoon interviewing candidates who are taking the entrance exam. Last night, I looked through the candidates' papers and was struck by the international flavour. These names caught my eye: Paglierani, Paz-Pena de Vire, Menneer, Lom-

nitz; but when I meet them today they are mostly very English boys from very English prep schools. I also note an increasingly aristocratic flavour which will worry some of my colleagues.

Thursday 27 October

Dine at the Garrick this evening as the guest of the Pooh Trustees. A.A. Milne[84] was a scholar at Westminster between the wars and left the school one quarter of his royalties, currently bringing us about £40,000 a year. I am here to represent the school at this occasional blend of good fare and whimsy. A worn teddy bear is on the centre of the table and in his speech, the chairman of the trustees addresses the bear as 'Pooh'. I sit next to John Lehmann[85], who talks about Virginia Woolf whom he knew well.

Friday 11 November

Speak about the significance of Remembrance Day in morning Abbey, after which I have to referee a confrontation between an angry parent and a housemaster. Both are emotional men and I fear an explosion. The parent starts in a quiet and calm tone that is deceptive. He says he does not want to rake up the past or to mention that the housemaster insulted him and victimised his son. For once the housemaster manages to keep his cool and the meeting ends on a note of rather unconvincing reconciliation.

---

[84] In my time, this was a useful annual bequest but when the royalities were sold outright to Walt Disney in 2000, the one quarter of the royalties was worth something in excess of £40 million. The generosity of one former pupil who hit the jackpot with his whimsical children's stories transformed the school's finances.

[85] Poet, publisher, editor and author.

Thursday 17 November

After Abbey, I see my Oxbridge historians and wish them luck in the exam. Then I talk to all the fifth forms together about subject choices open to them at O level. At lunchtime to Gordon Square for a meeting of HMC's direct grant schools. It is a difficult meeting because I have publicly opposed the Tory Party's proposed Assisted Places Scheme. The scheme would use taxpayers' money to subsidise places at independent day schools. I think that would be a serious mistake, but the heads of day schools strongly object to my making my opposition public when I am chairman of the HMC.

Friday 18 November

See a young master who joined us this term and the head of department. The latter is a very good schoolmaster whose judgement I trust. He thinks the young master hasn't got what it takes to be a success at Westminster and that pupils' chances in this subject are suffering as a result. We talk through all this with the young master but he refuses to accept that there is a problem and is far too confident of his ability to cope.

This evening, I am the guest speaker at the annual dinner of the Otter Swimming Club at the Café Royal. Half the diners are drunk before we sit down and the dinner is a rowdy affair throughout, with bread rolls thrown at the top table. I speak as briefly as I dare, trying to ignore the many interruptions and to avoid the bread rolls. And they say Westminster boys behave badly!

Saturday 26 November

The parents of a 15-year-old scholar come to see me. The story is this: the boy has been acting normally at school but disruptively at home. Two weeks ago, he took another scholar's post office book and withdrew £50. He made no effort to cover up his crime and was swiftly identified by the housemaster. Father is a civil servant, mother is a psychiatrist. Boy has now been at home for 10 days 'sorting things out' and has been seeing a psychiatrist who wants to see the boy on a daily basis for several weeks. Boy says he finds the pressures of life in a community intolerable. I suggest that he should return to school as soon as possible but as a day boy and parents agree that this is worth trying.

I then see a girl who is a candidate for entry to our sixth form in 1978. She is a good classicist. Father is a consultant surgeon and insists on saying in front of his daughter, 'She needs to meet some boys.' Parents!

Tuesday 5 December
I have decided that I cannot confirm the appointment of the young master who is having difficulty coming to terms with Westminster's pupils and this means he will have to leave at the end of term. I ask him to come and see me so that I can give him the news. An understatement to say it is a difficult interview. He does not see how there can be grounds for giving him notice after one term. He thinks his teaching and his rapport with the pupils are improving all the time and he hints that the head of department's criticisms are the result of a clash of personalities, not professional judgement. I am as sympathetic as I can be without budging an inch.

Friday 9 December
Two boys come to complain about my decision to give the young

master notice to leave at the end of term. They say he has excellent rapport with the boys in his classes. Later today, I receive a petition from 30 boys and girls saying that the young master's dismissal is 'unfair' and should be reconsidered. The young master has been rallying support but it will not change my mind.

Tuesday 13 December

Oxbridge results. Justin Byam Shaw is offered a place at Christ Church on the condition that he stays at school for two more terms to improve his classics. If he declines that offer, he will go to Bristol. I advise him to accept Christ Church's offer even though a planned trip to Australia will have to be abandoned, and after much discussion with father, he agrees to stay. Other Oxbridge results suggest a less good year for awards and a very good year for places.

Friday 16 December

The last day of the longest term on record. With depressing inevitability, Christopher Martin comes with a tale of woe. Christopher is a good schoolmaster and a good housemaster but he has an extraordinary knack of bringing me bad news just when I think things are going well. His tale is of Westminster boys who gate-crashed a party last weekend and behaved badly, drinking too much, stubbing cigarettes on the furniture and so on. I am annoyed to hear of such loutish behaviour but I am not inclined to do anything about it on the last day of term.

Lent Term 1978

Monday 23 January

The governing body meets this afternoon and at long last grasps the nettle of the bursar's retirement. The date is set for 31 December. Having lived with the present bursar for nearly eight years (how characteristic of our relationship that his name so seldom comes to mind) and having been frustrated so often by his clumsy handling of human relations, I cannot help feeling relieved that he is going. He will be 70 in December and stayed much too long (masters and the headmaster have to retire at 62). Yet he has good qualities that have kept the bursar's department on a tight rein. If we can find a new bursar who combines managerial skill with the ability to treat members of the common room with tact, the school will benefit enormously.

Saturday 28 January

Young scatterbrained is in trouble again for numerous peccadilloes and I have asked his mother to come and see me. She is sensible and will try to help us keep the boy on a reasonably even course.

Wednesday 8 February

I have called a common room meeting to discuss our policy on the treatment of girls in the sixth form. It is a good discussion. The general view is that we are too lax in insisting that the girls obey the same regulations as the boys and that this causes resentment among the boys and makes the girls feel they are not fully members of the school. One or two bachelors express disapproval of the attitude of the more extrovert girls but as the discussion develops, it appears that what really worries them is that these girls are challenging and changing the relationship that the masters have with the boys.

Friday 10 February

Mary Rose-Richards, a BBC researcher, is spending a week in the school. The BBC has decided to go ahead with a documentary on a public school first proposed nearly four years ago. They have short-listed three schools: Westminster, Bryanston and Marlborough. Much suspicion and envy, I suspect, among the schools not short-listed.

Tuesday 14 February

I hear that a father who has three boys in the school has committed suicide. The housemaster says the boys have not been told the manner of their father's death.

Friday 24 February

The head of modern languages tells me that a girl in his German set claims to have been seduced by a stranger in Oxford last weekend. The story lacks credibility and when the housemaster speaks to the parents, they dismiss the story as a complete fabrication. But why then has the girl made this claim? Is it because the parents' marriage is falling apart and she wishes to shout 'No'?

A different girl then comes to see me about a master who, she alleges, picks on her in class. She is rather emotional about it all, perhaps with reason, but when I ask the master, he complains that she tries to shock him by using four-letter words in class and then is upset if he is sharp with her. If that is the truth, he is right to be so.

Saturday 25 February

Simon Gray[86], who was at Westminster in the fifties, and whose play *Rear Column* has just opened in the West End, is quoted in a newspaper as saying of Westminster, 'it used to be one of the finest schools in the country and is fast becoming a small polytechnic'.

Wednesday 1 March

An interesting case. A 15-year-old scholar has told his parents he wants to leave and go to a comprehensive school. From his first term he has felt an alien in Westminster's affluent elitism and does not want to go on enjoying privilege. He says he finds his contemporaries in College 'rich and spoilt'. Father and great-grandfather were at Westminster; grandmother is a distinguished poet and critic.

Jim Cogan, his housemaster, thinks there is more to it than rejection of privilege, but when I see the boy I am impressed by his single-minded determination to leave. His left-wing convictions, which would have been commonplace in College a few years ago, now isolate him. I have no doubt he will do as he intends and leave at the end of the school year.

Thursday 2 March

At Latin prayers, I appoint two girls as school monitors. After

---

[86] Novelist and playwright. Lecturer, Queen Mary College, London, 1965 to 1985.

prayers, I see a Conservative MP who has two sons in the school. He is divorced and hardly on speaking terms with his former wife or with his elder son. The latter is head of house, a school monitor and an excellent person. He wants to try for Cambridge next term but father says he will not pay another term's fees because his new wife would not stand for it. In that case I will pay the fees out of the Headmaster's Fund. When he hears this, father lights a cigar and tells me how bad 'Margaret' is at communicating with back-benchers.

Saturday 4 March
Interview a girl who wants to join our sixth form. She is clearly very able. She is at St. Paul's Girls' School and the high mistress's report says she is 'very vulnerable and sensitive' but none of this comes through at interview.

Wednesday 8 March
Launcelot Fleming[87] conducts the confirmation service in the Abbey this morning with his usual freshness and sensitivity. A housemaster and his head of house arrive after the service. They suspect a boy in the house is selling cannabis. Housemaster is delighted that the house monitors have reported the matter to him, but the head of house worries about the monitors' position if this leads to expulsion. He says that boys and girls in the house would like to see the seller stopped but monitors don't want to be the ones who 'bring him to court'. How unchanging school-

---

[87] Bishop of Norwich; Dean of Windsor. Launcelot Fleming took our confirmation service every year. I have never known anyone who could talk with such conviction about Christian belief to adolescent boys.

boy morality is. I tell the housemaster to investigate further. This evening, I go round a boarding house with the head of house, Simon Peck, calling in at boys' studies and talking informally. It is too long since I have visited this particular house, and sure enough, over coffee at the end, one of the house monitors tells me bluntly that he thinks I am out of touch and should spend more time getting to know people individually. His name is William Cortazzi.

Wednesday 15 March
Struggling to keep ahead of history essays and various papers that need to be read and responded to. I do not like administration, and marking history essays is one of the least attractive parts of a history teacher's job. This afternoon, a three-hour meeting to select the 31 girls who will come into the sixth form in September. We favour girls of potential and girls from comprehensive schools rather than girls from established independent schools. Colleagues are in good form and take a lot of trouble to get the selection right. To dinner this evening with Justin Byam Shaw's mother and stepfather. One of the other guests has a girl at a country boarding school and says with obvious approval that you can smell the stables from the classroom block.

Friday 17 March
Young scatterbrain's parents who are separated and will shortly divorce come to see me. Father is an Etonian and takes an old-fashioned line. Sorting his adolescent son out is what he sent him to school for. He doesn't approve of parents being called in and lectured by the headmaster.

Thursday 20 April

Lunch with Shirley Williams. Her secretary telephoned on Monday. Just the two of us in a quiet restaurant in Holbein Place. I am not sure what the meeting is for. We spend a pleasant hour or so talking about current educational issues and I emphasise my opposition to the Tories' Assisted Places Scheme. I assume she thinks it is a good idea as Secretary of State to get out of the office from time to time and talk with people actually involved in education. She pays the bill and offers me a lift back to the school in the ministerial car.

Election Term 1978

Tuesday 25 April

The first full day of term. Willie Booth preaches very well in the Abbey service. He has grown in stature and confidence, and I realise how lucky I am to have him as a school chaplain. But the first day also brings an unwelcome problem. Piers Higson-Smith, the new captain of the school, tells me there is a rumour that a boy who left last year is selling cannabis on a fairly large scale and that two boys in the school have bought £100 worth. The names of both these boys are no surprise to me. Both live with mothers, parents being divorced. The former pupil who is said to be the supplier goes to Oxford in October. I set housemasters checking at once but it is a bad way to start the term. This afternoon, walk up to Vincent Square in need of fresh air, green grass and boys engaged in normal, healthy games.

Wednesday 26 April

Talk to the senior officers' course at the National Police College at Bramshill – some 20 officers from the UK and overseas. I would like to ask them about illegal drugs but I talk about education. They are lively and ask sharp questions.

Friday 28 April

After Latin prayers, spend much of the day trying to find out what substance (a good word) there is in this drug rumour. I am worried about Piers because it will be known that he is the source of my information, and by telling me he risks losing friends. As news of my enquiry spreads, a master looks in to say that when he was at a dinner party at the Reform Club, a fellow guest said he would never send a son to Westminster because it had been infiltrated by the drug culture. What nonsense! And yet it depresses me. I have spent seven years trying to dispel the druggy and permissive clouds that hung over Westminster's reputation and I will not let them return now. Another master asks whether I realise that some of the rumour-mongering about Westminster's drugs is encouraged by rival schools and especially by headmistresses who are losing girls to our sixth form. The competition for pupils can sometimes be a dirty one.

Tim Devlin, the director of the Independent Schools Information Service, comes to tell me that I am becoming isolated in the independent-school world because in my published articles I am critical of independent schools, especially of their support for the proposed Assisted Places Scheme. Heaven knows I could be critical if I chose to be. I have spent time and energy defending independent schools, sometimes when my heart was not in it. I write because I enjoy writing and being controversial but also because I want the voice of independent schools to be heard.

Saturday 29 April

A step further in unravelling the truth in the drugs rumour. The boy who is selling cannabis is not the one who has recently left, but a 16-year-old who takes O level this year. Of this I am now certain.

Wednesday 3 May

At 10.30am I see the 16-year-old who has been selling cannabis. He makes no attempt to deny it. Like a man who wishes several other cases to be taken into consideration, he says he has been dealing in drugs for a year. More recently, he has been trying to give up the trade and to limit his activities to doing favours for a few friends. When I ask him whether he smokes cannabis himself, he says that he does not. He claims that he does not make a large profit and he declines to say where he gets the cannabis from. He knows he will be expelled but remains cool, almost detached. As he gets up to leave, he says, 'Thank you for everything you have done for me.' I reply that I have not done much. 'No, but thanks all the same,' he says. It is all very polite. I say I am sorry it has ended like this, and in one sense, I am being sincere, but I am also relieved to be able to deal decisively with a clear-cut case of selling illegal drugs.

Thursday 4 May

Young scatterbrained is in trouble. He brought bottles of gin, rum and Cointreau into his boarding house at the beginning of term. He had been on holiday with his godmother in the West Indies and brought the bottles back with him. But when I tell the housemaster that I shall have to send the boy home for a week, he replies that I cannot do that. The boy's mother has just remarried and is on her honeymoon, so we shall have to wait until she returns.

Sunday 7 May
The expulsion of the drug dealer has caused other rumours to surface. One housemaster has been told by a boy that far more Westminster boys and girls smoke cannabis at parties at the weekend than the headmaster realises. The expulsion has also stirred up the common room. Middle-aged men who have done nothing to counter the drug culture now voice a hard line, saying that the school is doing too little, too late, that the headmaster is not acting vigorously enough and so on. Parents, too, react to the news. One father rings his daughter's housemaster, accusing the school of negligence and threatening that if drug users are not expelled immediately, he will take his daughter away and publish the reason to the world. I know the man and recall that he was once very critical of Marlborough's handling of his son, so I ring Roger Ellis[88], the headmaster of Marlborough, and ask him what happened. It turns out that the son was expelled from Marlborough for persistent stealing. That is useful information. If father threatens to give the press details of our drugs case, I will threaten to give the press information about his son's stealing.

All this reinforces my thought that I must conduct a thorough review of our policy on drugs. Sitting in the headmaster's stall in

---

[88] Headmaster of Rossall School 1967 to 1972, master of Marlborough College 1972 to 1986, chairman of Headmasters' Conference 1983.

Abbey matins, I use a dull sermon to decide that a more draconian policy may be needed but that I must consult first.

Monday 8 May

An angry master. A 14-year-old has walked out of his class. Master unwisely said to the boy, who was not attending, 'Do you want to stay in this class?' Boy answered 'No' and left. I know the parents; they are divorced. Resourceful mother does her best to control three teenage sons. Absent father – a recurring theme.

Thursday 11 May

I start consultation on our drugs policy. The school monitors' view is that the school appears to condone drug use because it does nothing about drug-taking at parties at the weekend. Housemasters recognise this problem but do not know how the school can control behaviour when boys and girls are at home. This is the nub of the problem. Westminster boys and girls are not especially prone to taking drugs but the unusual combination of day school and weekly boarding means that the boundary between school and parental responsibility is not always clear and is difficult to enforce.

Monday 15 May

I read through the papers on the boys taking the Challenge this week. One, a younger brother, reminds me that the peculiarly stupid and unpleasant father referred to the older brother as 'my daughter'. Perhaps not surprisingly, this older brother, who is 17, has developed into an effeminate, fey figure. Parents are divorced.

Tuesday 16 May

To the House of Commons to talk with Neville Sandelson[89], a Labour MP who was at Westminster just before the war. He wants his daughter to take her A level year at Westminster because the headmistress of her comprehensive school is hostile to Oxford, which she regards as elitist. How sad it is that heads should impose their own prejudices on their pupils.

Wednesday 17 May

The mother of a boy who admits to taking drugs at parties comes to see me. She is French, sensible and realistic. When I ask for her help, she replies that she would like to stop her son going to parties on Saturday nights but she cannot. She is on her own. Her son is 16 and she is small. It is as simple as that.

Thursday 18 May

This afternoon at the Challenge meeting, we elect 10 good Queen's Scholars. One has an unusual background. Father committed suicide when the boy was young. Mother remarried and the boy lives with grandparents in a small West Country village. This home is kindly but culturally impoverished: the only reading to hand is the *Daily Mirror*. For the last four years, the boy has been at a rather dim prep school, which he has outgrown intellectually. I suspect he is largely self-taught. He has scored the highest total in the Challenge in living memory, including 200 out of 200 in mathematics. He is a small, self-possessed and serious boy. It will be interesting to see how he fares in College.

---

[89] Labour MP for Hillingdon 1971 to 1981.

Friday 19 May

After Latin prayers, I spend an hour and a half talking with a 17-year-old girl who came into our sixth form from an all-girls' school. She has come to see me after her mother telephoned me yesterday. Girl has been drawn into the Saturday night party scene and has taken LSD. Mother said, 'I felt a pang in my heart when I remembered how excited I was that she would have the opportunity of going to Westminster.' The girl herself is yet another without a father; he was killed some years ago. I think this case worries me more than any since I came to Westminster, but the girl herself says that drug-taking away from the school is none of the school's business. She admires – or perhaps more than admires – a boy who likes to pose as a wicked figure; she would not be the first girl here who tries to save a bad lad from himself and gets drawn into his world. But this is speculation on my part.

After lunch, Maraid Corrigan, one of the two women who started the peace movement in Northern Ireland, talks to a crowded meeting of the John Locke Society. Her message is simple, even naïve, but she puts it across with such sincerity and unforced charm that the boys and girls are won over. It is a meeting between Irish appeal to the heart and the worldly young of London SW1 and the heart wins.

Wednesday 31 May

We get going again after the exeat and I set out to bring the drug investigation to a conclusion. Eight boys and girls admit to taking LSD, but all away from school and all only once and 'experimentally'. The temptation to believe them on that score is strong. Under the present regulation, they are not guilty of a school offence, but I can and do rusticate them nevertheless. Since the whole school knows, I must be seen to do something. As far as the regulations are concerned, I can either leave them as they are or change them to make it a school offence to use illegal drugs anywhere, anytime. I decide on the latter. I may not carry the common room and the parents with me, but the risk of damage to Westminster's reputation is too great. So I propose to reword the school regulations to make it explicit that any drug offence will normally be dealt with by expulsion and that this rule applies to both home and school and to both term time and holidays. I will speak to the school about these changes on Monday and also write to parents. A letter risks unfavourable publicity but it cannot be avoided.

Thursday 15 June
The end-of-term rush has started early this year. Boys, masters and visitors enter and leave my study with the rapidity of a French farce. One of the last is the boy I rusticated some time ago for writing a poison-pen letter to a master. Now he comes to accuse me of blackmailing one of his friends to give me information about drug-taking. He is a bit of a bruiser and does not mince his words. I tell him equally forcefully that trying to get to the truth about boys involved with drugs can indeed be a tough and unpleasant business. With that he seems to be satisfied and departs. He is followed by Duncan Matthews[90], a scholar who is 16 and has a year or so to go. We have a long chat about the school and about recent events. Is he angling for the post of captain of the school in January? I would not hold it against him.

---

[90] Captain of the school, Play Term 1979.

Thursday 22 June

I take the morning Abbey service and the organist plays a chant for the psalm that we have never heard before. So nobody sings and I can see senior colleagues scowling in their stalls. I fear it will be taken as evidence of falling morale. After a long day, Daphne and I dine with Ivan Ivanovic, who was at Westminster between the wars. He was a considerable athlete and represented Yugoslavia in the Berlin Olympics. He was one of those who refused to give the Nazi salute as he walked passed Hitler at the opening ceremony. I am woken at 2am by footsteps on the roof. I go out to see what is up and find two 14-year-old boys clambering along in the semi-darkness. I say 'Good evening' and they, only mildly surprised to see me apparently, say 'Sorry Sir'. I tell them that roof-climbing is dangerous and that they must come down through the headmaster's house and report to me in the morning. I admire their enterprise – it is what schoolboys should do sometime before they grow up, but they need a ticking off just the same.

Wednesday 28 June

Walk across the bridge to the Inner London Education Authority. Peter Newsam[91], the education officer, is worried about the quality of sixth form education in London, and I have suggested that Westminster might help by offering facilities and teaching. Peter likes the idea but says the political leaders of ILEA will veto any co-operation with an independent school. We dine with the Wolperts in Hampstead this evening and when we arrive,

---

[91] Sir Peter Newsam subsequently became director of the University of London Institute of Education.

their son Daniel, who is a day boy at Westminster, is assiduously doing his homework.

Friday 7 July

Spend two hours with Dave Moran who runs the Portobello Project[92] and has been helping young scatterbrained over his home and school difficulties. The boy comes as well and is as analytical as ever about his parents' divorce and his mother's remarriage. I am glad Dave Moran is helping him because I suspect that the housemaster has given up. However, the boy intellectualises everything in such a way that it is difficult to know what is going on in his mind.

Saturday 8 July

Alan Livingstone-Smith, a day-boy housemaster, tells me this story. One of his junior boys bumped into one of the school governors as he was leaving Dean's Yard yesterday. The governor tells the boy to tuck his shirt in. The boy does so but makes some smart remark which prompts the governor to lecture him on manners. The boy loses his cool and says that if he is late home, his father will smash the governor's face in. As this particular governor is very critical of discipline and appearance, the boy's words could have been better chosen. I tell Alan to play the thing down but to ensure the boy apologises. The boy is a rough diamond and clearly has no idea how important governors are. I smile to myself.

---

[92] A social regeneration project for young people based in West London.

Friday 14 July

The last day of term. At the final assembly I say goodbye to Denny Brock, the senior master. Denny has spent most of his life at Westminster as man and boy without becoming narrow in his outlook. He has been an outstandingly loyal and constructive man and I owe him more than I can ever repay for his friendship, support and help. I appointed him senior master in 1972 and it was one of the best decisions I have made. Denny never lost his head or did or said anything petty or mean. Of how few schoolmasters can that be said?

At the Election Dinner this evening, one of the guests I invited was the South African ambassador whose hospitality I enjoyed earlier in the year; but in Ashburnham Garden after dinner, some members of the common room say that they object to his being invited. I tell them that the Election Dinner is one of those occasions when people of different convictions can dine together. Privately, I think their objections are ridiculous.

Another school year has ended, my eighth at Westminster. Would I like to stay as long again, making it 16 years in all? But then I shall be 55 and who wants to employ an ex-public-school headmaster of that age? Either I try to find another job in the next year or two and leave Westminster before I am ready to leave, or I stay until my mid-fifties and risk both overstaying my welcome and being virtually unemployable. I do not know the answer to this riddle. The temptation to take the risk is strong because I have enjoyed my work at Westminster more than any other in my life and I fear that no other job, however modest or grand, will ever be so fulfilling or so richly varied.

1978-79
Play Term 1978

Thursday 7 September

Preparing for the term when I am visited by a former colleague who is headmaster of another independent school. He is very worried and with good reason. His governors met a few days ago and unanimously decided that he should be told to resign at Christmas. He admits that his informal and relaxed style of headmastering may have undermined confidence in the common room and this has been conveyed to governors. Three senior masters have written to the governors demanding that the headmaster should go. They have the support of the bursar and of recently retired masters who live locally and seem only too eager to stick their knives into the headmaster's back. The chairman of the governors, on whom he thought he could rely, is now equivocal. A headmaster will always have critics in the common room and on the governing body, which is why he must make sure that in both places he has others he can trust. It sounds to me as though in this case my former colleague has failed to do this. I will help if I can but I fear he has been politically naïve.

Friday 8 September

I have asked young scatterbrained to come and see me before term begins. We talk over the problems he had in his first year and I try to encourage him to avoid trouble when the new term starts. Does this talking to boys do any good? I suspect we fool ourselves into thinking that we have achieved something. I receive a letter from Prince Charles's assistant private secretary. The Prince is giving the Hugh Anderson Memorial Lecture in Cambridge in November on the theme of reviving the spiritual dimension in a materialistically urban society, and do I have any ideas?

Tuesday 12 September

A bright, fresh morning, just right to start the new school year. I like to be seen to launch the term personally; this is partly egocentricity, partly a defensive desire to be seen to be doing something, but principally a genuine belief that this is one of those times when the headmaster's public role is important. So I take assembly and read out the names of all the pupils, form by form, then preach in Abbey and afterwards speak to new boys and girls about Westminster and wish them well. It is satisfyingly exhausting, and because it all goes well, it gives me a sense of achievement. And in a characteristic Westminster way, I am soon brought down to earth. As we walk in to lunch, Jim Cogan tells me that he had to reprimand senior scholars for talking throughout my sermon.

This evening, I am one of six guests at a Bow Group[93] working dinner in Lord North Street to discuss Tory education policy.

---

[93] For young Conservatives.

The Tory MP, Keith Hampson, speaks for the shadow minister and to my surprise, has doubts about the party's Assisted Places Scheme, doubts that are echoed by other guests, including John Vaizey, who is now Lord Vaizey, of course, thanks to Wilson's resignation honours list.

Wednesday 20 September

Auriol Stevens, the education correspondent of the *Observer*, is fishing for a story to precede the annual general meeting of the Headmasters' Conference next week. I am cautiously indiscreet. I want to publicise the fact that there is plenty of opposition (not just me) to the Assisted Places Scheme even though this will make me unpopular with day-school heads who will benefit if the scheme is introduced.

This evening, an interesting meeting in Ashburnham drawing room. Four of our sixth formers, Emily Tomalin, Charlie Croft, Gabrielle de Wardener and David Heyman[94] – have produced a report on organisations in London that offer sex counselling to young people, and now they are meeting the representatives of those organisations, who are not altogether pleased by what the report says. One woman is angry because the sixth formers have described her organisation as unfriendly – 'we are known everywhere as a friendly service,' she cries. The sixth formers handle the meeting very well and keep their cool under fire. I am impressed.

Friday 22 September

Young scatterbrained has been caught smoking and drinking

---

[94] Now a film producer. Has produced the Harry Potter films.

vodka in the dormitory. So much for my advice before term started. The housemaster now says this is the last straw and the boy ought to be expelled. I sympathise with the housemaster but disagree. I speak to the house monitor who caught the boy drinking and what he says in interesting. The housemaster said that everyone in the house is fed up with young scatterbrained and wants to see him go, but that is not what the house monitor tells me. According to the house monitor, the other boys in the house know all about young scatterbrained's background and understand why he behaves as he does; they see him as an exception, not as someone who influences other boys or whose continuous breaking of the rules undermines the housemaster's authority. In that case, I shall rusticate the boy but warn him that my patience is almost exhausted.

Monday 2 October

Young scatterbrained has been caught smoking yet again and I decide that I cannot hang on any longer. He will have to go. I do not know whether we could have succeeded with this boy; perhaps if we had put him in a different house – but I doubt it. The behavioural problems have deeper origins and our failure to see him through adolescence is only partially our fault. One day, I hope, he will become the intelligent adult he promises to be[95].

Friday 6 October

After lunch, a girl in the Remove comes to see me about the expulsion of young scatterbrained. She accuses the school of being uncaring in its treatment of him. She says he was often

---

[95] Now a financial services manager.

drunk last term and no one took any notice; now the school turns round and throws him out. Why did no one show any concern earlier on? She then tells me that 'several times' the boy came up to her in Yard and put his hand on her breast. I am disconcerted but cannot see how that helps us to understand the boy's extraordinary compulsion to break the rules. I explain to the girl, how, over several months, different people did show concern and try to help but to no avail. She leaves in tears.

Saturday 7 October
I have driven down to Dartmoor to join one of the junior-school expeditions. This morning, I climb with the boys on Hound Tor. In the process, I knock myself about a bit but I am pleased to have a few bruises to prove I have done it. Then I drive on to another expedition caving in the Mendips.

I join a three-hour expedition to the underworld, which I enjoy despite my lack of fitness and occasional attacks of claustrophobia. A pint of cider and a pork chop with the boys and the masters in charge before driving home, reaching Westminster at midnight. I note that the masters – Cedric Harben and Robert Court – have just the right relationship with the boys on these expeditions, informal but not permissive.

Monday 16 October
In break, I have another go at the common room about punctuality. I dislike hearing myself using the familiar words and no doubt so do they, yet some members of the common room seem incapable of getting into their classroom on time. It is such a good common room in so many ways, much less inclined, I would guess, to form cliques than most common rooms, and

with enough mature and tolerant men and women to outweigh the occasional small-mindedness. But with all that, there are too many who see themselves as university dons, here to teach and to stimulate but not to be concerned with such matters as the school rules.

Leaving the common room, I find David Hepburne-Scott, the housemaster of Grant's, following me upstairs to my study. One of his junior boys is flatly refusing to do a punishment because he reckons it is unfair and David wants me to tell the boy he must. David has a knack of getting himself into these corners that is bordering on a specialised talent. But I have supported him all these years and I must go on doing so for the final months of his housemastership. I see the boy. The offence was so trivial I can hardly believe it, but I see no unfairness and tell the boy that he must do the punishment.

Friday 20 October

Emily Tomalin looks in. She wants me to invite a speaker on women's rights and a speaker on gay liberation to the John Locke Society. The former is easy to say yes to and the latter is easy to say no to. Why is this? Because women's rights is a subject much easier to defend in the face of the critics in the common room and among the parents than homosexual rights.

Thursday 2 November

See a father this morning whose 13-year-old son refuses to communicate with him. Boy is new this term and father wants me to see him. But meeting father, I can understand why the son finds communication difficult so I promise nothing. Boy lives with mother, parents having divorced when he was six.

Tuesday 7 November

This evening, a dinner in the Jerusalem Chamber in honour of the bursar, whose long delayed retirement is approaching. It is a good occasion, well attended by governors. I second the proposal of the bursar's health and manage to be both honest and generous to the old boy. How quickly old conflicts fade when your opponent is about to depart. In the candlelight, I smoke my cigar and recall some of the clashes between the bursar and myself and between the bursar and the common room.

Tuesday 15 November

Young scatterbrained's father comes to see me. He cannot accept that his son's problems have anything to do with the divorce. He says his son is just 'coming through the usual adolescent phase' but I have seen enough boys go through the adolescent phase to know that this one is unusual. Quite apart from taking his parents' divorce badly, I have the impression that his father has treated him as an adult since he was a child and that has not helped. I like father but I think he is deceiving himself.

Wednesday 22 November

Headmastering. I hear the sad news that Tony Davies has taken his own life. Tony and I were colleagues and friends at Harrow and left at the same time to become headmasters, he to a state grammar school, I to an independent school. He was a bachelor who lived with his elderly father in a large, Victorian headmaster's house. Father died and Tony was alone to face the pressures of turning the grammar school into a comprehensive school. What finally drove him to shoot himself I do not know.

Friday 8 December

Walking round the school this morning, I run into a young boy using four-letter words to a friend and reprimand him. Swearing among young boys is rife. What they say to each other in private is their business but what they say in my hearing is a different matter. Bad luck – he didn't see me coming.

Saturday 9 December

I have decided to make Roger Jakeman captain of the school in January and that will mean disappointing Duncan Matthews who wants the job and believed it would be his. But he is not ready for it yet and will have his chance in September. At the moment, I think Roger is the more mature and more reliable.

Thursday 14 December

The last full day of term. I await the customary minor problem and sure enough it arrives. Two senior boys have been fighting. They are from different houses and the housemasters spring to the defence of their own. This story emerges: one of the boys helped me with information when I was trying to unravel the drug rumours last term. The other boy threatened to beat him up so the first boy made a pre-emptive strike. Neither boy is hurt. I decide to play it down. The last thing the boy who gave me information wants is for me to make an issue of it.

Saturday 16 December

Drive down to Forest Hill where the local comprehensive school is making a film of my novel *The Custard Boys*. The school has a children's film unit which is very professional. The headmaster and I both have a role in the film. I play the local vicar – pupils, staff and parents are all involved. It is often said that only in independent schools are people prepared to give time to out-of-school activities, but this production gives the lie to that.

Lent Term 1979

Wednesday 17 January
The BBC has finally decided that it wants to make its documentary on a public school at Westminster. This afternoon the producer, Eddie Mirzoeff, the director, Jonathan Gili, and the researcher, Mary Rose-Richards, answer questions about the proposed programme from the common room. Publicly, I am uncommitted but I have already decided that the film must go ahead whether the common room and the governors like it or not. In the event, the BBC team are so quietly helpful and low-key, most members of the common room are won over. The team also meet the school monitors, who have no misgivings about the film.

Monday 22 January
I tell the common room in break that after taking various expressed doubts into consideration, I have decided to recommend to the governing body that the BBC filming should go ahead. When the governors meet, the majority support me, though I have to work hard to persuade them not to impose conditions, such as wanting editorial control, that the BBC would not accept.

Tuesday 23 January

I see Tristram Jones-Parry[96], who has become a day housemaster this term, about a 16-year-old who is said to be behaving very oddly. Parents are separated. I know the boy; he stands on the street and jumps out of the way of cars at the last minute (or rather not at the last minute, for his suicidal adolescence is an act). He wants attention and to be talked about. His doctor has referred him to a psychiatrist at the Westminster Hospital. I tell Tristram to keep an eye on him but I am not really worried. I happen to sit near him at lunch in College Hall. He fills his glass with water to overflowing as though he is too distracted to notice. The girl sitting opposite is very concerned, which is exactly what the boy wants.

Wednesday 24 January

I take the BBC producer and director to see the dean and we have a good discussion about the proposed film. This morning, the bursar showed me the draft of the minutes of the governing body meeting that agreed the filming should go ahead and I have amended the wording to make it clear that the governors have no say whatsoever in the film's final version. At 5.45, a long talk with Alan Livingstone-Smith[97] about his future. He has just missed being appointed headmaster of King's School, Worcester because when the governors asked him about his Christian faith, he replied honestly that he was sympathetic but not a believer.

---

[96] Joined Westminster staff 1973, a brilliant mathematics teacher, housemaster of Busby's 1979 to 1987, headmaster of Emanuel School 1994 to 1998, headmaster of Westminster School 1998 to 2005.

[97] Westminster. teacher and housemaster.

How many true believers are there among the heads of independent schools? Not many, I suspect, but a little hypocrisy goes a long way.

Friday 2 February
A father comes to talk about his daughter who joined our sixth form in September from St. Paul's Girls School. He say she is finding some of the work difficult and he wants me to know that this is not the result of any intellectual failing but of what he calls 'unrequited love'. When I check with the housemaster, he says the girl is fine and making good progress in all her subjects.

Saturday 24 February
To the Purcell Room to hear a concert of the music of Olivier Messiaen and George Benjamin. George left Westmister last year and is now reading music at King's, Cambridge. In his last year at Westminster, I gave him permission to go to Paris once a month to study with Messiaen. The concert includes two of his compositions, an octet and a piano sonata. I do not understand his music but I recognise his talent. What is more, he was a pleasant, good-humoured boy at school and has not changed.

Monday 26 February
The BBC start filming today. They have not told the boys, girls or the common room that for the first day or two there will be no film in the camera. When the excitement has died down, they will start filming in earnest. I have told them they can film what they like. It is a risk. How our rivals will rub their hands if it all goes wrong.

Saturday 3 March

Parents of a bright 11-year-old this morning. The boy, Daniel Glaser, is at a state primary school in north London. I have introduced a scheme for offering unconditional places to talented boys of this age to prevent them being snatched up by our rivals. Parents want Daniel to go to the Jewish Free School, which is a state comprehensive school, for two years before coming to Westminster. If I do not offer him an unconditional place, he will take up a scholarship at City of London School which has an 11+ entry. So I am happy to give the boy an unconditional place for two years hence. The competition for bright children in London is fierce and each school tries to outmanoeuvre its rivals.

This evening, I walk across the bridge to St. Thomas's Hospital to see a Westminster boy who has been knocked over by a car (not another adolescent daredevil, I hope). He is in casualty and the doctor says he is lucky to have got away with a broken leg. They have been unable to contact mother. When I telephone his home, mother is offhand; she will ring the hospital in an hour or two to see how he is.

Monday 5 March

At 4.15, the BBC film a meeting of housemasters and heads of department. It is rather dull until Theo Zinn makes a long, passionate and powerful speech about Westminster's failure (that is to say, my failure) to support classics. Can he have prepared this so as to record for posterity his warning that unless something is done, the classics that have been Westminster's glory in the past will die? The director, who is a classical scholar himself, seizes the chance to capture on film this eloquent defence of a classical education, and I have to restrain myself from responding to some of Theo's wilder criticisms of 'the powers that be'.

Thursday 15 March

I am showing an Australian headmaster round the school. In College, I knock on a senior scholar's door but when I try to open it, I find it locked. Sounds of hustle and haste within before the door is unlocked. The senior scholar looks embarrassed, as well he might. A girl from another house is working conscientiously at the desk. The Australian headmaster has seen it all before and tells me this story: at his school in Adelaide boys are not allowed to take showers during class time, but one boy did, and on hearing voices, hid in a cupboard. The headmaster was showing parents round the school's facilities. 'Plenty of cupboard space' the visiting father observed whereupon the headmaster opened the cupboard door only to reveal the naked boy within.

This afternoon, a four-hour meeting to select about 30 of the 6th form applicants to come in September. We sit round the table with all the reports and results of tests. The majority we select are girls, partly because few boys apply and partly because the girls are so much brighter and more mature.

Straight from this to a housemasters' meeting where an apparently uncontroversial subject – the letting of the school premises during the summer holidays – produces a thoroughly bad-tempered discussion. Two housemasters in particular make complete fools of themselves, accusing the new bursar of not consulting them before agreeing the summer letting, when nothing has been agreed at all. I thought with the departure of the old bursar this sort of meeting was a thing of the past, but it appears that for some housemasters the very word 'bursar' is a red rag to a bull.

Tuesday 20 March
It is my 48th birthday and it starts badly. Revd. Gary Davis is giving a Lenten talk up school instead of in the Abbey. Boys and girls have been warned to bring hymn books, but at least a quarter of them have not done so. When we stand to sing 'Come down O love divine', I see whole rows standing nonchalantly, hands in pockets, with expressions of superior detachment. I am angry because I know the visiting speaker cannot help but notice, so when the hymn ends, I ask Willie Booth to take the speaker out with him and then I give the school a rocket. It is followed by one of those satisfying silences.

In good spirits, because a show of force usually raises the headmaster's morale if no one else's, I attend today's meeting of the governors' executive committee. However, Sir Henry Chisholm's chairmanship is so sluggish, so lacking in any grasp of what needs to be decided, that by the end of the meeting my spirits have sunk again. Thank goodness for a good school concert in the Abbey this evening.

Election Term 1979

Thursday 3 May
I see Peter Harris, a new school monitor, for a talk before morning Abbey. He is a scholar and captain of cricket, an uncompli-

cated person, it would appear, though I doubt whether such a person exists. After Abbey, the boys and girls who edit the *Elizabethan* come to interview me. The same question every two years. Does the headmaster consult anyone before making decisions? If only he didn't have to. I have set up too many committees and working parties so that members of the common room come up the stairs to my study carrying all their files because they have lost track of which committee or working party it is this time. Or so they say.

Housemasters meet this evening and I introduce a discussion on the school's image, by which I mean its reputation among potential customers. The discussion initially gets bogged down in trivia – shirt tails hanging out and so on – but then lifts itself onto a more interesting plane. What is it about Westminster that really appeals to parents? The answer is that blend of intellectual excellence and liberal tolerance that, if we are not careful, can become concentration on only the most able and slack permissiveness. Playing to our strengths and not allowing them to become our weaknesses – that we all agree is the challenge.

Friday 11 May
A family doctor comes to see me about the mother of a boy in the school who is taking O level this year. Mother has married twice and both marriages have been, in the doctor's word, 'disastrous'. There are four children of which ours is the third. Mother was certified last year and spent time in a mental hospital but is now at home with a day and night nurse. She rings the boy's housemaster at three o'clock in the morning with fantasies about the son's lawless life. I have suggested that the boy would be better off at a country boarding school and the doctor agrees that

he must get away from mother, but both the boy and his mother think I am expelling him, which I am not. The boy's father is not in the picture at all; where he is and what contact he has with the boy, we have no idea. The family doctor will try to convince mother that boarding school would be better for her son.

When he has gone, I walk over to College to continue the discussion with the *Elizabethan* editors. I go to them rather than asking them to come to me because I want to escape from my study and prefer the informal talk on their territory.

Friday 18 May

Sheila Browne, the chief inspector at the Department of Education and Science, is visiting the school at my invitation to observe teaching at various levels, but she has to leave mid-morning to attend a meeting with Tory ministers on the Assisted Places Scheme. It is clear she has not seen a draft of the scheme and does not know the principles on which the scheme is based, so I seize the opportunity to point out its fundamental flaw. It is using taxpayers' money to enable parents to opt out of state schools without any check on whether there is any need for the child to move other than parents' wishes.

Lunch with Harold Wilson and Marcia at the Athenaeum. I have asked Harold about applying for the job of director of the British Council. He thinks it might be possible to make something of the job but he warns me that the British Council is full of 'second-raters' who have failed to make the grade in the Foreign Office. He is friendly but I am not sure how helpful he will be. I ask him about his choice of Edward Carpenter as dean of Westminster, and he replies that even before he won the election, he was determined to appoint Edward and had no difficulty imposing his choice on the appointments secretary at No. 10.

Return to school to teach my historians and then play football on Green[98] for the common room against the monitors. I score a goal. This evening, to a cabaret to mark the end of the week's music festival, which has been organised with impressive entrepreneurial skill by Simon Target. I was asked to perform in the cabaret. I hesitated a long time because other headmasters have made fools of themselves on such occasions and have lost credibility as a result (and in one case lost his job because he allowed himself to be put in the stocks and pelted with tomatoes). But Willie Booth has persuaded me to join him in a rendering of Offenbach's 'Gendarmes Song'. The audience is surprised to see me at all. Our act goes down well, thank goodness.

Monday 21 May

The Senior Debating Society meets in the John Locke hour to debate whether a scientific education is essential to the understanding of the modern world. It is an archetypal Westminster discussion with the articulate historians and English scholars easily defeating the scientists and mathematicians. Westminster has produced great scientists from Robert Hooke[99] to Sir Andrew Huxley[100], and the most popular subject is maths, but the ethos of the school is set by those who can use words well.

---

[98] The grass that fills the centre of Dean's Yard, hardly a lawn but more than a rough patch. In monastic days, it was the farmyard. Westminster boys and boys from the Choir School have the right to use it.

[99] At Westminster under Dr Busby; astonished his teachers by mastering the six books of Euclid in one week! The greatest mechanic of his age, he was the first to expound the true theory of elasticity.

[100] Winner of the Nobel Prize for medicine in 1963.

Thursday 24 May

Jim Cogan and I meet early to look through the Challenge results before the Challenge meeting at 11.15. There are some good scholars at the top of the list but it will be difficult to sort out the last two or three places. And so it proves when the meeting gets under way. It takes two hours to decide the 10 scholars and in the end I have to impose my preference for the last two places. I insist on excluding one boy whose marks were good enough but who was arrogant and unpleasant at interview and who was low down in the IQ test.

This evening, to Trinity, Cambridge for the Ascension Feast. An invitation to Trinity's grand occasions is just about all that is left of Henry VIII's decision to link Westminster to the grandest colleges in Oxford and Cambridge. I sit next to Steven Runciman[101], who speaks scornfully of the way young dons nowadays feel obliged to obtain a Ph.D, which he regards as a worthless degree. 'Are you a Ph.D?' he asks, and I am tempted to lie.

Sunday 3 June

A housemaster brings a 16-year-old to see me. The boy has been caught shoplifting in the Army and Navy Stores. He took half a dozen small items he does not need and can easily afford. On the surface, it is quite out of character but then nothing is out of character, so why did he do it? When I question him, he says he stole a book from Foyles last term. When I ask him why, he says he does not know. My guess is that it is a compulsion to take the risk and see if he can get away with it. The police are dealing

---

[101] Historian of the crusades.

with this so he will probably receive a caution. I add that there cannot be a next time if he wishes to remain in the school.

Thursday 7 June

Richard Woollett has been appointed headmaster of Wolverstone Hall, an Inner London Education Authority school in Suffolk. It is a job he very much wanted and to which he will bring good qualities. As housemaster of Busby's he has allowed the members of the house too much freedom, which has understandably annoyed his fellow housemasters, and he has been too anxious to convince the boys and girls that he is on their side. But he understands adolescence better than many in the common room and he will go to a lot of trouble to temper the wind to the shorn lamb. I shall now have to appoint a new housemaster of Busby's and a sixth form historian at short notice as Richard will leave in July.

Tuesday 12 June

I see Tristram Jones-Parry and offer him the housemastership of Busby's. This will cause criticism in the common room because Tristram has been housemaster of his day house for only two terms and there are others, more senior to him, who I know want to be housemaster of Busby's. But Tristram is the right man to take over this house at this time and I have never made seniority decisive in making appointments.

Saturday 16 June/Sunday 17 June

My decision to appoint Tristram housemaster of Busby's has leaked out and I spend some of the weekend smoothing ruffled feathers. The first man who comes to see me turned down a housemastership five years ago and now wants to know why he has been passed over for Busby's. I am about to tell him when he launches into a long monologue that is a statement of his case to be appointed. He is one of the best schoolmasters in the common room and cares more about the school than most of his colleagues do. He takes enormous trouble with individuals who need his help. He tells me he is a 'caring man', and so he is, but it is one thing to care for a favoured individual or loyal group of disciples and quite another to care for 70 boys and girls, all of whom are your responsibility but not all of whom will like you or share your enthusiasms – and that is something this particular man will find impossible to do. A housemaster (and even more a headmaster) has to sacrifice those closer relationships which imply that some are in favour and others are not. I try to explain this when the monologue comes to an end, but having stated his case, he does not want to hear. He is now happy to leave the decision up to me.

This evening, I take another man who had hoped to be housemaster of Busby's for a drink. The Adam and Eve is the scene of our conversation. He is clearly very disappointed because his ambition is to be a boarding housemaster. He is 37 and thinks opportunities for promotion are passing him by. He does not want to be head of science at another school, though he is well qualified. I tell him that a day house will be coming up in two years' time but do not make any promise. It is a constructive discussion but I can tell he is gloomy about his own future. We walk back to school talking of other things.

Monday 18 June
I announce Tristram's appointment to the housemastership of

Busby's to the common room. Immediately afterwards, one of the disappointed men gives me the cold shoulder as we pass one another in Yard. How childish it is. Why are schoolmasters so prone to this sort of behaviour?

At 4pm I see a boy who is completing his first year at Westminster. He came into the sixth form from a comprehensive school in west London. He says he is unhappy and disappointed by Westminster. He expected to find a stimulating intellectual atmosphere but claims to have found only cynicism and opportunism – boys copying one another's prep even at this level and laying hands on copies of internal exam papers so that they do not score low marks. No doubt there is truth is what he says, but I think he is generalising from a few cases or how could Westminster boys and girls achieve the final results that they do?

He is followed by a worried father whose 13-year-old son has taken to the punk scene after an enthusiastic first term. Father thinks his son has been influenced by disaffected older boys in the same house but then admits that his son mixes with a punk group at home. His son has changed his attitude to home and school overnight, but I tell father that neither he nor I can rediscover the enthusiastic young boy who came to us in January. When I speak to the housemaster, he is well aware of the problem and says it would be worth my seeing the father of an older boy who is a 'bad influence'. This father comes this evening. He is a bluff Australian who cannot accept that there is any problem. Then he mentions in passing that the boy's mother is away from home for a year taking a fine art course in Italy. It does not seem to have occurred to father or mother that her absence during her son's O level year might not be helpful. Father then admits that the boy has too much freedom as there is no one to check on what he is doing when father is busy. So, yes, he is into the punk scene in a big way and it is possible he is influencing the younger boy. I know this older boy; he has been involved in bullying and scowls his way around the school. Father reluctantly promises to talk to his son.

Monday 25 June
A Bulgarian boy arrives to spend a week at the school. He is 15, tall for his age and has an ill-fitting raincoat and the beginnings of a moustache. He is polite and rather distant.

The first big day of A and O level exams. I walk along the aisles between the desks to see that all is well and note one boy has written on top of the question paper, 'Government warning – exams can damage your health'.

Thursday 28 June
After teaching, I mark essays and start writing form reports. This afternoon, to the BBC to see the final cut of the documentary about the school. The film is 65 minutes long and my first impression is that it is a remarkably true and sensitive portrait of Westminster. There is no attempt to be snide or to disguise the problems of a school in the centre of London. It is the school we know. The film catches exactly the lively, intelligent, articulate flavour of the place as well as the tensions and anxieties that run beneath the surface – the worries about success and failure, about parental sacrifice, about uncertainties in our adapting to the presence of girls, about the rivalries between booming and declining academic departments. I tell the producer that I do not want him to change a thing because I think the gamble has come off. Some governors and old boys may not like the film but

it will do the school more good than harm. Then to Desmond Wilcox, the head of features, to discuss when the film should be shown. The programme planners want 4 September, but we agree that is too early as most school terms will not have started. We settle for 13 September.

Friday 29 June
Divorced parents come to see me with 12-year-old son. Father wants boy to try for Westminster. Mother, who has remarried and lives in the United States, wants him to finish his schooling there. I take the boy away to talk. He ismature and thoughtful about the problem though his solution is clearly designed to please both parents. He says he wants to start at Westminster and return to the States if it does not work. I urge him to choose one solution or the other because an attempt to keep both parents happy is likely to fail.

Michael Brearley, the England cricket captain, comes to lunch with the scholars. He is a classical scholar himself. We discuss the possibility of his teaching a few periods a week at Westminster. He says he wants to teach not classics but something in the overlap between psychoanalysis and literature. In the long run, he will be a psychoanalyst; in the short run, he will help to strengthen and stimulate our non-specialist studies. The one thing he doesn't want to do is to coach cricket.

This evening Daphne and I go to the Collegiate Dinner in Jerusalem. The Abbey clergy do themselves and us rather well. In a short after dinner speech, Edward Carpenter makes a plea that we should welcome the Vietnamese boat people. Heads nod in agreement but I doubt whether canons and the lay officers are keen to welcome any more refugees from distant lands. 'Thank you, Mr Dean, a splendid speech.' The English are the most un-ashamed hypocrites in the world, but perhaps that is the secret of our moderate and stable society.

Monday 2 July

Having applied for the post of director of the British Council, I hear that I am not even to be interviewed. It was a long shot and a half-hearted one but rejection hurts just the same. This evening, I tell Duncan Matthews that I would like him to be captain of the school next term. In its way a moving moment. He wants it so much and now I think he is ready to take it on. We are sitting in his study, drinking his coffee, which is a cut above mine, and eating his chocolates.

Tuesday 3 July

Dickie Dawe, the headmaster of our Under School, tells me this curious story. The parents of one of his leavers who is coming to us in September have been bothered by numer-ous visits from sales representatives they have not invited. It turns out that their son's enemy, who is a year older and in his first year with us, has been ordering various items on their behalf. It is an old trick but this week it took an unusual twist. The enemy put a card in a newsagent's window advertising thinly disguised sex services and giving the parents' telephone number, so that father and mother have been bothered at all hours of the day and night by men asking the price. Dickie expects me to do something about the culprit and I shall have to warn him off, but is it serious or just a rather sophisticated practical joke?

Wednesday 4 July

As the end-of-term rush gathers momentum and trivial incidents assume the character of crises, Jack Meyer[102] arrives with a Greek boy he is trying to persuade me to take next term. Jack founded Millfield School and left a few years ago to start another school in Greece. He is 74 and has lost none of his entrepreneurial skill. 'This boy will win a scholarship to Cambridge,' he says, handing me a bottle of Greek wine and another of Greek brandy, 'and he comes from one of the wealthiest families in Greece.' To the boy's mother, a widow who looks like Irene Papas, he describes me as the best headmaster in England. I catch mother's eye and we laugh together. The boy is a large 14 and is most unlikely to satisfy our academic requirements, but Jack had done as no doubt he promised and we part on a cheerful note.

Friday 13 July

The last day of term again. Owen Chadwick preaches at the end-of-term service on the theme of the Good Samaritan and he uses the phrase 'compassion and hurry don't agree'. That strikes home. Too often, a headmaster has to hurry one person out of the door in order not to keep the next waiting. Boys and girls are seen for a few minutes, colleagues for scarcely any longer. Committees and working parties follow one another without a break. And if pupils and teachers think the headmaster does not give them enough time, what about the headmaster's family?

---

[102] Founder and headmaster Millfield School 1935 to 1970.

1979-1980
Play Term 1979

Wednesday 5 September

A beautiful early September day. Daphne and I attend Mountbatten's funeral in the Abbey. It is an impressive occasion – meticulous ceremonial, controlled but deep emotion. There is, however, a moment of knockabout comedy. A British Legion flag bearer faints, taking a number of colleagues and flags with him. He is not content to lie down but tries to regain his place in the ranks, swaying this way and that like a drunken man and causing further confusion.

Sunday 9 September

Term starts tomorrow and one problem above all is on my mind. We do not do well enough by the 50 per cent who are not potential Oxbridge candidates. Boys who are not well motivated are not pushed hard enough which opens us to the charge that we are only interested in the scholars. I must make the common room face up to this problem and recognise that the pursuit of good A level results for everyone does not mean we are rejecting education for its own sake whatever that may mean. This evening, I go round to the deanery to discuss this problem with

Edward. Thank goodness I have a chairman of governors who understands and cares.

Wednesday 12 September

The term has swung easily into its stride. I see a 14-year-old who is at a Roman Catholic boarding school and wants to come to Westminster as a day boy. He says the bullying is very bad. Older boys hold younger boys' heads down the lavatory and pull the chain and black their backsides with boot polish. I am astonished to hear of this in 1979. It is like finding a Stone Age tribe living in a country you thought was civilised. Yet there seems no reason why the boy should have come up with this particular story when he could make a general complaint about bullying. Does the headmaster know this is happening?

This afternoon, I attend the first of the departmental meetings I have arranged to discuss how we can do justice to every pupil, not just the bright ones. This is the modern languages department. They say they recognise the problem but hasten to point out that their A level results, unlike those of some other departments, were better than last year.

Friday 14 September

Reactions to the BBC's film about Westminster, which was shown last night, are fascinating. The *Daily Telegraph* says the film is the best advertisement for public schools since Waterloo; the *Mail*, the *Express* and the *Evening Standard* are all very enthusiastic about the film and about Westminster as a school, and the *Guardian* only slightly less so. This is just as well because the informality and knockabout scenes will not have pleased traditionalists. Some fellow headmasters make contact to say that they think the film has done wonders for the image of public schools. I am, of course, relieved at so much favourable comment but I know that more hostile critics are biding their time.

Monday 17 September
As I expected, those who did not like the film now move in to attack. One in particular is worth quoting. It is from David Carey, an old boy and a governor whose idea of what a public school should be like is much influenced by the memory of his father, Bohun Carey, who was a housemaster and rugby coach at Sherborne before the First World War. Father was the model for 'The Bull', the character who dominates Alec Waugh's public school novel *The Loom of Youth*, a book that was thought so scandalous at the time that Sherborne refused to take Alec's younger brother, Evelyn, who had to go to Lancing. What David Carey writes is this: 'Thursday night did a lot of damage and I have already received numerous adverse comments from unattached folk. If the BBC were intending to depict independent education as a redeeming feature in our sad society they contributed nobly to the cause of the Labour party.'

I write a calm response drawing his attention to the many favourable comments but I know he will not let the matter rest.

Wednesday 26 September
After teaching this morning, I leave for Cambridge to attend the annual general meeting of the Headmasters' Conference. Cambridge is breathtakingly beautiful, especially Trinity where we are staying. Is there any more ravishing sight than Trinity Great Court in the soft September sun? But the meeting starts badly. I am at odds with the whole conference over the Assisted

Places Scheme. There is a debate on the scheme this evening at which Stuart Sexton, who devised the scheme for the Conservative Party, speaks in favour to warm applause. I know some headmasters have doubts about the scheme but will vote in favour all the same. It is a Conservative Party scheme and public-school headmasters are overwhelmingly Tory in outlook. I have to speak in the debate. I shall be accused of rocking the boat, but if I do not speak, I shall be accused of trimming my sails to the prevailing wind. I would rather be a rocker than a trimmer.

But I do not speak well. The audience of fellow headmasters is almost aggressively hostile and at one point I am shouted down. That must be a first for this well-mannered club. It isn't only my opposition to the scheme they don't like. Envy of the Westminster film and resentment at my being too much in the public eye fuel their impatience. I would happily let my opposition to the scheme drop, but I am convinced they are making a serious mistake by supporting it.

Monday 1 October
At noon I talk to all the boys and girls in the first A level year. They are all capable of good A levels and I want to encourage them to believe that and not to be satisfied if they think that their teachers have too low expectations of them.

Tuesday 9 October
The dean sends me a copy of a letter he has received demanding my 'immediate dismissal' for allowing the BBC film of the school to be made. It is from an elderly Old Westminster who lives in a flat in Eastbourne. I go round to see Edward and he tells me

not to worry. He says that as dean, he receives half a dozen cranky letters every day.

I see a 14-year-old who was caught with whisky on junior-school expeditions. He has been in too much trouble already and I rusticate him for two weeks. He is tearful. He is a natural leader and a naughty boy, a not uncommon combination. I must catch him before he goes for good.

This evening, a long session with Cedric Harben. He is 35 and is feeling frustrated: by his head of department with whom he does not get on, and because there is no prospect of a housemastership in the next year or two. He wants to apply for another job but what he really wants is to be reassured that I appreciate his energetic and diverse contribution to the life of the school. He is a good man and I reassure him.

Thursday 11 October

I take prospective parents round the school. Normally the registrar does this but if parents ask to see me, I am happy to do so. I take them into College but when I open a study door, we find a senior boy smoking. Blast!

Tuesday 30 October

Daphne leaves for Calcutta to work with Mother Teresa, who has asked her to take medicines, syringes, microscopes etc. It is a brave and enterprising project. This evening, I attend a meeting of the Liberal Party's Education Panel and lose my temper with a peevish anti-public-school man who trots out all the old clichés. I tell him he is talking 'bloody nonsense', which rather surprises the liberal faces round the table. They want a 'new initiative', a 'solution' to the intractable problem of public school.

I have to tell them that there is no solution, only the long-term improvement of state schools which will in time draw parents away from schools that charge fees. But they want something eye-catching to put in the manifesto.

Tuesday 6 November
A housemaster tells me that one of his sixth formers returned after the exeat with cannabis and sold some to another boy for £3. I am astonished that such an apparently happy and sensible boy should take such a risk. He is in my A level history set. It is easy to talk about having a firm and consistent drugs policy, but the better I know boys as individuals, the more difficult firmness and consistency become.

Later today, Christopher Harborne looks in, ostensibly to give me some literature about vitamin loss in cooked vegetables, a subject we discussed at lunch yesterday. But he has heard of my interest in him as a possible monitor and captain of the school in January. Two school monitors are staying on next term, but neither will make a good captain so I am looking at the next generation in which there are three good candidates – Christopher Harborne, Tom O'Shaughnessy and Toby Jones. I am having my supper when Christopher arrives and I guzzle my Stilton as he talks. He has come to let me know he is not afraid of high office but he does so in a way that is disarmingly naïve. There is none of the clumsy lust for power that characterises some boys. Whether his willingness to reach out for the top job is a virtue, I am not sure, but I am inclined to think it is.

Wednesday 7 November
I see the sixth former who is alleged to have brought

cannabis into the school and sold or given it to a number of others. He blithely informs me that the substance wasn't cannabis and that the whole thing was a joke. I ring my contact at the Home Office Dangerous Drugs Inspectorate and ask if he can arrange a quick analysis. He is very helpful and says the substance now in my possession will be collected as soon as possible.

At teatime, Bishop Launcelot Fleming comes to talk in our drawing room to the boys and girls who were confirmed last term. One of the boys has admitted being given and smoking the 'cannabis' now being analysed and is at risk of being expelled. He is also the current boyfriend of one of our daughters. At tea, he chats to me about this and that and offers me a cucumber sandwich. I hope to God the substance does not turn out to be cannabis after all.

This evening, Duncan Matthews appears and suggests in his avuncular way that I might be in need of a drink. So headmaster and captain of the school retire to the Cardinal, a pub behind the Catholic cathedral. He tells me there is so much gossip and rumour about the drugs case that a special assembly tomorrow would be helpful to clear the air. I decide to take his advice.

Thursday 8 November

At the special assembly, I tell the school exactly what is happening in the drugs case and that I am awaiting an answer from the Home Office. I spell out as clearly as I can what the policy on drugs is so that they cannot claim they did not know the consequences of being involved. I think the talk has gone down well, but a senior master tells me that in his opinion the school's reaction is 'universally cynical'. As if he knew.

The Home Office rings to say that the substance does not contain any cannabis or any controlled drug. I am very relieved. There were seven boys involved and the prospect of a mass expulsion was intolerable. I think I might even have suppressed the Home Office verdict if it had gone the other way. So rustication for the boy who sold the bogus cannabis to his friends and a week's gating for the rest.

Housemasters meet at 6pm and we have a good discussion about our entry procedure until Ronald French goes off at a tangent to say that recent cases of drugs and vandalism are the result of other housmasters' reluctance to punish those who are late for morning Abbey. This irrelevant outburst sours the atmosphere and I bring the meeting to a close. What a pain the man is.

Wednesday 28 November
I spend the day with the Transitus, a form of new boys, going into all their classes to listen and observe. I want to get to know them and also to get a feel of what it is like to be on the receiving end of their teaching programme.

They are an exceptionally able and lively group so it is no burden to spend the day in their company. The lessons run as follows: Latin, French, English, music, divinity and double chemistry. The teaching is good but Westminster masters talk too much. The boys and I have to listen to too many monologues. No wonder the boys are yawning in the last period before lunch and no wonder they come to life when they have to do a chemistry experiment. I note that some masters do not make it clear what the boys are supposed to write down and that in one or two cases did not know all the boys' names. I pass on these criticisms to the men concerned. Getting to know the name of every pupil in the class is one of the first duties of a teacher.

Thursday 29 November

Geoffrey Shepherd, an ex-housemaster who is now registrar, has stirred up a hornet's next by circulating to housemasters a list of boys and girls who smoke regularly. The list has been given to him by an informant. Housemasters are furious that he did not consult them before circulating the list. 'Who is the informant?' they want to know. I sympathise with the housemasters and am annoyed with Geoffrey, who as an experienced man should have known better.

Theo Zinn comes to see me and asks me to read a draft of an article that he has written for the *Elizabethan*. When he has gone, I do so. It is a hopelessly biased account of how true education has been sacrificed in recent years to the pursuit of A level grades. It is my turn to be angry. When I came here, the future of the majority of boys was sacrificed to the pursuit of Oxbridge scholarships for the chosen few. Boys who could easily have got good A levels ended up having to go to a crammer to take the exam again. I am amazed parents did not complain. Now that I am trying to make sure all boys and girls are given the same chance to do well, Theo feels that his precious little coterie of classical scholars is threatened. I shall not let his article be published unless a balancing article by me is published alongside.

This evening, to Jason Morrel's production of *Androcles and the Lion*. Jason is 16, the son of actors André Morrel and Joan Greenwood, so the theatre is in his blood. It is a delightfully inventive production and quickly washes away the frustrations of the day.

Monday 3 December

Ronald French claims to have conclusive evidence that a younger colleague, John Field, told boys that French was 'childish' and unfit to be a senior master with responsibility for discipline. Headmaster's action? It is like a problem set for a future headmasters' course. Field admits to an error of judgement and I tell him he must apologise. It is that stage of term.

This afternoon, to the Hall School for a governors' meeting. I am concerned that this north London prep school is not sending us as many boys as in the past. I learn that University College School in Hampstead is attracting boys who might have come to Westminster by giving them firm places at the age of 11. In that case, I will have to expand our unconditional place scheme and bully the headmaster of our Under School to accept an 11+ entry, which he is most reluctant to do. It is like a supermarket cut-price war and just as ruthless.

This evening, I am the guest of the school's Modern Language Society. They have asked me to introduce one of my favourite foreign-language films and I have chosen Jacques Becker's *Casque d'or*. It is as powerful as I remember when I first saw it at the Arts Cinema in Cambridge nearly 30 years ago.

Wednesday 5 December

See a potential scholar and his parents. The boy is obviously bright and we talk about the possibility of his taking the Challenge a year early. The background is interesting in terms of social mobility: grandfather was a plate-layer on the railways; father went to grammar school and is a lecturer. This boy will be a Westminster scholar and go to Oxford or Cambridge.

I lunch with Peter Newsam of ILEA and we talk about the

Assisted Places Scheme. He warns that a future Labour government could use the scheme as an excuse to withhold university grants from boys and girls at assisted places schools on the grounds that if all independent schools take money out of the state sector, the government will take it back in some other way.

Monday 10 December

In one of yesterday's papers there was speculation on who would be the next headmaster of Eton, mentioning my name as someone who would 'shake Eton to its roots'. I dislike this because it will make Westminster boys and girls think I want to leave and that Eton is a step up from Westminster. But I am not interested in Eton; it is not my scene.

At noon, I see Christopher Harborne and offer him the position of captain of the school, which he accepts. This afternoon, I inspect the former Grosvenor Hospital in Vincent Square. If I can persuade the governors to buy it, we could move our Under School there and expand its numbers. But the price is £600,000 and that would mean borrowing.

Wednesday 12 December

Up early to attend a leaving breakfast given by Duncan Matthews and Dickie Bannenburg, the prin. opp. Traditional English breakfast washed down with champagne.

Later, I welcome four educationists from the People's Republic of China. They are charming and seem genuinely interested in this local phenomenon, the English public school. They give me a delightful painting on bamboo and I, ill-prepared, give them a copy of the school prospectus. As we walk round, I introduce them to a number of boys and girls who are learning Chinese and our visitors are pleasantly surprised. Then I hand them over to Duncan and Dickie for coffee in Duncan's room in College. The four Chinamen in ill-fitting suits and caps are a strange contrast to the two senior boys who, rather more than is usual at Westminster, and – especially as Duncan is still wearing the pink carnation he wore at breakfast – look like young aristocrats at a Victorian public school.

Friday 14 December
Another term ends and I am less tired than usual, why, I do not know. More speculation this morning about my succeeding Michael McCrum as headmaster of Eton. It is momentarily flattering and also annoying because I resent the assumption that I would be pleased to be in the running. So at the end-of-term assembly I tell the school they should not believe everything they read in the newspapers.

Tuesday 18 December
I decide to apply for the headmastership of Eton. I was on the point of ringing up friends in the press to tell that I was not interested and would they please stop speculating. So what has changed my mind? I have talked it over with Daphne and with my two closest friends on the governing body, Edward Carpenter and Burke Trend. All were encouraging. Another governor I consulted sent an ambiguous answer on a card, 'We don't want to lose you but we think you ought to go.' Then there is the old problem that I cannot stay at Westminster till retirement and Eton does represent one of the career moves that makes sense. Ambition, too, plays a part but I also have my doubts.

I do not think Eton and I will have much in common. What finally made me swallow my doubts was a friendly letter from the provost of Eton in reply to my request for particulars of the job, a letter that did not explicitly encourage me to apply but seemed to imply that I should. So I shall.

This evening, I am on the panel of *Question Time*, a television version of *Any Questions?* In view of this morning's decision, I avoid being controversial. Neil Kinnock, Labour's education spokesman, is also on the panel and we get on well.

Wednesday 19 December

I lunch with the judges at the Central Criminal Court. It is their daily routine but for me it is a slap-up meal and I make the most of it. I sit next to a judge who is a former Westminster parent. I ask after his son and he tells me that he died of a brain tumour shortly after leaving Cambridge. He tells me he has another son, now aged 30, with Down's Syndrome, who was not at Westminster. I do not know what to say. The turkey and Christmas pudding are excellent.

Friday 21 December

The Oxbridge paper chase continues.

We have had another good year with 22 awards and more than that number of places, some of the latter the result of housemasters ringing round colleges all day until a place is found. If people wonder why schools like Westminster get so many boys and girls into Oxbridge, it is at least partly because the school takes so much trouble. This year, more than in the past, I am struck by the contrast between Oxford and Cambridge. Boys and girls of scholarship standard are lucky to obtain a place at

Cambridge, whereas less able candidates win open awards at Oxford.

I have no doubt that in most subjects it is more difficult to get into Cambridge.

Lent Term 1980

Friday 11 January

I receive a letter from the provost of Eton to say that I have not been placed on the short list for interview. How dare they refuse even to interview me? But as the day wears on, I feel more relieved than angry. How can I have imagined that Eton would appoint someone so keen on public controversy? Better to remain at Westminster where my views are accepted and where the opportunities to express them are greater.

This afternoon, a special meeting of the governing body decides to make a bid of £600,000 for the former Grosvenor Hospital in Vincent Square.

I am delighted that for once governors have had the courage and foresight to take a risk for Westminster's future. If our bid is accepted by the church commissioners and there is no difficulty over planning permission, we shall be able to treble the size of our Under School and have a proper 11+ entry from state primary schools. We shall also be able to run the two schools together financially with a common budget and balance sheet. If all this comes off, it will be one of the most important steps in Westminster's history for a long time.

Thursday 17 January

The new term swings easily into action. I take the morning Abbey service and then try to fill two hours efficiently before teaching my A level history set at noon.

I tend to fritter away the time, wandering out into Yard to talk to boys at random, drinking cups of coffee, any excuse for not getting down to the papers on my desk. I am certainly not a high-powered administrator; if there is an analogy for my style of headmastering, I think it would be the guerrilla leader who prefers to conduct business on the move.

Friday 25 January

A telephone call from Buckingham Palace invites me to lunch with the Queen on 21 February. That is good for morale.

Monday 28 January

Angus Wilson, the novelist who was at Westminster before the war, talks to the John Locke Society. He goes down well with the Westminster audience because he makes words work with fluency and humour. This afternoon, two mothers come to complain. The first thinks that her daughter has been badly treated by Newnham College, Cambridge. She is right. The college was cavalier in its handling of the girl's application last term but there is nothing the school can do about it now, except make a mental note not to send girls to Newnham in future. The second mother wants her son to have vegetarian meals which we do not provide. I can promise nothing. She then says that she does not want to complain because her son is very happy, but now that she is here there are one or two points, and she takes a list from her bag and puts on her glasses.

This evening, I take Michael Hugill to dinner at the Athenaeum. Michael is that unusual person, a public-school headmaster who decided to retire early so that he could return to his first love, which is teaching. He was headmaster of Whitgift School. I offered him a job because I knew him to be a good mathematician and because I welcomed the prospect of having a senior man in the common room – Michael is 58 – who understands the difficulties of the headmaster's position. We have a good talk during which we mention a mutual friend, Harry Rée, who was headmaster of Watford Grammar School and is now professor of education at York. According to Michael, Harry is one of two members of the Headmasters' Conference who has killed a German with his bare hands. Harry was a member of SOE[103] during the war. My own qualification for headmastering seems inadequate by comparison.

Sunday 3 February
To Nutfield in Surrey to attend the service of thanksgiving for the life of Joe Todhunter, who died of leukaemia last month aged 18. Joe left Westminster at the end of the summer term in 1978 and was due to take up a place at Brasenose College, Oxford last autumn. He spent only one day at Oxford and could not continue. He faced his illness and approaching death with a calm that was astonishing. The service of thanksgiving strikes just the right note and is attended by a number of his contemporaries from school.

---

[103] Special Operations Executive: sabotage behind enemy lines.

Tuesday 5 February

Routine meetings this morning with the director of studies, the chaplain and the captain of the school. I welcome a party of boys and girls from a comprehensive school who seem to regard their visit as a huge joke. This afternoon, wandering round the school, I meet Adrian, whose father has just written to say how unhappy his son is. Adrian denies this and he certainly does not look unhappy. And then I meet Richard, whose best friend has just walked out of the school saying he cannot stand the feeling of claustrophobia any longer. We meet for tea in College Hall and discuss his friend over a doughnut. Richard's advice to me is to avoid trying to force his friend to return. Both boys are 15. The missing boy's parents come to see me at 6pm. While we are talking their son telephones from home to say that he wants to come back to school after all.

Friday 8 February

After Latin prayers, I see a girl who wants to change houses because she finds the boys in her year juvenile and unsympathetic to her views. She says she wants to talk about issues such as abortion, racism and gay rights, but they only want to talk about football. I see the housemaster and he agrees that this may be an exception to the general rule that boys and girls are not allowed to change houses. To the Oxford Union this evening to speak against the motion that Oxford's admissions system is biased against candidates from comprehensive schools. The master of Balliol, Anthony Kenny, and I defend the system and lose by 13 votes.

Thursday 21 February

After teaching, I drive to Buckingham Palace for lunch. Our old car is sniffed at by a police Labrador, then into the palace for drinks. I stick to orange juice. The Queen, the Duke of Edinburgh and Prince Andrew join us and we are introduced. There are only eight guests so that both before and after lunch there is ample opportunity to talk with our hosts. The master of the household, Sir Peter Ashmore, hovers at pre-lunch drinks and post-lunch coffee to guide this guest to Her Majesty and that guest tactfully away. Unfortunately, for a short time I find myself talking to the Queen and the Duke in the company of a professor from Imperial College who is a bore and will go on about the increase in fees for overseas students. When it is clear that the Queen and the Duke consider the increase not unreasonable, he insists on pressing his case.

My chief impression is of the Queen's good humour and lack of hauteur. She is sparkling and amusing and good company. Lunch is modest but tasty. I almost pour French dressing on my lamb cutlet thinking it is gravy. I don't know on what basis individuals are chosen but I am pleased to have been because it is such a pleasant occasion, quite without stiffness or tension.

I return 10 minutes late for a meeting of the working party dealing with conversion of the Grosvenor Hospital into our new Under School. Governors look startled to hear that I have been to a private lunch at the palace.

Wednesday 27 February

I take Abbey and read and comment on John Donne's religious sonnet 'Batter my heart three-personed God'. A 15-year-old boarder is sent to me by his housemaster. The problem is this. He is doing badly academically with O level exams only a few months away and he has been in trouble for a string of minor offences. Housemaster is fed up but I suspect housemaster dislikes the boy and would be glad to see the back of him. Parents are abroad – father is in the army – and the boy's guardian is his aunt, an American with some counselling experience in American schools who fancies herself as a Freudian psychologist. Poor kid. The fates have loaded the world against him.

I talk to him but do not get far. He is baby-faced and according to some masters, foul-mouthed; they report his swearing loudly just as he disappears out of sight but not out of earshot. I am not sure what to make of him. He says he knows he must work harder and keep out of trouble so there is no point in my telling him. I tell him all the same, with a warning that unless there is an improvement, we may not take him into the sixth form in September.

Wednesday 5 March

I see the parents of a boy who has been told to leave another school. They are a nice couple but have come under a misapprehension. Boy was expelled for stealing. Parents say he was being bullied and think he stole to buy presents for the bullies. His headmaster has told him that I will consider the boy for a place but I told him on the telephone that would be impossible. So parents are annoyed and so am I. We all realise the boy's headmaster has misled parents deliberately to get them off his doorstep. Unscrupulous as all headmasters are at times, deceiving parents in that way is unforgivable.

Friday 7 March

I see a father who is, I think, without exception, the most unpleasant parent I have met at Westminster. I am predisposed to dislike him because he has already been very critical of the school. He has a 15-year-old with us and an older boy at Eton, and today he makes numerous comparisons between the schools which satisfy him that Westminster is in every way inferior. I am too battle-hardened now to be provoked but when he has finished, I say that as his son is taking O level this summer, now is the time to consider changing schools if father is so dissatisfied with Westminster. But no, that is not what he wants. He has made his point and just in case I have not taken it all in, as he leaves he gives me an aide-memoire of three sides of foolscap which purports to be a record of the housemaster's incompetence. It is a monstrously unfair document and I shall show it to no one. The boy is said to be vindictive and disliked by his contemporaries. He was dropped on his head as a baby, fracturing his skull, and is small for his age.

When father has gone, I start a three-hour meeting to select the successful candidates for September's sixth-form entry. I am impressed by the care and trouble that colleagues take over every case. If justice is not done, it is not for want of trying. We choose 38. Girls who may have done well in the academic tests but who were judged arrogant or off-hand at interview fall at this hurdle. We have plenty of good candidates and do not need to take risks.

Thursday 13 March

After school communion in Henry VII, I spend an hour with Alex Peckam. I have asked him to come and see me because he is a senior boy, taking A level and head of water (rowing), who for some reason I have not got to know. We pass one another in Yard without a sign of recognition. This is bad. My refusal to make him a school monitor has not helped. So now we spend an hour together drinking coffee and talking about our chances in the schools' head of the river race this afternoon, then about his university applications and finally about the philosophy of science which he hopes to read at King's College, London. Both mother and father are medical professors. The hour passes quickly and I feel we have at last made contact.

Monday 17 March

Teach a double period with my A level historians. They are getting weary after the term's work and the long drawn-out winter, and weary, too, I expect, of my going on about the admirable qualities of Cardinal Richelieu. I receive a phone call inviting me to be one of the judges for this year's Whitbread Literary Awards. I accept and am flattered to be asked. The judges get £500 each and I relish the prospect of extending my library with the best books of 1980.

This evening, we dine once again with John and Patsy Grigg[104] in Blackheath, a warm, relaxed and stimulating evening. A fellow guest is Arthur Koestler. Before dinner the wooden stool on which I am sitting collapses and Koestler insists that he heard the Griggs' dog start barking a fraction before the stool collapsed, as though I had communicated some form of early warning to the

---

[104] John Grigg was formerly Lord Altringham but renounced his peerage. Biographer of David Lloyd George.

animal. This enables Koestler to lead an interesting discussion about various forms of extra-sensory perception. But it is cut short by John Grigg, who points out that the dog, whose name is Slippers, barked because it heard the telephone in the hall ring just before the stool collapsed. We are all rather disappointed, especially Koestler.

Tuesday 18 March
To Oxford for lunch with the dean and senior censor of Christ Church. The university has ruled that no college may give more than 35 per cent of its places as awards and that effectively puts an end to Westminster's closed scholarships. I am delighted and tell my hosts. They thought the school would be upset, but on the contrary, the closed awards had become an embarrassment; they were a target for critics of the relationship between the old public schools and Oxford, and Westminster did not need them. Increasingly, able boys and girls refused to enter for a closed award because they wanted to show that they could win a scholarship in open competition.

I return to Westminster pleased with the day's business and find an envelope on my desk marked 'private and confidential'. At this stage of term, that can only mean bad news. Sure enough, it is from a house-master to say that three 14-year-olds have been caught in possession of cannabis. I light the gas fire in my study and sink into an armchair. I don't want another drugs case, not now at the end of term and certainly not involving boys who are only 14. I ring the housemaster and ask for details. Home for the weekend, one of the boys bought cannabis in Piccadilly. He brought it back to school on Sunday night and rolled a joint which he shared with the other two boys. A school monitor walked in on what they claim was a first time and an experiment. The prospect of having to expel three 14-year-olds is depressing.

Wednesday 19 March

I spend much of the day sorting out the drugs case. The three boys are shaken at being caught and fear expulsion. They cannot explain why they took such an unnecessary risk but it really does not need explanation. They are at the age of unnecessary risks. I believe them when they say they are not habitual dope smokers but they are not, I think, as innocent as their parents protest. How can I find a formula that will avoid expulsion yet maintain my hard line on drugs? Some of the substance has been kept and, recalling the case last term, I consider going through the motions of having it analysed and claiming that it is not cannabis after all. No one would be the wiser. But that deception will not do. I decide not to expel them on the safer ground that they are young and deserve a second chance. It is a risk because other boys may think the hard line need not be taken too seriously, but I rusticate the three boys and hope that will be enough.

This evening, to the school concert in St. Margaret's. There is a large turnout of parents and the concert itself is very good. It is tempting to see this as the true face of Westminster and the occasional case of drugs or stealing as an aberration, but it is the same school and the headmaster who thinks in terms of a few bad apples is fooling himself.

Election Term 1980

Tuesday 29 April

Tristram Jones-Parry, the housemaster of Busby's, comes to see me about a 15-year-old who has swallowed 50 aspirins and is in hospital. Boy told his housemaster and his parents that he could see no point in life; he has many talents, intellectual, sporting, and is an accomplished actor, but it all adds up to nothing for him at the moment. I telephone father, who says his son is out of danger. Father is trying to fix up a psychiatrist to see the boy before he returns to school.

This evening, I take David Hepburne-Scott to the Wilton Arms in Belgravia, a pleasant pub, out of range though rather small so that we are easily overheard. This morning, David said he wanted to see me urgently. 'What about?' I asked. 'Well basically, the common room are very unhappy,' he replied. He is not a common-room spokesman and I suspect that it is just he and some of his friends who are unhappy, but I know it is better to give him time than to ignore him altogether. To my surprise, he brings an attaché case with him to the pub; it contains two copies of the list of topics he wishes to discuss, one for him and one for me. I order two pints and tell him to start. He reaches inside his attaché case and brings out a hand-held projector and a number of coloured slides. What can this mean? Perhaps he has photographed colleagues in compromising situations but no, the slides are all of steam trains. Railways are his passion but I fail to see the relevance. Then he explains. These are the steam trains he hoped to see on the last day of last term but I had insisted that teaching should continue to the bitter end. 'And I supported you one hundred per cent,' David says. 'I said to myself, "He's the boss man and if that's what he wants, there's no room for argument."' But there were so many boys allowed off school to take part in a regatta and others allowed to go home early for various reasons that David reckons he missed his trains for nothing.

I take a deep swig of my beer. Is he going round the bend?

This and other complaints on his list I try to answer calmly but he keeps referring to me as 'the boss man' as though I am the white hunter and he is my native servant. The couple at the next table look at us a number of times. After two and a half pints he has finished. He packs his attaché case and we depart. Was it worth it? He is a senior master and an ex-housemaster so he deserves a hearing.

Wednesday 30 April

I see the mother of the baby-faced 15-year-old who was sent to me last term because of bad work and bad behaviour. Should he leave after O level or just change house? Mother thinks his naughtiness is the result of a clash of personality with his house-master. Housemaster thinks he is a dishonest and deceitful boy. Mother and I discuss changing school but come to no definite conclusion. A meeting of the Headmasters' Conference political and public relations sub-committee at the club this evening. Over dinner, Ian Beer tells me in confidence that he has been appointed headmaster of Harrow and will succeed Michael Hoban next year. That is good news. Ian is just the man Harrow needs to recover from Hoban's lazy and incompetent reign.

Tuesday 6 May

Willie Booth tells me he is worried about a rumour going round the school that a group of boys have got away with a financial fraud. As Willie is careful about what he passes on to me, I take this seriously. According to the rumour, the boys went round Belgravia pretending to be collecting money for an official Westminster School appeal on behalf of Afghanistan. They went from house to house carrying a bogus sponsorship form and collected anything from 50p to £5 from the trusting inhabitants. Apparently the name 'Westminster School' and my forged signature did the trick. Willie and I talk it over. We are amazed at their gall. But what of their morals? They are greedy for money and enjoy bringing off an imaginative coup. I doubt whether they need the money, but having money has never been a reason for not wanting more. I thank Willie and brace myself to start enquiries.

Wednesday 7 May

I take Abbey and teach. Last night, two of the women who had given money to the appeal for Afghanistan became suspicious and rang the school number. I rang them back and asked them to come in break today to see if they could identify any of the boys. They identify one 15-year-old in the first year of A levels. I telephone father and ask him to see me straightaway.

Neither the housemaster nor I are surprised that this boy is involved as he has a string of minor offences to his name. He had a very bad stammer and was teased when he first came to Westminster. He found it difficult to make friends and eventually teamed up with one of his worst persecutors. As a pair they got into a lot of trouble without going quite far enough to be sent home. Father is a decent, sensible and worried parent. He asks whether I am going to report this to the police and I tell him that I hope not to have to do so. With his agreement, I interview father and son together. I tell the boy that I know who his partners in crime were and he falls for it. With two more names, it will not be difficult to get all names of the members of the gang, though gang is the wrong word. They worked in pairs, each pair aware of the other pair's activity but not co-ordinating their routes, so that on one occasion, one pair followed another down the same street and, astonishingly, the women who came to the door gave money a second time. And that is when the two ladies became suspicious.

With the help of housemasters, I piece the rest of the story together. There were eight boys involved, all aged 15; three of them have bad track records and I have no doubt that they should be expelled. One of them is the baby-faced boy whose mother came to see me just a week ago. His housemaster was right after all; the boy is dishonest and deceitful. The problem is what to do with the other five. They are not bad boys, yet to let them get away with just a warning will be regarded with derision by the rest of the school, which is watching with interest. At 9pm, I attend Holy Communion in St. Faith's[105]. One of the five is helping Willie as a server and hands me the bread and body of Christ. After the service, I talk over the problem of what to do with these boys with the captain of the school. He confirms my view that something must be seen to be done. I decide to rusticate the five for two weeks and make them repay

---

[105] St. Faith's Chapel in Westminster Abbey.

the money personally to the women they cheated.

Thursday 8 May
To Woking crematorium for the funeral of Struan Reed, who left the school last July. He died suddenly and unexpectedly from a head injury sustained when he was very young. Willie Booth takes the service and a number of masters and boys who knew Struan well have come to the funeral. All the Reeds are very small in stature and the coffin looks like a child's.

This evening, to Brompton Square, where the London editor of *Time* magazine is giving a small dinner party – Lord Carrington, Rostropovich the Russian cellist, General Sir John Hackett and myself. I do not know what I am doing in this company but it is a thoroughly enjoyable evening with Rostropovich's entertaining stories about trying to buy contraceptives in a Japanese department store with his KGB minder acting as interpreter.

Friday 9 May
After Latin prayers, I see the father of one of the boys who was rusticated for his part in the fraud. Father's family are Prussian junkers. His reaction to his son's behaviour is unusual to say the least. He tells me that when he heard what his son had done, he thought about it calmly in the office, then went home, summoned his son into the study and hit him hard in the face. 'I have not done that for many years,' he adds.

Then I see, one by one, the boys who are to be expelled and their parents. It is difficult for them and for me. The first is an aggressive father who wishes to put the blame for what happened on the school and especially on the housemaster. 'There are no bad soldiers,' he says, 'just bad officers.' The next parents are separated and mother is desperately tearful. She has had to bring up two boys on her own. Father talks in a detached way about finding another school but mother cannot accept that it is fair for her boy to be expelled. 'He has never had a chance,' she says. The separation hit this boy particularly hard. The last couple are the most calm and realistic. Their son is the stammerer. We talk in a business-like way about getting him into a tutorial to take his A levels.

This evening, the *Guardian* telephones asking for details of the fraud. A boy has tipped them off already.

Monday 19 May

Rise early and go out into the school. The air is fresh and the sun is just touching the face of the buildings in Yard. I go into College Hall and talk to one or two boys over breakfast. No boy wants to see the headmaster at breakfast so I do this only rarely and try to make it look as though I am checking on the quality of the bangers and beans.

After teaching this morning, I welcome John Cleese[106], who has come to talk to the John Locke Society. He attracts the largest audience I can remember, larger even than for Enoch Powell or the Dalai Lama. He speaks well, avoiding the trap of being the funny man. An unpretentious, likeable man who is particularly interesting on his controversial film *The Life of Brian*.

---

[106] One of the original Monty Pythons. Best known, perhaps, for his television comedy series *Fawlty Towers*.

Tuesday 20 May

I take a history A level revision class before breakfast and then engage in the usual round of Tuesday morning discussions – director of studies at 9.45, Willie Booth at 10.30, captain of the school at 11.15. This evening, I go to Harrow to talk to housemasters of schools in the Rugby Group. There is a poor turnout and the evening would have been wasted if it had not been for the chance to talk with old Harrow friends over dinner. I travel back by underground and, changing trains at Embankment, run into a Westminster boy. It is getting on for midnight. What is he doing here at this hour? 'Oh, that is easily explained,' he replies; his housemaster gave him permission to join a dinner party at the house of one of his friends who is a day boy. I will check. We travel back to Westminster together.

Wednesday 21 May

A mother comes to see me about her son who is due to take our entrance exam in two years' time. The boy's half-brother – her son by a previous marriage – hanged himself at Oxford a short while back. He had been a scholar at Eton but came to Westminster for the Oxbridge term. Mother says he took his own life because he was depressed by the suicide of a girl with whom he was in love. She wants to be sure that the younger boy will be placed with a sensitive and understanding housemaster.

Wednesday 28 May

My father died this afternoon. He was not ready to die and could have lived a few more years, but he has been spared the deterioration of old age. He was 78. I was closer to him than to my mother, perhaps because I thought he understood me better and

I him. He was a good father. He had no religious faith other than a sort of generalised theism. His outlook on life was balanced, humane and unsentimental. He was perhaps too self-effacing. He was a good doctor, the senior radiologist at the London Hospital, but was not given the credit he deserved. With this in mind, I telephone a friend on the *Times* to see if he can arrange for an obituary to go in. He asks me to find one of my father's colleagues to write 300 words.

My older brother, my two younger sisters and I were lucky in our parents. They had a simplicity, reliability and loyalty to the family which, if Westminster parents are anything to go by, are increasingly rare.

Friday 13 June

I spend the day with a form of 13-year-olds, most of whom are in their second term in the school. Their second period this morning is physical education, which means swimming lessons in the local pool. I take my costume and join in the trials, imagining I can outrace these boys despite my age.

My arrogance is punished. I finish the four lengths with my heart pounding, only to find that three boys are comfortably faster. I remain quiet for the rest of the morning. By the end of the teaching day I am struck once again by how tiring it is to have to listen for so long. And these teachers are good; they know their subject. No wonder children play truant from a school where the teachers are both ignorant and boring.

Friday 27 June

I allowed one of the boys who was expelled over the fraud case to come back to school to take his O level exams and now have reason to regret that decision. In the elementary maths exam this boy persuaded the boy sitting at the desk in front to lay each completed sheet face up on the floor. The Oxford and Cambridge exam board has quickly spotted that one boy has copied from the other, though they do not know which way round.

When I hear the names I have no doubt. The board's policy is that a candidate caught cheating in one exam will have all his examination results cancelled. For the boy who has already been expelled and who clearly instigated this cheating, that may be a just punishment, but not for the other boy. I telephone the board and argue this other boy's case. At first, the board is reluctant to make an exception but they need our business and cannot afford to alienate a school like Westminster, so in the end they give way. The boy who laid his papers on the floor will have to take elementary maths again but all his other results will stand.

This evening, I see the father of the boy who had already been expelled. He cannot see what all the fuss is about. He always copied other boys' prep when he was at school. The man is a fool. He cannot see that his son has put another boy's career at risk.

As the end of the school year approaches, men of sound judgement take leave of their common sense. Stewart Murray, head of geography and physical education, is an old friend and loyal member of the common room, but he has allowed the disintegrating summer term to persuade him that the school is out of control. He says he would like to put a questionnaire round the common room asking whether members are satisfied with the behaviour, manners and appearance of boys and girls.

At this stage in the school year? The man must be mad. I tell him to forget it. The last thing we need just now is an excuse for the common room to put all their moans and groans on paper.

Friday 11 July

The last day of term goes without a hitch. At the governing body meeting this afternoon, the governors reject by a large majority a proposal that Westminster should join the Assisted Places Scheme. I am delighted. If they had voted to join, my position as a headmaster so publicly opposed to the scheme would have been difficult. The governors' opposition is led by Lord Trend, the former cabinet secretary, and by Lord Carr, the former home secretary, and once these two big guns made their position clear, the governors who favoured joining the scheme, like David Carey, backed off, though no doubt the subject will come up again in a year or two.

1980-1981
Play Term 1980

~ ༀ ~

Friday 12 September

I see two new school monitors at 8am to talk about the role before I appoint them at Latin prayers. I have, unwisely perhaps, tried to summarise the monitor's job on paper and have given each monitor a copy. On my way to Latin prayers, I pick up from my hall table an envelope marked 'private and confidential'. It contains a copy of my instructions for monitors with the phrase 'The headmaster's decision is final' underlined in red ink and written across the top 'L'école c'est moi?' So I go into Latin prayers wondering whether there is to be some public expression of dissent when the new monitors are appointed. But no, those days are over. I am too much in control.

After Latin prayers, I teach two periods, one with my Oxbridge historians and one with the top new boy form which contains all the scholars. One of the scholars asks me to explain logical positivism. I cannot and do not try. Never bluff with these boys; it is the quickest way to lose their respect.

This evening, I go round to College for coffee with Paul Castle, the new captain of the school. There is a row in College with 14-year-old scholars who have been in the school for a year throwing their weight about. We shut them up and then talk about Paul's future. He will go to Christ Church and then is keen on the academic life, by which he means university, though he would make an excellent schoolmaster.

Wednesday 24 September

I am in Edinburgh for the annual general meeting of the Headmasters' Conference. I don't look forward to these occasions any more because, although I have a few good friends, headmasters as a whole regard me with suspicion. This morning, I make a contribution to the open debate that follows the secretary of state's address on values in education. The tenor of the contributions from the floor is so self-satisfied and complacent that I cannot resist the temptation. I catch the chairman's eye, rise and say that we should be more concerned than we are about the low standard of honesty in our schools. 'There is not a single school represented here,' I add, 'where it is safe to leave an expensive calculator lying around for five minutes.' The journalists prick up their ears. The damage is done. Mark Carlisle, the secretary of state, responds kindly and constructively but colleagues seethe. Why did I not think of the press reaction? I was provoked by the holier-than-thou comments about the excellent moral teaching, especially in boarding schools, but my critics will think I am just headline grabbing. I spend the rest of the day fighting off angry colleagues who flatly deny that stealing is a problem in their schools. What liars they are. I learn later that even before the debate ended, one headmaster was called to the telephone to be told that two of his boys had been arrested for shoplifting.

If I felt unpopular last year over my opposition to the

Assisted Places Scheme, I feel an outcast now.

Thursday 25 September

Catch the 10.15am Flying Scotsman to King's Cross and mark history essays on the train. The morning press is not too bad, though one paper sent a reporter to interview young Westminster boys coming out of school yesterday afternoon.

'Is there a lot of stealing at Westminster?'

'Yes, quite a bit.'

Other headmasters will say that serves me right and will take the line, if their parents and governors ask, that this is a Westminster problem not typical of public schools as a whole. In which case I shall have to find some way of exposing their hypocrisy. I have made too many enemies. Headmistresses dislike me for advocating the transfer of girls to boys' sixth forms. Former direct-grant schools and the Tory Party dislike me for my outspoken opposition to the Assisted Places Scheme. Many people dislike my successful, but in their eyes, ungentlemanly use of the media and now they are furious because I have exposed what is well known anyway – that boys and girls in independent schools steal from one another and from the local shops.

Monday 6 October

I receive a letter from the *Times* agreeing to my suggestion that I should write an article on thieving in schools. The *Daily Mail* carries a front-page story about a Westminster boy's father whose wife's death is being investigated by the police. Allegations have been made that there was something suspicious about the circumstances of her death.

Friday 17 October

My article on thieving appears in the *Times*. It is not just about schools but it ends with this thought: 'The heads of independent schools might reflect that their claim to have a special concern for moral education will sound hollow if they pretend that there is no problem.' That is enough to provoke some backwoodsmen. Sure enough, I have just returned from Latin prayers to find Daphne doing her best to cope with a furious headmaster of King's College, Taunton. He telephones to say he, his staff and his boys are very angry about my article. How dare I presume to have what he calls 'the freedom of the press'? I am, he adds for good measure, 'forever tainted as a spokesman for independent schools'. I put the phone down because it is time to teach my Oxbridge historians. What a relief it is to be with mature 17 and 18-year-olds instead of with headmasters who so easily lose all sense of proportion.

After lunch in College Hall, I see a Jewish girl who is refusing to attend Abbey. She has been in the school for two years and it is rather late to discover that she has a conscientious objection. I have never allowed any boy or girl to be excused Abbey, whatever their belief or non-belief. It is the way we start the school day, and if you don't like it you are in the wrong school. I am not going to make an exception in this girl's case. She is followed by a boy who, having been offered an unconditional place at Trinity, Cambridge, says he has lost all motivation to work. He has a healthy contempt for open scholarships. I tell him not to worry; as the exam approaches his motivation will return.

This evening, to a prep school in Kent to talk to parents and answer questions about Westminster. Stealing is not mentioned. It is a lively session but the pouring rain and heavy traffic make for a dreary journey through south-east London.

Wednesday 29 October

A fine autumn day, breathtaking in its freshness and beauty. I see the father of a 15-year-old scholar who is under-achieving academically. Boy is at the silly stage, too young to be doing A level but too bright to be held back. Father is quietly concerned and sensitive. He says that his son read my novel *The Custard Boys* and liked it. Father believes that reading the novel has persuaded his son that the headmaster is not out of touch after all.

This evening, I see a young master who put a boy in detention for being late for class when the boy had been attending the weekly choir practice. The master is protesting against the timing of the practice by punishing the boy. Needless to say, he is in the wrong and I tell him so. He is a large, rather unsophisticated man who is inclined to do things as the mood takes him and disinclined to ask advice of older, more experienced men.

Wednesday 12 November

Dame Cicely Saunders[107] talks to the John Locke Society about caring for the terminally ill. It is good for the boys and girls to hear death discussed in such a practical, sensitive and unsentimental way. After lunch, I continue interviewing sixth formers individually, asking how their A level subjects are going and whether they have had any problems adjusting to the sixth form. Some are rather shy, others very sophisticated and end up inter-

---

[107] OM, chair of St. Christopher's Hospice.

viewing me rather than vice versa. Those who know that their work is not going well enter my study with a spring in their step and their explanations and excuses at the ready. It is only five or six minutes each but it is one of the most satisfying aspects of the job.

Thursday 27 November

The Oxford and Cambridge entrance exams are under way and I am glad to see that the history papers are straightforward. This morning, I drive to west London to talk to a hall full of sixth formers drawn from four comprehensive schools. It is not a success. I have been asked to talk about values in a changing society, but as soon as I start talking, some of the girls are reduced to giggles (by my accent?) and some boys talk among themselves. I struggle on, acutely aware of not making contact, but in a discussion that follows, the gigglers and the talkers are not short of interesting opinions, so much so that a shouting match develops between a group of white boys who hold unexpectedly right-wing views and a group of black girls who appear to be both more intelligent and more mature. Both sides make what in liberal, middle-class circles would be regarded as racist comments, but here seem harmless, even positively healthy because they are out in the open. As I walk away from the meeting, I see 'NF' painted on the wall, beneath which someone has written 'No Future'.

Friday 12 December

A quiet end of term. This evening I am a guest at a dinner in College Hall to celebrate the centenary of the founding of the Old Westminsters Football Club. It is so well intentioned and the welcome is so friendly but the speeches are far too long and in one case so crude that what should have been a pleasant evening turns into a nightmare. Endless recalling of past glories and legendary heroes is just bearable, but the speaker who proposes the health of Westminster's football is so deplorably crude that even the most boisterous diners are taken aback and glance at one another to see whether it is alright to laugh. The fool continues with one grossly obscene joke after another for an excruciating 15 minutes, and I am aghast at this demonstration of the English public-school ethos at its worst. The only consoling thought is that this man must have been educated at Charterhouse 40 or more years ago and that even the worst public school today could not turn out such an unattractive specimen. At last the speeches are over.

I sigh with relief and push back my chair, but thoughts of escape are premature. An ageing footballer rises unannounced and unwanted to make a speech of his own. Trapped by embarrassment and inertia, the audience allows him to ramble on in a gaga fashion, trying to list the men who played under his captaincy long, long ago. I can hardly contain myself.

Sunday 28 December

We dine with David and Patsy Puttnam. David's film *Chariots of Fire* is finished and has been chosen both for the Royal Film Performance and as a British entry for the Cannes Film Festival. Harold Wilson is also a guest. He has recovered from an operation but still looks weak and suffers from short-term memory loss. He cannot rememberwhere the lavatory is and twice heads for the front door before being caught and steered upstairs. But his grasp of historical detail is as extraordinary as ever. Out of the blue, he gives me detailed information about the six Westminster boys who became prime minister, and when I tell him that one of the best things he did when he was prime minister was to appoint Edward Carpenter dean of Westminster, he can recall every stage of his battle with the Church of England establishment. There was, he says, a powerful anti-Carpenter lobby orchestrated by John Hewitt, the man in Downing Street responsible for advising on Church appointments but Harold favoured Carpenter and so – according to Harold – did the Queen, although officially she was not allowed to express an opinion. The church lobby fought very hard to block Carpenter but the Prime Minister had the last word.

Lent Term 1981

Tuesday 13 January

A very cold morning to start the term. I see Nicholas Barker about his son Christian. By way of an opening gambit, Nicholas says, 'The school has made a balls-up of Christian's education.' Nicholas is Sir Ernest Barker's son. We have known one another for 20 years, ever since he worked in publishing for Rupert Hart-Davis[108] and helped to prepare my novel *The Custard Boys* for publication. Now we sit together staring into the flames of the gas log fire, brooding on the difficulties of seeing our own children

---

[108] Director of Rupert Hart-Davis Ltd, publishers 1946 to 1968.

through adolescence. I ask whether there are any members of staff Christian respects, and with the two names Nicholas gives me, I will try to get the boy back on track.

Tuesday 3 February
A housemaster has found a quantity of cannabis in a sixth former's possession. The story is this: the sixth former bought the cannabis from another boy for £30 before Abbey yesterday morning. I see both boys individually. The buyer is rather a sad misfit, underachieving, parents on the point of divorce, his life centred on records and punk out of school. The seller is altogether different. He is a smooth, intelligent, articulate Anglo-American with father in New York and mother in South Kensington; he claims he sold dried nettles as a joke and that someone must have swapped cannabis for the nettles. He says he intended to return the £30 in a day or two. No mitigating circumstances in either case. After consulting housemasters, I decide that both boys should be expelled. I fear that when the seller's father hears the news, he will be on the next flight of Concorde accompanied by his attorney. It is that sort of family, so I alert the school solicitor just in case.

Monday 2 March
After Abbey, Ronald French comes for one of his routine and predictable moans about his colleagues' failure to impose discipline. To Cambridge this afternoon for a meeting with Easterling and Robson, the former and present tutors for admission at Trinity College. They know I share their enthusiasm for abolishing the post-A level entrance exam at Oxford and Cambridge that gives public-school boys and girls such an

advantage because so few state schools can afford to run a post-A level class. And they share my enthusiasm for getting rid of scholarships at the university because they encourage schools to concentrate on potential scholars at the expense of the others.

We meet in Robson's rooms overlooking Great Court, a set that was designed and financed by the Duke of Somerset who wanted his son to live in style at the university. Then I meet up with Daphne for dinner at the union, where I am speaking against a motion welcoming the Assisted Places Scheme. Neil Kinnock and I are opposing the motion, which is being proposed by Rhodes Boyson, a Tory MP and education spokesman, and by Alan Cooper, the headmaster of King's School, Macclesfield, a former direct-grant school that wants the assisted places to fill the gaps left by the abolition of the direct grant. Alan Cooper spends most of his speech attacking me for writing articles in the newspapers and appearing on television. 'Most headmasters prefer to spend their time in their schools,' he adds, at which Neil leans over to say, 'He doesn't like you, does he?' Cooper's personal attack on me helps to lose his side the debate and Neil and I win easily.

We give Neil a lift home. He talks about the effect of the recession on the poor families in south Wales; but when Daphne, who has recently returned from Calcutta, describes in detail the poverty in parts of that city, Neil falls silent. At his request, we drop him off in Parliament Square where it is pouring with rain.

Tuesday 3 March
The Pancake Greaze[109] at 11am this morning is one of the few

occasions left in the year when there is a chance of my losing control of the school. In one sense, it is a formal event with the dean (accompanied by the verger) and myself in our red cassocks, but in another sense it is an invitation to anarchy because as the boys fight for a piece of the pancake, the spectators could get carried away, making it almost impossible to restore order. It never quite goes that far but the fact that it could keeps us on our toes. The winner this year is a sturdy 13-year-old called Todd Hamilton. The dean presents him with a golden guinea, which will be exchanged later for a five-pound note

This afternoon, a difficult hour with a 16-year-old who has made a number of attempts to kill himself. He left the school last term for hospital observation and treatment and now wishes to return. His father, who is approaching 80, supports his son's wish and so does the psychiatrist who has been treating the boy, but I do not believe it would be fair on the housemaster and on the boys and girls in his house. When I spoke to the psychiatrist, he said it would be in the boy's interest to return to the school – but what about the interests of the other members of the school community? I remember all too well the effect of a young boy's suicide when I was headmaster of Taunton. We had no forewarning then but now we do and I do not think I would be justified in taking the risk. I explain this to the boy and he says he understands. We talk about the merits of various tutorial

---

[109] An ancient custom of unknown origin. Jeremy Bentham, who was at school 1755 to 1760, refers to it in a letter but the custom is probably much older. The chef tosses a large pancake over the bar up school and one boy from each form joins the scrum to fight for the largest piece. The scrum continues for one minute and the winner receives a golden guinea from the dean, which is exchanged later for modern currency.

colleges where he could take his A levels.

This evening, to the Athenaeum to speak at the annual Shrove Tuesday dinner for Old Westminster lawyers. Sir Michael Havers proposes the health of the school and I reply. Havers was at Westminster just before the war and is now the attorney-general in Thatcher's government.

Monday 9 March

Heavy rain all day. Some boys take no notice of the shallow lakes on Yard's uneven surface; they step deliberately into the water to show that they don't care. Before the war, a rolled umbrella was part of the school uniform but now, not a single umbrella in sight. Some girls hold their books on their head to protect their hair from the rain. I see boys and girls before Abbey – this one with good work to show me, that one with an appeal against a housemaster's punishment.

Tuesday 17 March

To the Hall School in Hampstead with the registrar, Geoffrey Shepherd. The Hall is one of our best feeder prep schools so we are not so much on a recruiting drive as on a visit to correct disinformation about Westminster spread by our rivals for the best boys. No public school headmaster would admit to spreading disinformation, but feedback from parents suggests that it happens frequently. Geoffrey and I are old hands and manage to imply that boarding schools in the country are more likely to be dens of vice than schools that are in touch with the real world.

Election Term 1981

Friday 24 April

In morning Abbey, I allow myself to be irritated by a boy standing in the front row with his hands in his pockets refusing to sing. It is my pride that is offended, not my religious sensibilities. I catch him on the way out and tell him that he will have to sing in future, to which he replies, 'I don't want to be impertinent but I don't believe in God.' I threaten to ban him from Abbey, which is the silliest thing to do, but I recover quickly and tell the housemaster to move this boy to some obscure corner and replace him with a hearty singer.

Wednesday 29 April

I keep thinking I must describe in detail a typical headmaster's day.

I rise at 6.30 and spend an hour before breakfast drafting a paper for the governing body on the need to make changes in our academic curriculum, changes that will in turn have implications for manpower, the largest single item on our budget. Westminster governors do not usually have strong views about what subjects should or should not have priority on the timetable unless they have been lobbied by heads of academic departments.

At 8am, I open the mail. My secretary dislikes my doing this. I think she feels that in some way it downgrades her status but once I am at my desk, I am impatient to get on with the day's business. A parent writes to say that she understands from her son that the bursar is cutting down on the money spent on school lunch at the same time as incurring unnecessary expenditure providing fitted carpets for his office. I recognise at once the voice of her son's housemaster. What are the facts? The bursar's office has just had a new carpet but there has been no cut in expenditure on school lunch. The only connection between the two is in the housemaster's disgruntled imagination.

Two boys to see before Abbey, one with good work to show me, the other wanting to know whether he can go on a junior-school expedition this weekend when he has already been gated for frequenting a pub under age. I hurry through the cloisters putting my gown on as I go, unprepared to take morning Abbey. As it happens, my off-the-cuff comments on the lesson are not heard because without warning us, the Abbey clerk of works has arranged for repairs to the roof to coincide with the start of our service. It is a 'one-off' not worth complaining about.

I teach three periods this morning (that is not typical) and then welcome Dr Nicholas Rawlins, a research fellow at University College, Oxford, who is talking to the John Locke Society about the undergraduate course in psychology and about his own special interest: the study of anxiety. We go to College Hall for lunch.

This afternoon, I continue interviewing boys and girls in the Remove about their university and career plans. It will take me three weeks to interview all 120 of them. At 4.30, I see at parents' request, an Eton boy who has been expelled for driving his housemaster's car down the high street. He is said to be a good linguist who wants to do Russian. Is that the reason for my interest or is it the fact that he is the heir to a dukedom? When he has gone, Cedric Harben comes to see me. He is a good man and a good chemistry teacher and will become housemaster of Rigaud's in January, but my heart sinks when he takes out a typed list of points he wants to raise. After just under an hour and with a wonderful feeling of release, I escape and walk out into Little Dean's Yard to see what is going on and to talk to any boys and girls who are around.

This evening, I go up school for the bishop of London's farewell party. Gerald Ellison has been a good neighbour and has made many friends inside and outside the church. The hall is crowded and the speeches are too long. A clergyman faints and is carried to a chair where water is flicked in his face in what looks like the parody of a religious ritual. I have arranged to play fives after the party with three boys. My partner and I lose but it is just what I need after a long day. Home to bath, complete this diary and go to bed soon after 11pm.

Thursday 21 May

I am working late when a headmaster colleague telephones with this sad story. A master at a famous boarding school was recently suspected of molesting young boys. The headmaster sent him a note to say that he wished to see him 'on an important matter' the following morning. The master never arrived for his appointment. Later that day, his body was found near the railway a mile or so out of town. He had thrown himself in front of a train, which severed his head and carried his trunk down the line.

Monday 15 June

After Abbey, I go up school to check on the internal exams for the Lower Shell and, walking between the desks, I notice that young X has chemical formulae written on the palm of his hand. I tell him to come and see me after the exam, but when he arrives, I cannot pin him down. He never meant to use the formulae, of course; he wrote them on his hand last night when he was revising and forgot to wash them off. There is no way I can prove otherwise and he goes off with a ghost of a smile on his face. He will have a successful career in some job that requires a quick wit and a ready tongue.

Thursday 25 June

An important meeting this afternoon to discuss what our policy should be if boarding numbers continue to fall. When I came to Westminster in 1970, there were 292 boarders and 190 day boys, making a total of 482. This year, 1981, there are 218 boarders and 300 day pupils, making a total of 518. We have been able to compensate for the fall in boarders by increasing the number of day boys and girls but the large increase in total numbers has put great pressure on our limited space. Unlike many other schools, Westminster has nowhere to build a new day house or a new classroom block and buying existing buildings in this part of London is way beyond our financial resources. So if boarding numbers continue to fall, we shall be in serious trouble.

I have circulated a paper to colleagues explaining why the solutions used by other schools that face this problem are not open to Westminster. We cannot, as other schools do, try to reverse the decline in boarding by recruiting overseas or by lowering the academic entry standard for boarders. Westminster is a weekly boarding school and could not cope with large numbers of boys from the Far East who have nowhere to go at the weekend. Westminster is also a school whose most powerful appeal to parents is that it is one of the leading academic schools in the country. If we lower the academic standard for boarders, our reputation will be undermined.

I have invited all the key players to discuss this problem and although there are the usual hobby horses and the predictable disagreements between the hawks and the doves, between those who think the answer is more discipline and those who believe that Westminster's liberality is what attracts parents who would otherwise have sent their children to a country boarding school, from my point of view the discussion goes well. When the meeting ends, I am confident that these professional men and women have taken on board that Westminster's future depends on how successful we are at attracting more boarders of the right academic calibre.

Friday 10 July

I went to bed too early thinking that I had stayed up long enough to deter last-night-of-term pranks. This morning at 6.30, walking from my house into Yard, I meet Bill Drummond[110], the clerk of works, whose more than usually lugubrious expression tells me that I made a mistake and that the pranksters were only waiting until the coast was clear. Bill leads me into Yard and points up at the roof of Ashburnham House. There for the world to see in large white letters is the message 'No Nukes, Fuck Defence'.

My first thought and Bill's is that whoever did this took one hell of a risk. From the steeply pitched roof of Ashburnham House it is a straight fall for three storeys to the paving stones

---

[110] Bill Drummond was a 'character' and one of my most valuable allies on the non-teaching staff. He knew instinctively when the headmaster should be told and when it was better for an end-of-term prank to be dealt with off the record.

below. It required a very strong nerve to hang suspended on a rope while painting the letters. One slip, Bill tells me, and he or they would almost certainly have been killed.

Our next thought is a purely practical one. The pranksters chose last night to get their message across because today is Election Day, the last day of term, when Yard is filled at different times with parents collecting boys and girls, governors coming to this afternoon's governors' meeting and distinguished guests attending this evening's Election Dinner. It is essential that we find some way of removing this graffiti as quickly as possible. A few young early risers look up on their way to breakfast as Bill and I ponder our options. Can the graffiti be washed away or painted over, and even if it can, who is going to take the risk? Not for the first time, Bill Drummond comes up with the solution. He suggests we hang a tarpaulin from the top of the roof to cover the letters. The risk is much reduced and the problem of how to clean the roof can be left to the holidays. I tell him to go ahead. If people ask why the tarpaulin is there, we can think of a vague statement about repairs or cleaning.

After this, the end of term goes smoothly and as far as the graffiti is concerned, the least said the better. We have outmanoeuvred the pranksters by quickly removing their message from view, though they will have the satisfaction of having pulled off a remarkable steady-nerve stunt. I am interested to know who was responsible but have no intention of starting a witch-hunt.

In Ashburnham Garden after the Election Dinner, guests, governors, colleagues, senior boys and girls and scholars enjoy a drink and a quiet talk. There are rumours of riots in Brixton and some in the garden say they can see the sky across the river is lighter as though buildings are on fire. It is only the following day when I am writing this journal that I am fully aware of the contrast. While young Westminster boys were being congratulated on their Latin and Greek epigrams, their contemporaries south of the river were throwing petrol bombs at the police and looting local shops.

1981-1982
Play Term 1981

Sunday 13 September

I have done 11 years at Westminster and sense that it is vital to show that I still have the energy and the enthusiasm needed for the job. If people, that is to say governors or parents or members of the common room, have the slightest hint that I have lost interest or run out of steam, I shall be vulnerable. The term starts tomorrow and I am ready. The key question in this new school year is whether I am seen to be effectively leading the fight-back against the decline in the number of boarders.

I try without much success to write a sermon for the beginning-of-term service on Tuesday morning. What the boys and girls need is practical advice, not high-brow philosophising. This evening, housemasters and heads of department meet to sort any problems that arise as a result of A and O level results. The most difficult cases are those of boys and girls who want to have a shot at Oxbridge even though their A level results do not suggest they have a chance of success. Our policy is to let them have a go unless they are obvious non-starters.

A sharply critical review of my book *The Public School Revolution* by Auberon Waugh appears in today's *Sunday Telegraph*. The book was published two weeks ago and has received plenty of good reviews, so Waugh's hostility comes as a bit of a shock, all the more so because it is not so much a review of the book as an attack on me personally and my reputation as a maverick in the education world.

Wednesday 16 September

When William Frankel, a former editor of the *Jewish Chronicle*, talks to the John Locke Society about the Israeli case, Omar Qattan, a Palestinian boy who is trying for Oxford this term, tackles him vigorously but Frankel handles the questions well and wins respect.

Thursday 17 September

This evening, a meeting of housemasters and heads of department to resolve any conflicts over choice of college by Oxbridge candidates. It is a case of trying to prevent too many good candidates applying to the same college. After 11 years, I know the strengths and weaknesses of individual colleges better than anyone and rather enjoy being the final arbiter when there is a clash.

Jim Cogan waits behind after the meeting to tell me that frustration and anger with the bursar are already evident after only a few days of the term. The bursar's personality leads him to try to wriggle out of a corner instead of admitting that he has made a mistake, thus losing respect and getting himself into deeper trouble. I do not relish the prospect of another conflict between the bursar and the common room so I draft a letter to the bursar – why a letter? Why not tell him to his face? – to say that I am aware of some friction between his department

('department' – another evasion) and the common room and have asked the president and secretary of the common room to see him to discuss how such friction can be avoided in future. The headmaster is a referee between the different interests in a school and, like the referee, he is frequently accused of making wrong decisions.

Friday 18 September

The first Latin prayers of term. The school is so large we cannot find seats for them all and a number have to stand at the back. I appoint new school monitors and then lead the singing of the psalm and chanting of the paternoster, versicals and responses. I am not a classical scholar and could not translate every phrase but Latin lends itself to this sort of robust community ritual. I love to hear the school's responses; the boys and girls take part more willingly than they do in Abbey. I am fantasising, of course but 'Et libera nos a malo' ('and deliver us from evil') always seems to be sung with particular force.

Monday 21 September

In Abbey this morning, I talk about Voltaire's response – 'a terrible argument against optimism' – to the Lisbon earthquake on All Saints' Day in 1755. It is my contribution to Willie Booth's week of reflections on the problem of suffering. Teach Oxbridge history sets on historiography and then see the parents of a girl new this term who says her chemistry master never explains anything. I promise to speak to the master concerned. When they have gone, I pack a case and set off for the annual general meeting of the Headmasters' Conference in Oxford. After last year's furore over stealing, I have resolved to say nothing that could possibly be quoted by the press.

Tuesday 22 September

HMC's annual dinner in Christ Church hall. We use Christ Church not because it is one of the grandest colleges, but because it has enough bedrooms to accommodate us all. However, there is no doubt that the hall at Christ Church is where public school headmasters feel most at home. This evening, the hall is filled with 250 headmasters and guests. The headmasters shine like black cats in their dinner jackets. After dinner, they light up cigars and listen to the speeches and as they lean back in their chairs and blow smoke up into the vastness, I am reminded of First World War cartoons of war-profiteers. Throughout the day, we have been criticising the government's cuts in education but this evening, we can't help feeling pleased that the cuts have not applied to us. The handful of female guests look ill at ease, as well they might, for the headmasters are for the most part patronising or rather clumsily flirtatious. After dinner, I go for a walk to cool my head and, pausing to look in the window of a second-hand bookshop, I see a copy of my book *The Public School Revolution* for sale. It is only three weeks since it was published.

Wednesday 30 September

The classics department has asked for an urgent meeting. When they are settled in their chairs, Theo Zinn reads out the charge against me. In *The Public School Revolution* I give the impression, he says, that classics at Westminster is on the decline which, they believe, is untrue. At the best of times I would have found it difficult to listen to his whinge but now I am anxious to catch a train to Haywards Heath to talk to prep school parents about boarding at Westminster. So instead of letting Theo talk himself out I keep interrupting him. He and Denis Moylan believe that classics should receive special treatment; but why do they need the headmaster to discriminate in their favour if classics is not on the decline? It is a frustrating meeting and gets us nowhere.

This evening Geoffrey Shepherd and I talk and answer questions from a large audience of parents at Cumnor House Prep School in Haywards Heath, Sussex. For two decades at least, Cumnor House has supplied us with a steady stream of boarders, but that stream has dried up and we do not know why. Cumnor House's headmaster, Nick Milner-Gulland, is an Old Westminster and tries to encourage parents to consider boarding at his old school, but parents tell him that if their children are going to board, they want a boarding school nearer home so that they can easily travel to watch matches, attend plays and concerts and so on. Some also say they want full boarding, not weekly boarding, and others admit that they are not convinced that Westminster does enough to protect its pupils from the temptations of London. Nick suggests that when we talk to parents we concentrate on this last point and so we do. How successful are we? Only the number of candidates from Cumnor House in the next few years will give us the answer.

Monday 5 October

I teach my Oxbridge historians for the first hour and a half after Abbey. Then a Thames Television producer comes to ask if I will take part in a programme arguing the case for the abolition of Christmas. He offers a fee of £500. It is crazy. Several hours' work on an article for the newspaper earns me £100. For a year's work on a book I am lucky to earn £1,500. And he is offering me £500 for half an hour's discussion on television. It is out of all proportion and I shall accept it without hesitation. After lunch, I see a mother whose story makes bad listening. On Saturday night her son, who is a 16-year-old boarder, invited too many friends to a party at home, and many others arrived uninvited. She called the police, who cleared the crowd outside the house. She was shocked by the behaviour of boys and girls from Westminster and from other schools. I ask why her husband did not help and she tells me that he was away for the weekend. She wants to blame Westminster for the chaos and damage but although I am angry at the boorish behaviour, I do not accept that the school is to blame. We are at loggerheads. I tell her she was responsible for allowing such an open-ended party when her husband was away. She tells me that the behaviour of Westminster's boys and girls reflects the school's failure to give a lead on matters of morals and manners. I do not feel like trying to find a formula that will enable us to part on good terms so she leaves as disgruntled as she came.

This evening, I walk round to Barton Street where a small number of girls are boarding with a master and his wife. Officially, this is an experiment but if we can find the space, we can expand girls' boarding as another way of countering the fall in boarders.

Friday 23 October
I receive a letter from Shirley Williams asking me to speak at a meeting on education in Crosby where she is standing for the SDP in a by-election. She is trying to overturn a 19,000 Tory majority and obviously hopes I might be able to counter those who accuse her of destroying the grammar schools. I would

like to do it but I need to consult Edward Carpenter and Burke Trend first. They will protect me if other governors are critical. I shall not consult the Headmasters' Conference because I do not care what they think.

Monday 2 November
Over the exeat, I heard from Edward Carpenter and Burke Trend. They both advise me to say no to Shirley Williams because they think the risk of being misquoted by the press is too great and that Westminster might suffer from articles along the lines of 'Why is a public school headmaster defending one of the leading opponents of selective education?' I shall take their advice.

At Latin prayers this morning, I offer a brief apology for a crack I made about CND at Latin prayers before the exeat. I don't think the headmaster should use such a one-sided occasion to attack beliefs that some boys and girls hold dear. After prayers, some senior boys catch me in Yard and tell me that in their opinion my apology was a mistake. I am not quite sure what their argument is but it appears that they think the headmaster should never apologise, certainly not in public. Interesting.

The mother of a scholar comes to see me. Her other son is very unhappy at Bryanston (he is the third or fourth unhappy boy from Bryanston this term) and wants to come into the sixth form at Westminster next year. Why is he unhappy? He has been badly affected by his parents' divorce. How does he get on with the other boys in the house? He stole the house pocket money, which made him equally unpopular with the housemaster and the boys. I say that he can take his chances with all the other candidates for sixth-form entry and that there are no special favours for the brother of a boy already in the school.

This evening, drifting round the school, I call late on Tristram Jones-Parry, the housemaster of Busby's, and we have a drink together in his study. We have both been concerned about a 16-year-old boarder in Tristram's house who is increasingly disaffected. Tristram asks whether I know the circumstances of the boy's father's death. I do not, so Tristram tells me. When the boy was six years old, his father called him into his study. Father asked the boy to close the door. Then he took a revolver out of the desk draw, and shot himself in front of his son.

Thursday 5 November

This afternoon, the Duke and Duchess of Kent visit the school. They are interested in their younger son, Nicholas Windsor, coming to Westminster. I would have thought that being in the centre of London would raise questions about security for a member of the royal family. A pleasant, polite couple. I have arranged for a master to go round the school ahead of us to sweep away any scruffy or punk figures with the result that we meet only the most respectable-looking pupils. I am congratulating myself when Julian Mann[111] appears, looking even more eccentrically dressed than usual. He slinks past, making no acknowledgement of our presence. The Duke eyes him with surprise, while I reckon that any chance of Lord Nicholas Windsor coming to Westminster has vanished.

---

[111] After Peterhouse, Cambridge, he worked as a journalist before being ordained and is currently vicar of a parish in Sheffield.

Sunday 8 November

After the Remembrance service in the Abbey, I walk over to the RAC for a swim. A 15-year-old boarder challenged me yesterday to a race over 100 yards freestyle. He is a constant source of irritation to his housemaster; nothing serious, just adolescent naughtiness combined with an exasperating gift of the gab that enables him to talk his way out of many a tight corner. And here he is, sitting on the side of the pool and dangling his legs in the water. We race and for three lengths I keep up, but on the fourth he sprints away, kicking his legs hard and leaving me struggling in his wake.

Monday 16 November

The high mistress of St. Paul's Girls' School telephones to ask whether I can send some Westminster boys to a dance that her girls are organising. I reply that I am not prepared to do this. I don't like boys being used as cannon fodder any more than girls. The high mistress rings off abruptly.

Wednesday 25 November

Boys to see before Abbey. Nothing serious, so a warning is all that is needed. In Abbey, I talk briefly about an 18th-century Westminster boy, Augustus Montagu Toplady, whose hymn 'Rock of ages cleft for me' we are singing this morning. A divinity prize was founded in Toplady's memory and I mention that one of the winners just before the war was Tony Benn. Coming out of Abbey, a senior boy walks alongside me in the cloister and says that he thinks it was 'inappropriate' to mention Tony Benn's name in the Abbey.

Michael Quinlan, who is the senior civil servant in the

ministry of Defence, talks to the John Locke Society about Britain's nuclear deterrent and puts the case against nuclear disarmament. He is brilliantly clear and cool and must have raised doubts in the minds of boys and girls who support CND.

This evening, Geoffrey Shepherd and I drive down to Dulwich College Preparatory School which – despite its name – is one of the main providers of boys for Westminster. Our aim here is to persuade more parents to think in terms of weekly boarding. There is a large audience of 200 or so and from the lively question-and-answer session, Geoffrey and I think we have at least awakened parents' interest in the possibility of weekly boarding. We return in a rather self-satisfied mood, convinced that Westminster is the best of all possible schools. However, driving towards Parliament Square we spot three of our girl boarders on the pavement, one of whom is smoking. We stop and question them. They say they have their housemaster's permission to walk round the block because it is a warm night. The smoker is standing with her cigarette inexpertly hidden behind her back. I make a mental note to tell the housemaster not to give girls permission to walk round the block at 11 o'clock at night and tell the girls to see me in the morning before Abbey.

Friday 27 November

Shirley Williams won Crosby in the by-election, overturning a huge Tory majority. A 15-year-old boy to see before Abbey. He ought to be sent home but I settle for a warning and the reason is this: last week his mother told him that his father was not in fact his real father. Real father apparently disappeared soon after the boy was born. I am not sure whether the real father and mother are divorced and I do not think it is my business to ask. Stepfather (if indeed that is what he is) pays the boy's fees by writing enormously successful non-fiction books.

Thursday 3 December

This evening, the Rigaud's Society holds a dinner in College Hall in honour of the housemaster, Ronald French, who retires this term. It is an occasion out of a novel by Evelyn Waugh or Tom Sharpe – rowdy, good-humoured and just managing to avoid anarchy. Ronald enjoys every moment of it. He sees himself as the last of the great Westminster housemasters, which is nonsense, but this evening's gala performance no doubt confirms his self-deception. When he replies to the toast, he talks of the importance of discipline while one of his house monitors is sitting in front of him smoking a cigarette. That scene accurately captures the man: talk of discipline while turning a blind eye to what his favoured boys are doing. He wants a reputation for being a strict housemaster who is popular with boys, and such is the gullibility of many boys and parents that he just about succeeds.

Friday 4 December

A letter from a parent who needs help to pay the fees. He is a highly-regarded writer but you need to be a bestseller to keep up with Westminster's fees. When I speak to the housemaster, he tells me that the father pays the fees not by writing but by playing poker. He recently won £900 in one evening – perhaps his luck has run out.

Tuesday 8 December

Snow and for once it has settled and shows no sign of melting. A housemaster rings: 'Should we stop the boys snowballing?' Certainly not. It is good to see them having an excuse to let off steam.

Thursday 17 December

The first Oxbridge results look good, though the element of lottery at Oxford is more marked than ever. The difference between Oxford and Cambridge? Cambridge entry is less of a lottery and Cambridge colleges are less susceptible to the sort of family connections that can still influence your chances at Oxford. It is the last night of term and, after last term's roof-painting episode, I have arranged for an all-night vigil to deter any end-of-term prank. Masters who thought it was unnecessary are now (at midnight) enjoying coffee and sandwiches in the common room and making a patrol of Yard and other school buildings every half an hour. But all is quiet on this bitterly cold night.

Friday 18 December

I spoke too soon. At 1.30am, two boys were spotted on the roof of Ashburnham House. We leave our coffee and sandwiches and rush round to Ashburnham House like keystone cops. Then up the stairs and out onto the roof where we arrest two Oxbridge candidates who, having finished their exams, are preparing some prank. They look rather taken aback to be arrested by a posse of masters. They have no paint with them but I recognise them as two of the boys suspected of being responsible for the anti-nuclear message on this roof in the summer. We escort them back to their house and I tell them to report to me at 8am. They are both leaving today and I can do no more than send them home straightaway with a letter to parents saying why.

After breakfast, I am told that 23 boys and girls (including one of our night climbers) have won open awards at Oxford and Cambridge, a record as far as open awards are concerned. The school needs that to maintain its reputation as an academic high-flyer and I need that to keep my critics at bay after 11 years as headmaster.

Monday 21 December

Keeping things in perspective. A father who comes to see me about his son's lacklustre academic performance this term tells me that whenever he worries about his son, he remembers an aristocratic lady who had complained to him, along the following lines: 'My son has been expelled from Eton for an offence that I thought had become acceptable since Wolfenden, my daughter has been sent down from Oxford for failing her exams and my cat has been raped by a hare.'

Loose ends at Oxbridge, mostly disappointments but not all. X applied to Christ Church for English. The college turned him down and he was not picked up by his second or third-choice college. I heard on the grapevine that Keble was looking for an English candidate so I telephoned the college and persuaded the tutor for admissions to look at X's papers. I hear today that Keble has given X a place.

Lent Term 1982

Tuesday 19 January

On the first day of term, a governing body meeting in Jerusalem, most of which is taken up with a lively discussion on the relative merits of Oxford and Cambridge. It is provoked by the list of open awards in my headmaster's report. Someone asks why there are more awards at Oxford than Cambridge and why almost all the awards in science and mathematics are at Cambridge. The dean of Christ Church springs to Oxford's defence. It is 20 years out of date, he says, to think of Cambridge as superior in science and mathematics. I think he is wrong but remain silent because I want to hear the views of the numerous distinguished Oxbridge academics on the governing body. But the dean of Christ Church has not finished. There is no element of lottery in Oxford's entry system. 'Oh yes there is, there is bound to be,' says Lord Trend, rector of Lincoln College. It is a serious and civilised debate and although I have often been frustrated by the geriatric bumblings of Sir Reginald Sharpe and Sir Henry Chisholm, on this occasion I realise how lucky I am to have so many governors of high calibre.

Saturday 23 January

When I return to my study after Abbey, I receive a telephone call to say that the bursar, Kenneth Stevens, died during the night of a heart attack. It is so unexpected it is hard to focus on the news. We were not close, headmasters and bursars seldom are, but we shared many problems and confidences, particularly in relation to the governing body. I telephone his wife and she seems down-to-earth about it all, asking whether I would be kind enough to let the governors know and put a notice on the common room board. When I have put the phone down, I think about the consequences of Kenneth's death. Though he was an improvement on his predecessor, he was still remarkably maladroit in his relations with other people. I am sorry for his wife and daughter who have never really become part of the Westminster community and will now have to find a new home. As far as the school is concerned, we shall start the search for a new bursar and pray that this time we get it right.

Monday 25 January

I go over to the bursar's office, where the chief accountant and I look through the papers on Kenneth's desk to see if there is any urgent business. Meanwhile, the common room's reaction is understandably mixed. The uncompromising nature of death's decision stops them in their tracks, but only briefly; like me, they are thinking ahead to a time when there is a bursar the common room can get on with. This evening, a long talk with George Weston, the new captain of the school, mostly about who we should appoint as school monitors.

Friday 29 January

After Latin prayers, I see a 17-year-old who is an A level candidate and has lost all his motivation to work. He switched from science A levels, which he thought he hated, to arts A levels, which he thought he would love, and in the process has lost all interest in his work. He is difficult to reach because he seems to be only half conscious. His eyes look elsewhere. A loner, shy and uncertain; the adopted son of an evangelical Anglican clergyman with a smart West End parish. I do not get very far with him and with his eyes darting around the room, I am not sure he has heard a word I said.

Monday 1 February

Talk to Rory Stuart's English set about the arguments for deism and then welcome back Simba Lyons, the former bursar, who is going to hold the fort until a new bursar is appointed. We never got on well and in 10 years he never used my Christian name, but now, as we shake hands, he says, 'Hello, John.'

Thursday 4 February

Dr George Birdwood comes to talk to housemasters and matrons about illegal drugs and smoking. He is at his best, informative about the present scene, balanced in outlook and low key in delivery. He is just what we needed. He talks regularly to the boys in the lower school and is at the end of a telephone if I need advice. I was lucky to find him. We talk for a while after the meeting and I tell him that the amount of drug use here is difficult to judge, though the impression is that my hard line has had the effect of reducing the number of boys and girls using drugs. We both realise, however, that the hard line makes monitors and others less willing to pass on information, so the impression of less drug use may be a false one. We just don't know.

Friday 12 February

Instead of Latin prayers this morning, Charles Sewart, Isobel Nyman and Miles King play the first movement of Mendelssohn's piano trio. I am so proud of them. They play superbly and appear to hold the school's attention by sheer expertise.

This evening, I drive to my old school, Bishop's Stortford College, for a common-room dinner in honour of Leslie Soady, the senior master who is retiring after 36 years on the staff. He arrived at the school in 1946 when I was 15 and we soon clashed over a number of issues, especially my wish to resign from the army cadet corps of which he was the commanding officer. He refused to accept my resignation, so one night, I took a group of friends out on bicycles to the cadet corps' weekend camp and cut down all the tents while the inmates were fast asleep. We just about got away with it and cycled back to school. Leslie Soady must have had a good idea about who was responsible but he could not prove it. And now he is sitting beside me at his farewell dinner, a kindly, ageing man who stoops and looks frail. Should I tell him? I think not.

Friday 19 February

Bill Drummond, the clerk of works, interrupts my breakfast. Some boys have removed the Greaze bar and hidden it somewhere beyond Bill Drummond's searches. That takes some doing because the iron bar is heavy and padlocked to the wall. If it isn't found before the Greaze next Tuesday, we shall look foolish. I go up school for Latin prayers and after making announcements, I say 'I see the Greaze bar has been temporarily mislaid. As Mr Drummond and I took precautions to prevent this happening, I must, reluctantly, congratulate those responsible. Now the deal is this. I do not want Mr Drummond to spend the weekend looking for the bar and replacing it. If those responsible speak to him and arrange to help him replace it before Tuesday morning, that will be that. But if the bar is not back before Tuesday morning, there will be no Greaze and I shall then treat its disappearance as a serious matter.'

It works. By mid-morning break, the culprits have contacted Mr Drummond and arranged to help him replace the bar.

Thursday 25 February
A useful housemasters' meeting this evening to discuss what we should do about the half-dozen boys who look as though they will not obtain five O levels, which is our qualification for entering the sixth form. When it comes to the point, we find it hard to insist a boy should leave when we judged him to be Westminster material three years ago. We agree that parents should be given as much warning as possible. Then I change into a dinner jacket and drive to a party at Lord Rayne's home in Hampstead. Max Rayne has a boy in the school. It is a very upmarket affair with the Kents and other members of the royal family, hereditary and life peers by the dozen, fashionable ladies, cabinet ministers, leaders of the arts and industry and – somewhat improbably – me. I do my best to appear at ease but need the Dom Perignon to dispel the sense of being in the wrong place at the wrong time. Max Rayne looks as much a fish out of water as I do and I warm to him. I meet some pleasant people, some of whom know me. I also meet some people who, when they discover who I am, clearly have no intention of being stuck with such an unglamorous figure as a schoolmaster and quickly move on. I hang around for an hour or so and then drive home.

Friday 26 February
Interview applicants for the temporary English post and find one who should do rather well. The monitors' meeting after school goes over the familiar ground of setting up an elected school

council. The captain, George Weston, and most of the monitors are too sensible and too protective of their own positions to argue in favour of a school council, so I can sit back and give the radical minority enough rope to hang themselves.

This evening, I take housemasters to a buffet supper at Dulwich College Preparatory School, where the head, Hugh Woodcock, has invited housemasters from Westminster, Tonbridge and Alleyns to discuss with his own staff any problems of entry to the senior schools. It appears to be useful and it is interesting to observe the polite competition between the schools. At the end of the evening, I rise to say thank you on behalf of all three schools but no sooner have I sat down than the headmaster of Tonbridge makes a short speech expressing Tonbridge's appreciation of the evening and the headmaster of Alleyns, not to be outdone, follows suit. An interesting example of headmasters' fear of being outdone by the heads of rival schools.

Wednesday 10 March

Confirmation service in the Abbey this morning. As ever, Bishop Launcelot Fleming gives the service a depth and sincerity so that it is a moving occasion, despite being a small congregation lost in the vastness of the Abbey. After lunch, I see Angela Rogers, the secretary of the Haywood Foundation[112], and find her sympathetic to my idea that the foundation should fund sixth form scholarships for girls from state schools. I undertake to send her details of a scheme that would provide these girls with a springboard to Oxbridge and other good universities.

---

[112] One of the few charitable foundations prepared to pay the fees of girls who want to come to Westminster in the sixth form.

When she has gone, I play fives with George Weston as my partner against Peter Southern[113] and David Cook.

This evening, to the Westminster Cathedral Preparatory School on a recruiting drive. We are selling the idea of weekly boarding to parents who could easily send their sons to Westminster as day boys. Back home by 10.30pm to mark history essays.

Thursday 18 March

Drive to Oxford with Jim Cogan and Eddie Smith, head of mathematics. The dean of Christ Church has invited us because the college is worried about the falling number of Westminster applicants for places and awards. The historic connection between Westminster and Christ Church is strong, despite the ending of closed scholarships, but it cuts no ice with today's Westminster boys and girls. Their choice of college is influenced by: a) the feedback they have received from Westminster boys already at Oxford; b) the advice of their academic mentors (so Peter Southern may say to his historians that Magdalen and Merton are the best colleges for history at Oxford) and c) family connections with the college. The fact that 16 deans of Christ Church have been educated at Westminster means nothing to a Westminster boy who is trying to make up his mind.

We lunch with the dean and a number of admission tutors. Unwisely, I mention that some Westminster boys are put off by the Christ Church image, which is aristocratic and snobbish. The dean counters by saying that the Westminster image is 'arrogant and slightly dissipated'. After exchanging images, we

---

[113] Headmaster of Christ's Hospital 1996 to 2007.

get down to business. We can't force boys and girls to apply for Christ Church but I say that it would be easier to persuade boys and girls to apply if we had a clearer picture of the college's strengths and weaknesses, so perhaps the tutor for admissions could visit the school to talk to all our Oxford candidates, and this is agreed.

Election Term 1982

Tuesday 11 May
A lovely fresh summer day. Most of the morning is taken up with interviewing scholarship candidates. It is difficult to assess these bright young 13-year-olds and I have found over the years that the interview is no guide at all to the boys' performance in the scholarship papers. The parents reflect Westminster's changing clientele – more millionaires, fewer academics.

Tuesday 18 May
The fine spring weather continues and raises morale. The bursar selection committee interviews six possibles today and finds only one that is worth seeing again. Interestingly enough, he is also the only one without a service background. Between interviews we gossip or talk about the candidates and I find myself unnecessarily sensitive to remarks by governors on the committee about how sensible of this or that candidate to think of leaving after 10 years in his present job. This is my twelfth year as headmaster of Westminster and my ears may hear

hints that were never dropped.

On the other hand, it may not be just my imagination and if governors are thinking it is time I was moving on, I can't blame them. But what am I to do? I have written to Sir James Hamilton at the Department of Education and Science asking his advice and I am going to see him on 15 June. I am sure the right policy for me is to be active in seeking a new job without losing impetus here. I am not worried. I am too well known to be shunted by the governing body, but I want to leave before it is obvious to everybody that I am running out of steam.

Thursday 3 June

A surprisingly constructive housemasters' discussion for this stage of term. After this, I change quickly and rush to the Dorchester to attend the de la Rue dinner for the diplomatic corps. It is an enjoyable evening to which a number of public school headmasters have been invited, including Dom Philip Jebb[114] of Downside, who sits opposite me at dinner. As I walk back to my car after dinner, I hear shouts behind me and I turn to see a tall man with a handgun who shoots twice – crack, crack like a children's firework – and an Arab falls to the pavement in front of me. There is much shouting and confusion. A surprising number of men draw small hand guns from inside their dinner jackets. I hear that a Palestinian has shot the Israeli Ambassador emerging from the hotel. His automatic weapon (a machine pistol) lies on the ground near his body together with a brown leather shoulder bag in which it must have been hidden. I am not sure what to

---

[114] Headmaster of Downside 1980 to 1991.

do. Should I remain standing by the body or move away? Philip Jebb appears and kneels beside the mortally wounded Palestinian to administer the last rites. Eventually, a policewoman tells us to move on. I ought to feel excitement but I do not. Although I was so close to the attempted assassination and to the killing of the assassin, I am not involved.

Tuesday 8 June

I spend some time this morning entertaining a prep school headmaster and his wife. We need some more good boys from his school so I give him the deluxe tour, in the course of which I discover that there is a time, roughly noon, when the houses all look spick and span because the cleaning ladies have just finished and gone home. As I take my visitors round College and Grant's they keep commenting on the tidiness of boys' studies and making favourable comparisons with Winchester and Marlborough, which they have visited recently. We can't time all parents' visits at noon but prep school headmasters should always be invited to see Westminster at the moment in the day when the houses look orderly and clean.

Friday 11 June

Tristram Jones-Parry comes to see me about a boy in his house who has had some sort of breakdown and gone home. This is the boy whose father committed suicide in front of him. He had, until today, been making a success of finding (or do I mean 'fighting'?) his way through adolescence and has been a much less surly presence in Yard. What has gone wrong? A psychiatrist has seen him and arranged for him to go into the Middlesex Hospital. Both Tristram and I wonder about drugs but if there is any evidence, the psychiatrist will find it. The boy is doing A levels now and still has a number of papers to take.

Tuesday 15 June

To the Department of Education and Science to see Sir James Hamilton. He is a delightful and friendly Scot whose advice I have sought about my own future. Are there any interesting jobs in his gift? There are not but he is prepared to mention my name when asked about possible candidates for other jobs. He is particularly keen to encourage me to think about the principal's job at a polytechnic; that had never occurred to me but I will give it some thought because I like Hamilton and trust his judgement.

Interviewing applicants for the modern languages post this afternoon. Not bad but where have all the schoolmasters gone? They are well qualified but there's not one of whom I would say, 'There is a born schoolmaster.'

Saturday 19 June

Interview common entrance candidates all morning. This afternoon to a memorial service for Dr. R.L. James in Harrow School chapel. Jimmy James appointed me to Harrow and taught me most of what I know about schoolmastering. As personalities, we had little in common, yet I am conscious that his example of how to run a school is the one I turn to most. Jimmy shunned publicity, hated committees and was the very opposite of a hands-on headmaster. He ran the school from his study, where in winter he appeared to spend the whole day standing in front of the fire reading the *Times*. He was always happy to see you and never gave the impression you were interrupting some important work. When masters come to see me, they almost always start the conversation by saying, 'I know you are very busy, headmaster, but…' Daphne and I were very fond of Jimmy and his wife Bobbie. Sadly, the memorial service fails to capture Jimmy's character or to do justice to his peculiar genius for appearing to do nothing while running a very successful school.

Wednesday 23 June

Two Soviet educationalists visit the school. How serious they are, but when they return to me for a glass of sherry before lunch, they relax and say how much they envy our traditions. This evening, Daphne sees dark figures on the roof of the school. The IRA? No, much more likely to be Westminster boys. I go downstairs, hurry across Yard and, using the master key, gain access to school. They have probably seen me coming and made good their escape, but when I climb up the ladder behind the stage and onto the roof, three black figures are crouching in front of me and dangerously near the edge. This is no time for games of hide and seek; I tell them to follow me down, and when we are all safely back in Yard, I say, 'Report to my study at eight in the morning.'

Thursday 24 June

See the night climbers. For two it is a first offence (or the first that has come my way) and they can be gated for two weeks. But the third has been gated twice already in this school year. He goes in for an ugly type of bullying that the police would call 'demanding money with menaces'. He threatens younger boys, saying that he will beat them up if they don't pay. My mistake was in not expelling him for that more serious offence.

Wednesday 30 June

It being the silly season, two boys are found entering a girls' boarding house[115] in the early hours of this morning. They are 15-year-old scholars and, knowing them as well as I do, I guess that their intentions were frivolous rather than passionate, but I shall see them after lunch and find out.

I receive a letter from the school solicitor, Mallory Hollis. Some days ago, Lord Adrian wrote to Mallory to say that he would have to resign as a governor of the school because he was not a member of the Church of England. The school statutes do make this a requirement but until now no one has taken this particular requirement seriously; during my headmastership the governors have included at least two agnostics and the governing body itself unanimously agreed that scholars need not 'profess the Christian faith'.

It is preposterous that membership of the Church of England should now be insisted on as a qualification for membership of the governing body. Mallory Hollis's view is that although the school statutes could be changed, they should not be because of the school's close association with the Abbey. But the school has long ceased to require scholars or masters to be members of the Church of England and even the headmaster can be a Roman Catholic. The Church of England requirement was part of the school's modern statutes which were drawn up in 1869. I drop a note to the dean to say that I would like him to start the

---

[115] Girls' boarding started in a piecemeal fashion (the governors were not told that we had started) but by 1982, there were enough girls who wanted to board to convert one of our houses in Barton Street into a girls' boarding house.

process of getting the statutes changed.

After lunch, I see the two scholars caught trying to enter the girls' boarding house. They say it was just a prank to leave a pair of men's shoes outside the door of one of the girls' rooms. That is probably the truth. I warn them that at many schools, breaking into a girls' boarding house would mean automatic expulsion. That would be an exaggerated response in this case but they need a jolt and so does public opinion. I ought to send them home for the rest of term but one of the boys, Ben Hamilton[116], is an outstanding oarsman and a key member of our most successful Junior 15 VIII in years and they still have some high-profile races to come. I shall have to settle for gating them for the rest of term.

Thursday 15 July

The last full day of term and the familiar round of boys and girls to see about poor sixth form exam results, and masters keen to get their complaint or request in before the holidays. The last night of *Twelfth Night* in Ashburnham Garden. It is Richard Jacobs's first chance to break into the magic circle of Shakespeare producers and he does it very well. I set my alarm for 2.30am and go down into Yard to find Cedric Harben still up and glad to see me. A fire had been started in his house day room an hour or so ago. By chance, the flames were spotted almost straightaway and the fire put out. Another end-of-term prank? Possibly, but it is frightening to contemplate the consequences if the fire had not been put out quickly. Cedric, who

---

[116] Balliol College, Oxford, and then a television journalist.

has only recently taken over the house, is understandably shaken. We stand in Yard discussing what should be done. There is little doubt that the fire was started deliberately. Cedric suspects a boy who is leaving this term after a dismal school career, but we can prove nothing. I tell Cedric to question the boy first thing but to play the incident down as far as the boys and girls in the house are concerned. He asks whether I will say anything about it at the end-of-term assembly and, after some discussion, I tell him that I will not mention it at all. Arson is no joke but it will do nothing but harm to the school if boys and girls go home today and tell their parents that 'someone tried to set fire to one of the boarding houses'.

Friday 16 July
Cedric telephones me early to say that the boy he suspected is outraged to be accused and clearly has no intention of changing his story. We will have to leave it there for the moment. The last day of term follows its traditional course and happily all goes well. Even the governing body seems to have caught the spirit of good sense. Following the lead of the dean and Burke Trend, the proposal to remove the Church of England qualification for membership of the governing body is approved without a single dissenting voice. David Carey, who is all for keeping the qualification, goes along with the rest because he is above all a 'trimmer', not a man of principle.

In the garden after Election Dinner, as senior boys and girls talk quietly with governors and distinguished guests, I am struck once again by the beauty of the place. Arrogantly, I look on this small garden surrounded by school and Abbey as the centre of civilisation. I am so lucky to be here but my days are numbered.

Monday 19 July

Lunch with David Carey. Over coffee he raises, ever so tactfully, the question of my future. I tell him the truth; I have registered my interest in finding another job both with Colin Peterson at the Cabinet Office and with James Hamilton at the Department for Education and Science but somehow I doubt whether these approaches will produce a job. I explain to David that although I have done 12 years at Westminster, I am still only 51 and that is far too young to retire. David would much enjoy playing a key role in finding my successor. I don't begrudge him that pleasure but it is one he will have to postpone as I have no intention of allowing myself to be hurried out of office.

1982-1983
Play Term 1982

Tuesday 14 September

Quietly and smoothly, the new school year is launched. The autumn weather is warm and golden. The boys and girls look suntanned from holidays abroad, tidy and fresh and short-haired, the latter being the current fashion which for once co-incides with the headmaster's expectations. Before assembly, I stand on the steps of school, listening to the hubbub within while masters ask me to make this or that announcement. From time to time, a shout can be heard above the hubbub as one of the more experienced hands greets his friends across the hall, a public performance rather than a private gesture.

Friday 17 September

At Latin prayers, I appoint new school monitors, among whom is Alexandra Perricone, the first girl to be a head of house. The blazing September weather continues. The first rush of the beginning of term is over and the community settles down easily to an even pace. Morale appears to be good. Taken together, the A level and O level results are the best the school has ever produced. The demand for places continues to be strong.

I am too experienced to believe that this mood of optimism will last indefinitely and sure enough, after break, Theo Zinn appears on my threshold. Exactly what it is that exercises him is, as usual, difficult to identify in his rambling monologue about his timetable for next year, the problem of keeping order with the junior forms and his anxiety about his cat. Eventually, it turns out to be the fact that he does not want to retire at the same time as his friend Denis Moylan, who is the number two in the classics department and almost as much of a legendary figure as Theo himself. Theo wants his retirement to stand alone and says that there are bound to be 'certain events' to mark his departure. He wants to go out in style but not in tandem with Denis. He suggests that I should ask Denis to retire a term early, but I say that is something for him to do and this agitates him even more. The irony is that when it comes to the day, I doubt whether his leaving will be regarded by others as such a significant event as he anticipates. There is no doubt that he has been one of the great classics teachers but he has outlived his time.

Thursday 30 September

The housemasters' meeting follows a pattern. We are due to discuss this year's Oxbridge entry but first I ask whether there are any short points anyone wishes to raise before we tackle the main business. This approach usually disposes quickly of minor points that do not merit a place on the agenda, but not today. A new housemaster remarks that one of his new boys finished his station so early, he had time to go home for tea even though he is a boarder. Why are games allowed to finish so early? Why are some members of the common room allowed to opt out of supervising games? Is our credibility as a boarding school likely to survive if parents find their boarding son coming home for tea in Kensington on a games afternoon? We are soon off on a wild-goose chase through the complex maze of problems that face a school in the middle of London. I decide to let it run.

Thursday 14 October
Justin Albert reports to me before Abbey for being too often late for school. His father is an American lawyer and Justin has inherited some of his father's deft footwork. Late for school? Not intentionally, headmaster, but the buses are so unreliable.

Flu jabs this morning, a simple enough exercise but Ronald French who is supposed to be in charge, seizes the opportunity to criticise the school doctor who is a few minutes late, the school monitors who do not bark loudly or often enough and the pupils in general who are unpunctual and indifferent.

Then I see parents of a boy at Eton aged 14 who say he is being bullied. Bullying these days is not by the older boys but by the same age-group or sometimes by the next year up. It would be rare to find a 14-year-old being bullied by a 16 or 17-year-old. When I ask this boy what form the bullying took, he replies that other boys deliberately blasphemed in chapel because they knew he would be shocked. I'm afraid he would not find Westminster boys less insensitive and tell him so.

This evening to Camden Town Hall to join a meeting on education organised by the National Union of Teachers. A panel of eight, including myself and Neil Kinnock, answer questions from the floor. It is very much a left-wing occasion and the first questions are all aimed at me. How can I justify working in the 'commercial sector' with 'privileged children'? I reply that in a free society the state should never have a monopoly of education.

They are not won over, of course, because they have absorbed the left-wing ideology in which what used to be called the public schools are the root of all the evils in society. Then they go for Neil Kinnock who in defending himself overdoes the populist, welsh-wizard act. When he realises that this is not going down well, he switches from fine generalisations to unnecessary detail, citing clauses and sub-clauses in previous education acts as though detail was bound to triumph where rhetoric failed.

Wednesday 3 November

I see two 14-year-olds who have been making life difficult for a young woman who is here as a temporary French teacher. She is vulnerable and they have attacked. I tell them what I think of that and warn them that if they are reported to me again for this offence, they will be sent home. I doubt whether they have any sense of guilt. In their view teachers should know how to keep control and if they don't, that is their problem. Do they feel sympathy for the temporary teacher? Not at all. As A.C. Benson, the celebrated Eton master, wrote, 'The pathos of the situation touches the pupils not at all.'

A mother and son to see. Boy is at Oundle and wants to leave for no very clear reason. I am not encouraging. Westminster is prepared to consider genuine refugees but not those who are applying just because they think the grass is greener.

To the office of Enigma, David Puttnam's film company. The governors have agreed to give me a sabbatical term in the New Year and David Puttnam has agreed to let me accompany him to Thailand, where he is making a film called *The Killing Fields*. This morning, I meet the film's director, Roland Joffe. I like him at once and we are soon in animated discussion about the script, which I have read over the exeat. What exactly I shall do in Thailand and how long I shall stay remains to be seen but it will make an interesting start to my sabbatical in January.

After lunch, a meeting with the art department. Christopher Clarke is doing a good job as head of department but it appears that one of his part-time assistants often sends the sixth form set back to the house instead of teaching them. I tell her this must stop. She is under the illusion that Westminster boys and girls work if they are given a private study period.

Thursday 4 November
In the first two periods this morning, I take two new boys' forms, one after the other, to talk to them about the problem of drugs. These talks are part of my drug-prevention strategy. I try to make them as informal as possible, so they are held in our drawing room with boys sitting on the floor and me, gownless, in an easy chair. It is interesting to see the contrast in the reactions of the two forms. Transitus A is the scholars form and they listen in silence, asking and contributing little, overawed by the subject or by me. Transitus C, the bottom new boy form are talkative and interested and much more prepared to reveal their knowledge of the subject and its slang. My aim is to inform and deter. I want to build up in these 13 year-olds the basis for resistance to temptation if and when it comes along and to warn them of the sort of circumstances such as the unsupervised party when temptation is most likely to appear.

This afternoon I am told that two of our Colts football XI have been attacked and injured after a match against Pimlico Comprehensive. It is an ugly incident, not just pushing and shoving; chains were used and our boys have deep cuts on their heads.

I ring the police. It turns out later that the attackers were not from Pimlico Comprehensive but were well known local thugs. Pimlico and ourselves are equally anxious to prevent any aggro between our two schools, so it is a relief to discover that in this case, Pimlico pupils were not involved.

Friday 5 November
At 8.30am, I see Paddy O'Hara, who has been sent to me for persistently refusing to go to bed on time. Paddy is 16, Irish and a sweet-talker even by Westminster standards. I warn him of the danger if he goes on refusing to obey his housemaster. He says he understands.

After Abbey, I see David Poole and ask him to be captain of the school in January. It is no surprise to him, nor will it be to anyone else because for once there is no question as to who is the best candidate. He accepts my offer and we talk about his role over coffee.

This afternoon, some boys come to see me about starting a poetry society. No problem, but I wish they would get on with it. They have been going to start their society for several months and had better start now before the idea of a poetry society be-comes a joke.

At the end of a long day, I go for a swim at the RAC and find Paddy O'Hara about to dive in. He greets me as a club acquain-tance and is quite un-put-out by the memory of this morning's confrontation. We do some lengths together and I give him a lift back to school.

After supper, I play fives with the outgoing captain, George Weston, against two history men, Peter Southern and David Cook, and go with them all for a pint afterwards in a local pub.

Monday 22 November

Theo Zinn comes to see me this morning straight after Abbey. He looks upset and I fear some classics timetable problem has resurfaced, but once he has sunk deep into one of my armchairs, he launches into a long and sad story of how he has lost control of the 15-year-olds in his O level Latin set.

He does not want to go on teaching them. I refuse to give him permission to hand over this set to someone else. Instead, I tell Theo to send the two worst offenders to me. Theo says this is the first time in over 30 years that he has had difficulty with a form but his memory deceives him. With his small classics sets in the upper school he has always maintained an easy and relaxed discipline. Who couldn't! But he has had difficulty before with some of the less motivated boys in O level sets.

Wednesday 24 November

I see the two main trouble-makers in Theo Zinn's form and warn them off. I find myself trying to sound angrier than I feel and I use the words 'I have no patience with silly boys', which is both badly phrased and untrue. If there is such a character as 'a wicked boy', then I have no patience with him, but I am not sure he exists, except perhaps in the form of the persistent and cruel bully or the professional drug dealer.

Thursday 25 November

Simon has been caught smoking yet again. The problem is not what it seems. His persistent breaking of the rules will lead to expulsion unless we can change his direction. He is 16, first year sixth studying classics. Nice but ineffectual parents. Housemaster has exhausted all responses, boy has been warned several times and rusticated. I agree with the housemaster and mother that he should be withdrawn from the school for a few days to have psychiatric tests. That avoids expelling him, but how realistic an approach, it is I am not sure. As a personality, Simon is likeable if a little gauche, an odd character to find among the scholarly pupils who sit at Theo Zinn's feet.

Monday 29 November

This evening, to the Carlton Club in St. James's for a dinner that the governing body's executive committee is giving for Simba Lyons, the former bursar who stepped in at short notice when his successor Kenneth Stevens died in January. I park in St. James's Square and walk down King Street. Outside the Carlton, an ambulance is parked and I can guess what has happened. Simba arrived by taxi and was found to be dying in the back when the driver turned to tell him the fare. He is taken to Westminster Hospital but dies at 8.45pm. He was 75 and a rather lonely widower. There are worse ways to go than suddenly on your way to a dinner in your honour.

His death leaves us in a tricky position. Eight governors, the present bursar and I gather in the private room, not sure whether to disperse or go ahead with the dinner that has been prepared. Bishop Knapp-Fisher says that we should disperse immediately but this no doubt morally correct answer is greeted with little enthusiasm. Some governors have come a long way and the prospect of a good dinner is not easy to forego. So we sit down after the bishop has said a prayer for Simba's soul and enjoy an excellent meal. How Simba would have chuckled if he could have foreseen this valedictory occasion. He liked good food and good wine as well as anyone. After the meal we stand, heads bowed, our port half drunk, our cigars smoking in the ashtrays, as the bishop insists on leading us through the Lord's Prayer. One or two governors stumble over the words but the bishop's lead is firm (he was, after all, bishop of Pretoria in South Africa) and we arrive at the 'Amen' more or less in unison. Then we sit down, take up our cigars and resume our conversation.

Thursday 30 November
I have applied for the job of secretary-general of the Arts Council and this morning I go along for an interview at 3 Smith Square, the home of the chairman, William Rees-Mogg. The interview is fun, though I come away doubting whether they think I am the man for the job. I am not sure that I want to leave Westminster yet and I expect this comes through at interview, yet it is time I started to look for another job.

Monday 13 December
I thought I had seen the last of Theo Zinn for this term but here he is, anxious that his cat will be disoriented by structural changes in his flat during the Christmas holidays. Theo must have seen the glazed look in my eye because for once he departs promptly. Daphne tells me that she knows all about this as Theo telephones her regularly about his anxieties over his cat.

I hear from the Arts Council that I have not been selected for the job. I am less concerned about this than by the fact that the short list was leaked to the press and in one paper I am described as 'the dark horse'. The common room will know I applied but there is nothing I can do about that.

Friday 17 December

I get up at 2.30am to go on the night watch and all is quiet. I do not return to bed but take the opportunity of the silent hours to clear my desk. I am going on sabbatical leave next term and Jim Cogan will be acting headmaster. I am sure he will do it well but it is a comfort to know that David Poole, who is sure to be one of the best captains of recent years, will be staying on too.

Sabbatical Term 1983

Two weeks in Thailand as the guest of the film producer David Puttnam. My role – not very clearly defined – seems to be to work on the script and do some occasional scriptwriting. The film, *The Killing Fields*, will be directed by Roland Joffe and produced by David. Have I really got anything to offer this very different world? I suggest the script is overburdened with four-letter words and that they should be cut down. The scriptwriter clearly thinks I am just being a typical headmaster. Despite such disagreements, I am overwhelmed by the kindness, openness and professionalism of the film people, who have the true hospitality of nomads. In the evening, we sit at large tables in the tropical night talking about anything but the film.

From Thailand to New York, where I am the guest of Robin Lester, the headmaster of Trinity School in Manhattan. I have known Robin for many years and he has suggested that I should take one class a day of the senior boys and girls at Trinity in return for board and lodging in New York. I am happy to do this because it gives me the run of New York while enjoying the cut and thrust of debate with some very bright New York teenagers. Trinity is an expensive school, so the boys and girls I am arguing with are from affluent homes. I thoroughly enjoy my eight weeks in Manhattan and then, with Daphne, spend a week at Baylor University in Texas and a few days with my brother, Angus, at his home in Vancouver.

I return to England, very much refreshed but also rather impatient with some of the problems that I know are awaiting my return. There is a strong common-room lobby in favour of abolishing Saturday morning school as St. Paul's and Dulwich have done. I am not in favour. It will further encourage the collapse of boarding. Who is going to pay our boarding fees for a five-day week? I am impatient too with the pressure from the Under School to put in our application to start the Assisted Places Scheme.

Election Term 1983

Monday 25 April
The new term and back to the old routine. I am torn between eagerness to show I have lost none of my energy and enthusiasm and a strange feeling that I do not belong, that I should never have come back from my sabbatical. At the common-room meeting this morning, I aim to give the impression of a man who has returned rejuvenated and excited by new ideas but heaven knows whether I succeed. This evening, an Eton Group

headmasters' meeting and dinner at KCS Wimbledon. Good to be with headmaster colleagues again because we can laugh together at the absurdities of the job.

Tuesday 26 April

After a term away, I am determined to make my mark. After preaching in Abbey, I stalk round the school like a Virginian gentleman returning to his plantation after a long trip abroad. Have the boys and girls noticed that I have been away? David Poole, the captain of the school, has noticed. Over coffee we talk about any problems that need to be tackled and about his choice of university. Should he accept the firm place he has at Bristol to read the subject he wants, which is religion and literature, or should he have a shot at Oxford as his parents want but where there is no comparable course? I advise him to accept the firm offer from Bristol.

Tuesday 3 May

This evening, we give a party for 40 or so Harrovians to celebrate the publication of Daphne's book *A World Apart* on Thursday. It is such a happy occasion. Schoolmasters are particularly attached to those boys they knew well in the first years of teaching; master and pupils are only a few years apart in age and something like a genuine friendship develops, so it is good to see them and to pick up with ease the old ties.

Wednesday 4 May

Jim Cogan has alerted me to the possibility of a general moan in the common room about poor discipline in the junior forms, hence the common-room meeting this evening. The meeting starts badly and it is my fault. I ask David Hepburne-Scott, as a senior man and a good disciplinarian, what he thinks the problem is. I should have known better because David has 'lost interest' and is no fan of mine. His jokey answer nearly ruins the atmosphere. He says he used to expect high standards of discipline but has given up doing so as it is so obviously something that the school no longer cares very much about. I am angry and say that there is not much point in continuing to be a teacher if he has ceased to care about these things. This has a rather good effect and the meeting takes off on a constructive course. But it will further sour my relationship with a colleague and it could be dangerous because he will join the ranks of the disenchanted. A headmaster will always have enemies, yet he must do his best to see that they do not unite against him.

Thursday 5 May
Daphne's book *A World Apart* is published by Butterworths today. I pick up the first hint of possible trouble in a diary piece in *The Times* this morning. I am not unduly worried but I do not want Daphne to be exposed to attacks if the public school establishment gets the whole thing out of perspective. It would be ridiculous if the book was regarded as a criticism of public schools, which it certainly is not. Some boarding school heads are so paranoid about bad publicity that they would complain if there was an article in the press criticising boarding kennels for cats and dogs.

Friday 6 May
I am interviewing the boys and girls in their A level year, a process that takes several days to complete. Most of these boys and

girls I know well but there are a few I hardly know at all. They have slipped up the school unnoticed and I do not want them to say in a few years' time, 'The headmaster? – we never spoke to him.' Some are absolutely clear what subject they want to study at university and what career they hope to follow; others have no idea at all on either count.

This evening, I take a party of our heads of department to the Hall Prep School in Hampstead to meet their staff. It is a useful evening that is only slightly soured by one of their language teachers whose son was expelled from Westminster for stealing. We manage to avoid mentioning the subject, but I catch her watching me, as though I am the Night Porter with a murderous past.

Tuesday 10 May

The attacks on Daphne's book gather momentum and there is a note of real unpleasantness that surprises us both. The headmaster of Wellington School in Somerset, John Kendall-Carpenter, accuses Daphne of being 'a sick woman'. Is that how one headmaster speaks publicly about another headmaster's wife? Even more disappointing is the reaction of Tim Devlin, director of ISIS, the Independent Schools Information Service. I have recently written to ask his help in presenting the case for independent schools in a Channel 4 television debate. His reply comes today. He cannot offer me any help because Daphne's book and my views on the Assisted Places Scheme make me an unfit person to speak on behalf of independent schools. What on earth has got into the man? He would not have got the job of director of ISIS without my help and I have always regarded him as one of the few people who can keep all the hysteria about bad publicity in perspective.

Feeling frustrated by the stupidity of some independent school headmasters, I take the train to Shrewsbury to talk to the common room about changing values in our schools. It is good to find a window seat and enjoy a few hours of privacy. Simon Langdale, the headmaster of Shrewsbury, is to meet me at the other end but at first I don't see him or he me. At last, I find him sitting in his car marking essays. 'I am sorry,' he says, 'but one can't afford to waste even ten minutes these days.' I warm to him at once. He is an exponent of headmasterly one-upmanship. His common room are lively and a pleasure to talk to. Like Lord Milner, Simon has gathered round him a kindergarten of bright young men and I am envious. I have recruited some excellent young teachers but not enough. At Westminster, the large group of disgruntled ex-housemasters can still dominate the common room.

Wednesday 11 May

An early train to London and a chance to think about what might happen if the criticisms of Daphne's book continue. They ought to die down but I fear some people – journalists, fellow headmasters who would like to see me brought down a peg or two – may have an interest in fanning the flames. There is, I suspect, an undercurrent of misogyny. Some men hate women who dare to comment on the male world and nothing is more typical of the male world than the English public school. I arrive home in time to welcome Dr Oleg Kerensky, son of Alexander (former Russian prime minister), who is talking to the John Locke Society about his reflections on the Russian Revolution. This evening, a common room meeting to discuss all the boys in the Upper

Shell, that is, all those who are taking O level this term and making choices for A level courses. There are one or two boys whose chances of qualifying for the sixth form are small, but that is very rare at Westminster.

Thursday 12 May

Parents, masters and boys to see this morning. Daphne has gone to see her lawyer just in case the reactions to the book should turn really nasty.I have already intercepted one or two unpleasant letters addressed to Daphne, unsigned of course, and pretty unbalanced in tone. Experience has taught me to spot the poisonous-pen letter by looking at the handwriting on the envelope. The name and address written in scrawl or in capital letters is almost always a sign of unbalanced contents. I spotted one this morning and sure enough, the unsigned letter read: 'For a woman in your position to have written such an appalling load of titillating filth in your book *A World Apart* indicates personal weaknesses of a particularly prurient kind.' When I ring Daphne's lawyer, he gives me some free advice, on the lines that I am not responsible for what my wife may write. That is all very well, but it does not solve the problem of my relations with the common room and the governing body. If governors and masters think Daphne's book is damaging the school and it is known that I not only encouraged Daphne to write it but wrote some passages, my credibility as headmaster could be undermined. But I cannot believe that the book is bad publicity for public schools. The idea is preposterous. Nevertheless, as a precaution, I will see the dean and telephone Burke Trend in Oxford to make sure that they are aware of the problem. The dean confirms that he read the manuscript before Daphne's agent and wholeheartedly approved of the book. The only suggestion he made was to write a last chapter, 'Looking Back', which Daphne did. He also confirmed that he had shown the manuscript to Burke Trend. Whether Burke read the whole manuscript I do not know, but he did not apparently find anything that he objected to.

Sunday 15 May

This evening, I go round to the deanery to see Edward concerning school business and am surprised to find him uncharacteristically worried about the impact of bad publicity that Daphne's book has attracted. It is obvious that some senior members of the common room and some governors have expressed their concern about the harm that the publicity is doing to the school. I point out that much of the publicity has been favourable and that a well-known novelist, Susan Hill, wrote a very good review for a leading newspaper, only to have the review returned because the paper wanted the book to be attacked not praised. I also tell Edward that some of the hostility directed at the book is really intended for me. It is me the hawks in the independent school world want to bring down in full flight, not Daphne. We talk late into the night. What interests both Edward and myself is that Daphne has received so many letters of support and agreement from men whose experience of boarding school confirms so much of what Daphne describes. Far from disapproving of a woman writing about boys' boarding schools, they welcome it.

Monday 16 May

Not summer, not even spring. After Abbey, Jim Cogan briefs me about attitudes in the common room towards Daphne's book. A few, he says, are seizing the opportunity to argue that my position as headmaster is no longer tenable; they think I should resign so that a new headmaster can be appointed for the beginning of the new year in September 1984. The majority (according to Jim) believe that it would be ridiculous for me to resign and that the fuss over Daphne's book will soon be forgotten.

Tuesday 17 May

The governing body meets in Jerusalem. They will be discussing Daphne's book under any other business when I have left the meeting. That does not worry me unduly. What does worry me is that the Under School committee has put forward a proposal that the Under School should apply to join the assisted places scheme. If the governors approve, the first assisted places boys will move on to Westminster School at the age of 13 in two years' time. In other words, that is the moment when I shall have to resign on principle because I have always been totally opposed to the Assisted Places Scheme. Now all depends on how governors vote when they come to this item on the agenda.

Chilled white wine and cold salmon. The discussion on whether the Under School should apply to join the assisted places scheme is sensible and appears to be going well. I speak forcefully (too forcefully I think in retrospect) against the scheme and I am confident that we shall win a close vote. But we do not. The governors are in favour of the Under School joining the scheme by six votes to five. For the record, these governors were on the side of the angels: Burke Trend, Gordon Pirie, Edward Knapp-Fisher, Michael Baughan and the dean himself. Unless the governing body changes its mind and depending on how slowly the bureaucracy in the assisted places scheme operates, I shall be resigning as headmaster of Westminster sometime in 1985 or 1986.

Later this evening, at about 10.30, the dean calls and asks me to go round for a nightcap. When we are settled, he tells me that the governors discussed Daphne's book for an hour or so after I had left the meeting and came to the conclusion that there is no possible case for dismissing me or asking me to resign. They also asked Edward to convey to me their opinion that in view of the governors' vote in favour of joining the assisted places scheme it would be wise for me to start looking for another job in the next year or so. That is not an ultimatum, just advice.

Wednesday 18 May

I talk at length today with David Poole, the captain of the school, Jim Cogan and Willie Booth. I am taking soundings about the reaction in the school to the brouhaha over Daphne's book. The answer is that there is not much feeling about the book in the school and I have the impression that if it were not for disgruntled senior masters stirring the pot, the book would soon be forgotten. Members of the common room and members of the school want to get on with their own lives. Daphne's book is a skirmish in the ongoing struggle for power that characterises all schools. The boys and girls do not understand all the shifting alliances but the members of the common room do and play their part.

One of the more interesting aspects of the school's reaction is that no boy or girl has tipped off the press. That is unusual, as Westminster pupils are not slow to ring up the national papers.

Daphne has gone to Oxford to stay with the Trends.

Thursday 19th May

I think the crisis, in so far as it was a genuine crisis, over Daphne's book has passed. There will be some minor aftershocks, I am sure, but the power of the book to hurt us has gone. I go to bed early and sleep soundly.

Tuesday 24 May

This evening at 9pm, I am working at my desk when John Grigg rings to say that they are expecting us for dinner. We rush down to Blackheath and what an excellent evening it is. John and Patsy Grigg and their other guests cannot get their minds around the fact that *A World Apart* poses a problem.

Over dinner, we are reduced to mirth, almost hilarity, by our inability to understand what it is about Daphne's book that causes so much offence. Anthony Sampson, who was a scholar at Westminster in 1940 and whose son has just joined us, simply cannot grasp what all the fuss is about. It does us both so much good to hear someone who knows the school well, both as a former pupil and as a parent, explode with laughter at the suggestion that the book has in some way done the school harm that as we drive home in the early hours, our spirits are higher than for a very long time.

Friday 3 June

I have a heavy cold and have to force myself through the day – Latin prayers, teaching A level historians, chairing a long meeting on switching to a five-day week – so that by the late afternoon I am worn out. There is no escape from the treadmill, however, because this evening there is a dinner in College Hall to say goodbye to the three masters who are leaving at the end of term. The first is a man I have sacked because he is clearly unable to control, let alone teach, Westminster pupils. This is his first job and I am convinced that, like Mr Chips, his best hope is to be given a second chance in a different school where his limitations are not known. The master chosen to wish this man well has the good sense to keep it short and the audience welcome both his brevity and his wit. The second, who is also going with my blessing, presents an intriguingly difficult problem because he is disliked by the rest of the common room. The master chosen to sing his praises does a good job, proving once again what hypocrites school teachers are.

Last is Theo Zinn, who speaks about Denis Moylan's qualities as a schoolmaster and as a colleague. So far so good; but then Denis replies in an extraordinarily dull speech that means little or nothing to his younger audience. In its way, it is as arrogant a performance as I have heard in a long time because it assumes that the heroes of his distant past will fascinate those sitting nearby. No wonder the latter are soon talking among themselves.

Thursday 9 June
Appoint acting school monitors to cover the A level period. They are on trial, so it will be interesting to see how they get on. I vote SDP. Exit polls predict a Tory landslide but I am too tired to stay up into the early hours.

Friday 10 June
The Duke of Kent comes to tell me that he would like his younger son, Lord Nicholas Windsor, to come to Westminster. That will be one in the eye for those croakers in the common room who argued that Daphne's book weakened Westminster's ability

to attract pupils. I rather like the Duke. He is direct, unfussy and open.

Saturday 11 June
Three problems.

1. A 13-year-old is being teased in a way that is difficult to prevent. The teasing takes the not-unfamiliar form of implying the victim is homosexual. This morning a note addressed to the boy in class is intercepted. The note reads: 'What does fuck mean?' I go into the class after break. I do not believe in collective punishments, but in this case the teasing has been going on too long, so I threaten the form that they will all suffer if the boy responsible does not come forward. At the end of morning school, a tiny mouse of a boy appears at my study door to confess. I am so relieved, I nearly forget to be angry with him. I hand him the note he wrote and tell him to show it to his parents explaining why I have ordered him to do so.

2. A mother of a 14-year-old telephones to seek my advice. She is allowing her son to give a party this evening. Her husband is abroad and she has just discovered that her son has invited 50 friends. What shall she do if the party gets out of hand? There are many things I could say but at this stage, I say simply that, if things get out of hand, she should telephone me and I will bring a couple of the tougher housemasters with me to restore order. One day my bluff with be called.

3. A stranger telephones to say that his 15-year-old daughter has left home and is spending the weekend with a Westminster boy whose own parents have gone away for the weekend. I ask the boy's name. Then I telephone the housemaster and tell him

to check the home number because the chances are that the boy will answer the phone himself. He does. 'Why aren't you in school this morning?' The boy mumbles a lame excuse about not feeling very well. I know the boy well; he is an unpleasant and spiteful young man who is leaving at the end of term because he has been involved in a lot of trouble, never quite bad enough to merit expulsion, but always in such a way that someone else gets hurt. It is not my business who he spends the weekend with but it is my business if he cuts Saturday morning school and lies to his housemaster.

Monday 13 June

Michael Marland, the head of North Westminster Comprehensive School, telephones. I was due to speak tomorrow to his parents and staff about the state schools and independent schools working together but after last week's general election the National Union of Teachers' members on his staff met and passed a resolution saying that it would be an insult for me to visit their school and that they propose to picket the meeting. Michael apologises but says he will have to cancel the meeting. So much for free speech.

One of our best modern-language teachers writes to say that he wishes to resign at the end of next term. There is no doubt he is a good teacher of French but this is offset by his prickliness in the common room and I shall not be altogether sorry to see him go.

Tuesday 14 June

This evening to a meeting of the Headmasters' Conference political and public relations sub-committee. I have been summoned to appear before them to explain my attitude to a) the Assisted Places Scheme; b) Daphne's book; c) my all too frequent appearances in the media. They are fellow headmasters, together with Tim Devlin, the director of ISIS, and, with the exception of Tim, I do not think they really want to be quizzing me when they could be having a good gossip over dinner. It all ends amicably and I walk home across St. James's Park in the dusk. Out of the corner of my eye, I see this cameo of Westminster life. A Westminster boy is lounging on the grass with a girlfriend smoking a cigarette. He sees me and, dropping his cigarette into the grass, lies back on top of it. It is almost, if not quite an heroic gesture.

Friday 8 July

Despite lobbying for the other candidate by my allies, the common room elect Ronald French as their next president. This is not good news. Although the president of the common room has no official authority, Ronald French is quite capable of interpreting his role as speaking on behalf of the common room to the governing body and therein lies the danger: governors may think he represents the views of all the staff, but I know he does not. When the vote was taken in the common room, the result was a tie, so that the outgoing president had to exercise his casting vote. As the outgoing president was Denis Moylan, Ronald French was home and dry.

Friday 15 July

I set my alarm for 1.30am and get up to join the patrol of masters for the last night of term. I have no doubt that I should show more leadership qualities and insist that younger masters patrol in the small hours, but the truth is I rather enjoy it. So from 2am until 4.30am I spend two and a half hours working in my study and going out every half-hour or so to see that all is quiet. Time to think too. The dean has warned me the hawks on the governing body, notably David Carey and Michael Baughan, are going to raise the question of discipline in the school at the governing body meeting this afternoon. Although I am angry with the hawks for not consulting me first, I suspect there is more to this than meets the eye. I don't suspect a plot, but when your critics in the common room and on the governing body appear to be moving in concert, it is time to get your defences in order.

I am sitting on the low wall outside Ashburnham House when I notice movements in the shadows on the far side of Yard. They are easily caught. Did they really think they would be invisible? They decline to say where they were heading and I am not inclined to press them for the truth. I am suddenly wide awake, which is more than I can say for Andrew Mackay, an 18-year-old who staggers into Yard from some party or other. I decide to send them all off to bed before dawn lights up this unsatisfactory scene.

It develops into a very warm day, making the dean's uncharacteristically obscure sermon at the end-of-term service very difficult to follow. Then straight into the final assembly at which I speak in praise and gratitude of Denis Moylan's 32 years service to the school and especially of his gifts as a teacher. When he was appointed to the staff in 1951, his reference from his former school said of him: 'He is quite outstanding in the classroom.' That is still true of him 32 years later. Many boys and girls must owe their love of classics as well as their good A level results to Denis's teaching but sadly he remained a narrow-minded man whose life followed a routine of walking from the school to the Oxford and Cambridge Club for dinner and thence to his rooms in Pimlico. Prompt at 8.30 in the morning, he reappeared in Dean's Yard to start the school day. He was a lonely man, a bachelor with few close friends and I do not know what he will do with himself in retirement.

This afternoon, the governing body meets in Jerusalem. The bursar has provided a highly unsuitable meal and a heavy claret wine, with the result that most governors find it difficult to concentrate. David Carey and Michael Baughan raise the question of bad discipline under any other business. As I have been forewarned, I do not find their criticisms difficult to deal with. When I suggest that it would have been more helpful to raise the matter with me directly rather than at a governing body meeting, several governors say, 'Here, here,' and that effectively ends the discussion.

No doubt the hawks on the governing body and in the common room will return to this question in the new school year but there is no reason for me to be threatened by them. Westminster's reputation has never been higher and the governors know this. Unless I lose confidence in myself, my position as headmaster is secure.

1983-1984
Play Term 1983

Saturday 10/Sunday 11 September

The longest hot summer of the century ends in wind and rain. We have swum and surfed in Cornwall. I have applied for the directorship of the London School of Economics and written to influential friends asking for help in finding another job. It makes sense to look around. Smooth flight path into the term.

I see two possible candidates for captain of the school. A is the more senior. He is rather tense but well-meaning and clearly wants the job. The other boy, B, is that rare person who is obviously right for the job and mature beyond his years. He will not be 17 until November, but has already got excellent A levels and is trying for Oxford at the end of term. I shall appoint him. At 6pm on Sunday, the meeting of heads of department and housemasters to sort out the large number of Oxbridge candidates who are returning. It is good to see these colleagues again; so many of them are high-quality professionals – more secure, less quirky and thin-skinned than at any school I have ever known.

Monday 12 September

An angry letter from the father of the disappointed candidate for captain of the school. He is a backbench Tory MP and he and his wife have all sorts of political and Oxbridge connections and are used to getting their own way. They come round to see me this evening and needless to say it is a difficult meeting. We part, if not on friendly terms, at least still talking to one another. Otherwise, the term has got off to a good start, though I hear that Ronald French, the new president of the common room and no fan of mine, gave a characteristically provocative performance at the common-room meeting that followed mine. He will want watching. I write a sermon for tomorrow and sleep well.

Wednesday 21 September

At Latin prayers up school, I speak to the school about behaviour at the weekend. It is outside our control but parties gate-crashed and so on damage the school's reputation. Westminster pupils do have something of a reputation for wild behaviour and when added to the accusation of intellectual arrogance, it does not make them popular. Lunch with Tony Howard, the editor of the *Observer*. He is one of the people I have written to for advice about finding a new job. He promises to sound friends in the BBC and to see whether there might be an opening for me as an occasional columnist on his paper. He urges me to join the National Union of Journalists. Return to my study for an 'open-door' session. Between 4pm and 6pm any boy or girl can drop in to raise whatever they like. The queue and the questions extend beyond 6.30pm.

Friday 23 September

I take Abbey and provoke angry protests by my comment on the lesson. Jesus, asked whether tribute should be paid to Caesar, answers 'Render unto Caesar the things that are Caesar's...' I say that I find this a clever but evasive and unsatisfactory answer. The fact that I am critical of Jesus causes great rage among a few members of the common room and one of them writes me a characteristically silly letter, posing as the defender of true religion in a godless school. I return an unprovocative answer but he is not satisfied and writes to the dean to complain. As it happens, I prepared nothing for Abbey this morning and my comments were off the cuff when I heard the lesson, but I still think they are valid. But I must not underestimate the harm one hostile master can do and I will prepare my Abbey homilies in future.

Otherwise, a routine day. A Canadian headmaster to show round, historians to teach, colleagues to see, monitors to meet.

Saturday 24 – Monday 26 September

On Saturday afternoon, I fly to New York. Bus to Central Station and walk to the Algonquin Hotel where I am booked in for two nights. The BBC has brought me over to film in the Bronx High School of Science as part of a programme on selective schools. Bronx Science is an oddity: a selective high school within a non-selective school system. At 14, some 7,000 boys and girls take a test in maths and English and about 800 are selected. The 3,000-pupil school teaches arts as well as science but the excellent science programme gives the school its name and reputation. I spend the day visiting classes, talking with pupils and staff, and getting the feel of the community. It is the quietest school I have ever been in. The 3,000 high school students go about their business speaking in purposeful, low voices. The teaching is traditional, didactic and many teachers seemed unwilling to encourage any dialogue with these gifted boys and girls. But the school is an eye-opener to me. No discipline problems, no graffiti (not quite true because I was relieved to find some graffiti towards the end of the afternoon), hugely successful results, almost all leavers going on to good colleges.

I fly back overnight on Monday and go straight to the AGM of the Headmasters' Conference in Cambridge. Having been their chairman, I am now something of a black sheep or rogue elephant and I leave the Conference early to return home.

Thursday 29 September

Our 1st XI earn a draw with Repton, a school that takes its games very seriously. A reporter from the *Times* is covering the match and this will help to counter the image of Westminster as just an intellectual hothouse. At 6pm, housemasters meet and I cannot help reflecting on how lucky I am with the present team. I tell them I have received a letter from the MCC completely undermining the governors' allegations last July that our boys' behaviour had been bad. When I read the letter, I rubbed my hands. I will circulate it to the governors without comment. It is important not to score easy points; the letter will speak for itself.

Monday 3 October

Instead of Abbey, Daniel Glaser, a sixth former, plays two pieces for the flute. Daniel is the all-rounder of whom headmasters dream. He took our scholarship exam from a comprehensive school and easily did well enough to have been in College but he chose to be a day boy honorary scholar. He is not only bright, but sane, a good musician and a keen oarsman who rows in the Junior 16 VIII. What more could you ask?

Tuesday 11 October

This afternoon, to Vincent Square to watch our 1st XI play Winchester. An interesting thing happens. The game is hard and exciting and ends in a 1-1 draw. As the teams leave the field, the Winchester master approaches in the grip of an almost uncontrollable rage. I cannot imagine what has got into him. It turns out that he is furious with the hard, abrasive play of our boys.

'I have not seen anything like it since I watched football on Hackney Marshes,' he says. Hackney Marshes? I am at a loss. It doesn't sound a very suitable place for football. He accuses our boys of cheating, of physical intimidation, of questioning the referee's decisions, in short, of 'playing like professionals'. I am rather pleased. For years I have tried to persuade Westminster boys to play harder football as they are so often knocked off the ball by more robust country schools. 'This is not what public-school football is about,' the Winchester master tells me. I make soothing noises because he is our guest and he is clearly very angry, but I watched the whole game and cannot honestly say that it occurred to me that our players were anything other than fully committed. I think part of his wrath is at being held to a draw by a team that he may have regarded as a soft touch. I am not perturbed. Our team played hard but not dirty and it was a pleasure to see Westminster boys refusing to be pushed around by another school.

This evening, to St. Thomas's Hospital to talk to students and doctors on 'Independent schools and the politicians'. A pleasant dinner after in the consultants' dining room.

Friday 14 October

This evening, a long meeting about whether we should – like St.Paul's – abolish Saturday morning school. It is a frank and constructive discussion and I am proud of my colleagues as they hammer away at this complex and potentially divisive subject in such a mature fashion. At the end, the majority favour a five-day week while recognising that the price of making the change may be too high. Let off steam with a vigorous game of fives with a colleague against two senior boys.

Monday 17 October

Two boys arrive with a petition signed by 265 boys and girls asking for a change in the regulations to allow smoking outside the school. Although I am very unsympathetic I agree to consider it. Bruce Kent, the treasurer of the Campaign for Nuclear Disarmament, comes to talk and draws a good audience if little support. The boys and girls are not hostile but neither do they believe in the unilateralist stance. Kent is agreeable and articulate but they are not convinced. Despite the anti-nuclear graffiti on the roof three years ago, CND has few supporters at Westminster these days.

Wednesday 19 October

A talk with Willie Booth. He is worried that a division is opening up in the common room between the croakers – as Wellington called them – and the rest. The croakers are a small group of the disaffected and disappointed, with the master who complained to the dean about my godless of-the-cuff remarks in Abbey at the centre of the group. He is leaving at the end of term but I cannot ignore the danger that Willie is warning me against.

Frank Singer, the American English Speaking Union student, comes round for a talk. He likes Westminster and is enjoying the English teaching in particular. However, he says he is shocked by the open racism of some of the boys. Frank is Jewish and I ask whether the boys are anti-Semitic but he says no, the racism is directed against West Indian and Asian immigrants. He finds it all in marked contrast to the USA where – he says – that sort of blatant racism is a thing of the past. What he says does not altogether surprise me; racism is widespread among the English of all classes and schoolboys are less inhibited than their parents about expressing it or perhaps they are just less hypocritical.

Friday 21 October

The final of the music competition raises a typical problem. The new director of music has revived the house choirs and persuaded every house to enter. That is fine but some of the entries are robust rather than tuneful and each house is cheered on by its supporters. As the first item on the programme it has its dangers, particularly when the adjudicator is an Old Westminster and there are a number of parents in the front rows. There are moments when the rowdiness becomes embarrassing and I am uncertain whether to go forward and rebuke the supporters. Any public occasion may challenge the headmaster's judgement in this way but the rowdiness subsides and I do not have to intervene.

Wednesday 2 November

I have invited Rabbi Hugo Gryn to spend the morning in the school. He talks in Abbey, teaches three senior history classes on the Holocaust and speaks to the John Locke Society on

'Religious and philosophical responses to prejudice'. He is in excellent form, communicating agony with wit and dissecting bigotry with deft strokes. Westminster now has a larger Jewish population than when I arrived in 1970. This is partly because I removed the 'Christian faith' qualification for scholars which has helped to dispel our former reputation for anti-Semitism. However, we make no concessions to any non-Christians when it comes to compulsory attendance at morning Abbey. Hugo tells me that Jewish parents are put off Westminster by Saturday morning school.

Interviewing candidates for the modern-language job this afternoon. One or two good ones but it is the old story – the perfect candidate does not exist, though one continues to believe in his existence. A parents' meeting this evening to brief parents of new boys and girls about our academic organisation. It goes well. The only miscue is made by a colleague who bewails the influence of 'these wretched computers' with the minister for information technology sitting in front of him.

Thursday 3 November

A disgruntled prep-school headmaster to see. He has complained that Westminster has not communicated what it is looking for in the way of candidates, so I give him a lot of time and walk him slowly round the school, talking with boys (carefully chosen), going into classes and so on. Most of his boys go to St. Paul's and we want some of them.

This evening, after a particularly constructive housemasters' meeting, I go to Jerusalem for a dinner in honour of Sir Reginald Sharpe who is retiring – thank God – from the governing body. It is all good fellowship and warmest thanks. I sit quietly and do my duty but cannot share the hyperbole. Rex Sharpe has never been one of my supporters and he has at times been obstructive on such subjects as the admission of girls.

Wednesday 16 November
Horace Lashley comes to talk to the John Locke Society about his work for the Commission for Racial Equality. He makes a poor impression. He is from Trinidad and has lived most of his life in this country. He lectures the boys and girls on the failure of the British to recognise the passing of imperial status but the Empire means nothing whatsoever to them. Over lunch he is touchy because a girl says to him that black athletes are better sprinters because they have a lower centre of gravity. If only he had more of a sense of humour he would have won more friends.

Friday 18 November
I find Alasdair Coles, the captain of the school, and his monitors celebrating his 17th birthday with a champagne breakfast in Little Dean's Yard. It has become the traditional way to mark the captain's birthday but it provokes sour comments from some members of the common room. I like the idea; it has style. Nevertheless, it does mean that the chaplain has to read the lesson in Abbey because the monitor on duty seems unlikely to make sense of a Pauline epistle after two glasses of champagne.

Lunch in Rigaud's where young Hassan Fadli tells me his solution to the problems of his people in Palestine. He is particularly interesting and intelligent and I wonder if he will use his talents in the Palestinian cause or, like father, make his way in business.

A London Schools Music Fair here this evening. All goes well until a Westminster group finishes playing, whereupon all the Westminster audience depart. As the next item is a steel band from a comprehensive school across the river, the exodus makes a bad impression and I shall have to speak to them about it.

Friday 25 November
Wet and close; the flagstones in the cloisters sweat. I am told this about one of our Oxford history candidates, a day boy in Ashburnham. He went to Spain with his parents after A level in the summer. A house guest was a girl reading history at Cambridge. The boy fell in love and went with the girl for a trip to the Pyrenees. But something went wrong. It appears that she tried to seduce him and he was unable to respond. He returned to England fearing that he was homosexual or impotent, and could not concentrate on his work for Oxford. When the exams came, he made a poor showing and after the last paper yesterday, he went out to drown his sorrows. Sometime yesterday evening, he was found vomiting in Parliament Square by two policemen who charged him with being drunk and disorderly. He was placed in a cell in Cannon Row with an Irishman who had been arrested for indecent exposure. This morning the boy appeared at Horseferry Road Magistrate's Court and was fined £10. Meanwhile, the family and the school are moving into action to persuade New College to interview him despite his poor papers. I know the family well and I am sorry that the boy has not done himself justice.

Friday 2 December
I go to the common-room dinner this evening without much

enthusiasm. It is a black-tie affair in College Hall to say goodbye to Theo Zinn. After 33 years as head of classics he certainly deserves a good send-off and he has invited a number of former colleagues and friends. I have clashed with one of the latter before and do not like him, but he is Theo's guest and I must put up with him. When we stand to drink Theo's health, this man says loud enough for all to hear, 'To the departure of John Rae.' I am too surprised to react and then too experienced to show any emotion. The dinner proceeds as though nothing has happened. It is an extraordinary incident and even Ronald French, the president of the common room, is shocked enough to offer me an apology. What slings and arrows headmasters have to be prepared for.

Monday 5 December
In Abbey, a boy trumpeter plays Handel, a sharp, clear sound to wake the dead and us on this Monday morning. Teach two history periods back to back and then welcome a Soviet historian, Oleg Rzheshevsky, who has come to talk to the modern-history specialists about the Great Patriotic War. He is a military historian, an army colonel and an admirer of my supervisor Michael Howard[117]. Hard-line, fluent in English and highly intelligent, he is very impressive. It is good for the boys and girls to hear about the war from the point of view of a Soviet and Marxist historian.

I see the parents of a boy who is continuously in trouble of

---

[117] Sir Michael Howard, professor of war studies at King's College, London; Regius professor of modern history at Oxford; fellow of All Souls. Supervised my Ph.D. thesis on the treatment of conscientious objectors in the two World Wars.

one sort or another. Father is a doctor of Arab origin and speaks with an over-precise upper-class accent. His look and manner suggest a streak of fanaticism. Mother is posing as an English milady but is probably Irish. Most odd. They are helpful and constructive but I don't believe in the sincerity of their response; I know that the local authority regards the children in the family as at risk because father whips them. Social Services are in touch with the housemaster. Boy comes to school clean and well dressed but home, we are told, is grim. It is hardly surprising the boy is an awkward customer and I have probably made matters worse by telling parents that their son is on a final warning.

Tuesday 6 December
Drive down to Charterhouse to watch our 1st XI in this the oldest school soccer fixture. A very cold afternoon with frost under the soft surface of the pitch. The match ends in a draw, 2-2, which is satisfactory as far as Westminster is concerned but the Charterhouse boys make a bad impression. They swear on the field, 'fuck' and 'shit' being in frequent use, and their spectators are yobbish and unsporting in the manner that used to be so characteristic of Lancing. For once, Westminster boys appear well-mannered by comparison. Drive back in winter sunset and dine this evening with Roland Joffe, the film director.

Thursday 8 December
The director of music appears early with this tale to tell. He was policing an informal concert after school yesterday. A senior boy got involved in some pushing and shoving with another boy and was told to leave. But he refused to go, so the director of music told him he would be reported to the headmaster. The boy is in

his A level year and is the key defensive player in the 1st XI. I must support the master and be seen to do so and the only certain way to achieve that is to send the boy home for a few days. But the 1st XI play the Old Boys on Saturday and we want to win to stifle old-boy criticism of current Westminster sporting standards. I am tempted to settle for a ticking-off but I know it won't do. It will be good for the common room and the school to see me put the demands of discipline before the needs of the 1st XI, so I rusticate the boy until next Tuesday[118].

Housemasters meet for the last time this term; we are all too tired to do much and too good colleagues for any aggro to occur. I reflect again on how lucky I am with this body of men now that the awkward squad are no longer housemasters.

Friday 9 December

This evening, Daphne and I go to a house play. I am appalled. Daphne walks out after 10 minutes; I leave less pointedly at the interval. The play, *Ubu Roi*, is a string of four-letter words. I am amazed that such a good housemaster has allowed this to be produced, indeed, has a part in the play dressed up as a bear. I am embarrassed more than for many years at the thought of parents' reactions. An error of judgement on the housemaster's part – but what an error. Yet he is a good man and a loyal colleague. I will speak to him but I must prevent others making a major issue out of it.

Thursday 15 December

---

[118] In the event, the 1st X1 match against the Old Boys was cancelled because the pitch was unfit.

A sixth former appears to tell me of an incident on Saturday night. He tried to gatecrash another Westminster boy's party. When refused entry, he slugged the other boy in the eye, causing a heavy bruise. He claims the other boy said, 'We don't want any Jews.' I suspect he has made that up to cover himself but I tell him anyway that provocation does not justify that sort of violence.

I hear that the captain, Alasdair Coles, has won an open scholarship to read medicine at Oxford. That is really good news. This evening, I join colleagues on the patrol for last night of term.

Friday 16 December
It is 4.31am. I have not gone to bed. Rumours of a major last-night prank have kept me up – no doubt exactly what the rumour spreaders intended. All is quiet. I write notes for my farewells at assembly later this morning. Two men are leaving. Although Theo Zinn has sometimes been a difficult colleague when trying to defend the privileged position of Latin and Greek, he is one of the great senior classics masters of his time. The other man who is leaving is the critic of my Abbey homily and has alienated most people in the common room by his intemperate attacks on me, on senior colleagues and on Westminster as a whole. I shall send him on his way with as much good grace as I can muster. It is essential to preserve the public fabric of goodwill on these occasions; to speak ill of a colleague at his final assembly would be as disapproved of as speaking ill of the dead at a funeral. Everyone knows the truth but this is an occasion when they do not want to hear it. Above all, a headmaster can only gain by being magnanimous. I must not overdo it, of course, but walk the thin

line between truth and hypocrisy.

5.35am. Still all quiet but I am now too wide awake to bother going to bed. Time to reflect. What do I really think about my own future? I will take a worthwhile job if it comes along. Meanwhile, I must tactfully but firmly kill speculation that I am leaving, for nothing undermines support for a headmaster so easily as the belief that he is packing his bags.

5.50am. Bill Drummond, the clerk of works, appears and relieves me of my night watch. What a curious life I lead. But if reincarnation turned out to be the norm I would not chose a different one.

Assembly at 9am. The farewells are said. Afterwards, colleagues tell me how much they were appreciated. I wonder whether it was the truth or the lies that really impressed them. I am told later that one of the senior classic boys was in tears when I was speaking about Theo Zinn.

The term ends quietly but there is one sour note that illustrates everything I hate about the English Establishment. A has failed to get into Magdalen College, Oxford, to read law. Mother and father want to pull out all the stops to get him a place at another college. Nothing wrong in that but it is the way they go about it and their assumption that their son has a right to a place at Oxbridge that alienates me. Father has influential friends in politics, business and academia; he lists his contacts at Oxford and wants me to do the telephoning. 'Our Euro-MP has a brother-in-law who is the Provost of Oriel,' is the sort of line. He also suggests that I approach Lord Dacre, Master of Peterhouse, Cambridge, because he took a friend's boy last year who had failed to make Oxford. And so on. Meanwhile, mother implies that the school is at fault and that any system that fails to recognise her son's quality must be inefficient or corrupt. The fact is that Magdalen was much too competitive a college for this borderline candidate with only three Bs at A level, but parents insisted because of the family connections with the college. She says she will get her brother, a prominent Magdalen man, to ring the president of the college. She sees nothing wrong in twisting every arm to get her son into Oxford. I must stop myself reacting against the son because I so much dislike the parents' attitude; the children of this world suffer enough at the hands of their parents without me adding to their disadvantage. I ring a couple of law dons and discover that the law field is very strong this year and that it is very unlikely that a college has a vacancy.

Lent Term 1984

Saturday 7 January
The father and mother who are determined to get their son into Oxbridge bring me up to date on their lobbying. Mother's brother has persuaded Arnold Goodman at University College to look at the boy's papers. The Euro MP did indeed write to the Provost of Oriel. Lord Dacre at Peterhouse has replied cautiously to father's approach. 'If we can find a place for him, I shall be delighted. I fear there may be a difficulty with the law tutor since we seem to be particularly pressed in that subject but we shall see. I have sent the papers to our Tutor for Admissions with as strong a recommendation as it is decent or prudent for a head of house to give.' Nicely phrased. Meanwhile, father has

lobbied Asa Briggs at Worcester and Robert Blake of Queen's. If this boy gets into Oxford or Cambridge, it will be a triumph for the network. I would like to see him get in despite the lobbying but I cannot help hoping that the lobbying will fail.

Monday 9 January
To the Imperial War Museum this evening where I am a trustee. We are giving an informal dinner for the prime minister. I find Margaret Thatcher more sympathetic as a person than I had expected, noticeably relaxed both in conversation and in her off-the-cuff speech after dinner.

Wednesday 11 January
My long and determined stand against the assisted places scheme returns to haunt me. The press has got hold of the fact that Westminster's governing body has decided that our prep school should join the scheme and journalists ring up all day to know whether this means Dr. Rae will resign. I realised that something like this would happen so, after consulting Burke Trend and the dean, I issue a statement to the effect that I still have doubts about the scheme (a euphemism of course; I still oppose it root and branch) and will watch the 'limited experiment' in our Under School with interest. I fear some newspapers tomorrow will take a 'will Rae resign?' line but fortunately the key governors support my statement. They don't like the publicity, of course, and they will be thinking that I am too accident-prone for comfort. In some ways, it would be good to be able to resign over this as a matter of principle, but who at the age of 52 and concerned about his family and his pension can afford to have principles? Still, this very public reverse means I am on the

303

defensive and that is unwise. A man on the ropes has numerous sympathisers but few real friends.

Thursday 12 January
The *Daily Telegraph* carries this sentence in its report: 'Last night there was speculation about Dr Rae's future at the school he has run for 13 years, after such a disagreement with the governors.' But in the same article, the dean is quoted, denying that there is any question of my resigning.

Tuesday 17 January
Trouble with press photographers who want pictures of Nicholas Windsor on his first day at school. No doubt it will die down quickly enough. A fine, cold day in place of yesterday's downpour. What a difference it makes for the start of the new term. I speak to the new boys after lunch and find myself taking a more moralistic line than in the past: remain true to the ideals and values your parents have taught you now that you move into the wider and tougher world of a public school. The fact is that I do not want them to be corrupted by this new world; I want them to make the transition from youth to manhood without the disenchantment, alienation or over-indulgence that overcome some boys. I think that deep down I yearn for a lost world of Edwardian public-school stories – sentimental, striving for the fight, naïve and uncynical. I read a biography of Robert Birley[119] in the holidays. How I wish that I was a good headmaster in the sense that he was. But I am not a gifted teacher like Birley. And

---

[119] Headmaster of Eton 1949 to 1964.

I am not a Christian idealist like Arnold[120] or an innovator like Sanderson[121]. Yet when I see these new boys looking up at me so wide-eyed, so expectant and hopeful of my leadership, I wish I was a more traditional headmaster. Although I can articulate fine sentiments, I am really a pessimist, a deist, an opportunist and a fixer. I can do some aspects of the job well and I really care about these boys and their lives but I have too many doubts to be the hero they need.

Wednesday 18 January

The chaplain, Willie Booth, comes to talk about pastoral matters and tells me this. Yesterday, a senior boy was coming back from our boathouse in Putney and saw an elderly lady climb onto the parapet of Putney Bridge. He rushed forward to prevent her jumping but could only take hold of her coat which came off as she plunged downwards. Her body has not yet been found. The boy blames himself for not saving her even though he did more than the vast majority of people would have done. Thank goodness the school has in Willie a genuine parish priest who can help this boy.

Saturday 21 January

The boy on whose behalf so much lobbying has been done, so many strings pulled, has been given a place at Christ Church, Oxford. Well, well! I don't begrudge the boy his good fortune but this saga illustrates the nature of inequality. A boy without family connections and only three Bs at A level would not have managed to wangle a place in this way. If it was widely

---

[120] Dr Thomas Arnold, headmaster of Rugby 1828 to 1842.
[121] FW Sanderson, headmaster of Oundle 1892 to 1922.

known, it would undermine Oxford's claims to be aiming at fairness in their entry.

Monday 23 January

Pouring with rain. At 8.15, a meeting with the catering officer to discuss menus for our four dinner parties this term. He is black-coated, striped-trousered, well-hair-watered and primed with excellent dishes to suggest. Then new monitors. Do any of them have any reservations? No, they want the job. It still carries prestige. At 9am at Latin prayers, I appoint them formally and publicly. After Latin prayers, I see S and his parents. The history is this: for two terms, he has been breaking the law – smoking, disrupting classes, using bad language in public – and numerous warnings from the housemaster have not deterred him. Last Saturday, he was abusive to a young member of staff in front of the form, refusing to be disciplined and using a string of four-letter words to reinforce his case. There is little more to be said. No school or headmaster can tolerate that. He is 15 and will now have to go to a tutorial to complete his O levels. It is a relief, when they have gone, to teach my A level historians.

This evening, Daphne and I are guests at a party given by the US ambassador in honour of Dr Henry Kissinger. A relaxed and enjoyable occasion. Neil Kinnock greets me by saying, 'I'm sorry we didn't have a chance to scrap the Assisted Places Scheme before you got hooked.' A shrewd speech by Kissinger, dryly witty.

Thursday 2 February

Teach two history sets. How I enjoy teaching the French Revolution. It has all the elements of a great and exciting historical event – hope, idealism, violence, disenchantment and despair. I enjoy it because it lifts me out of routine cares and frustrations. I hope I manage to communicate some of this enthusiasm to the boys and girls.

This evening, to Trinity, Cambridge for the Candlemas Feast. Ah, this is the life. The hall in candlelight, stimulating company, good food, excellent wines, the college choir singing the Latin grace. I am the guest of Henry Chadwick who as dean of Christ Church, Oxford, was a governor of Westminster for 10 years. He is now regius professor of divinity in Cambridge. We talk about difficult members of staff and he assures me that no member of the Westminster common room could match some of the more awkward members of the senior common room at Christ Church. If Dean Liddell thought he had difficulty with Charles Dodgson alias Lewis Carroll, it was nothing compared with the personal vendettas and vitriolic correspondence that Henry was subjected to at Christ Church. But he misses the undergraduates and tells me that I will miss the young if I leave Westminster. I know he is right. 'The staff are superfluous,' Henry adds, 'but the young are essential.' Daphne drives me back to town and we are home soon after midnight.

Monday 27 February

Latin prayers. How I enjoy these occasions. Like an old trooper, I tread the boards and play upon the audience, a warning here, a joke there. They see through it all but it is part of our relationship, headmaster and school. After Latin prayers, some anxious parents. Their son is at Colet Court, the St. Paul's Prep School, and is subject to the usual moral pressure to go to St. Paul's. Parents want Westminster. Will I give their son an unconditional place? Yes, I will, because I know he is a very bright boy.

307

Possible heads of science to interview this afternoon. There are three internal candidates but I am looking outside. An outside candidate must be better than just good: he must have some extra quality: sparkle, energy, vision, ambition and so on. None of the men I see today is better than good.

This evening, to Lambeth Palace for a meeting of Nobody's Friends, the dining club I was surprised to be invited to join. It is the lay and clerical Anglican establishment. The dinner is good and I enjoy the company of the archbishop of Canterbury sitting beside me, but I can't think why I joined except that Edward Carpenter and Burke Trend are both members. After dinner, we discuss the admission of women to membership and some very odd backwoodsman's views are expressed, notably by three former headmasters – Frank Fisher, Tom Howarth and Oliver van Oss. The latter is particularly pompous, reducing the discussion to farce, an old trick that headmasters use when faced with pupils or masters demanding change. I say a few words in favour of admitting women but it is decided that there will be a postal vote and I guess the backwoodsmen will carry the day. In the obscurity of the closet, the bishops and deans will vote for the cosy status quo.

Tuesday 28 February

More heads of science to interview and among them, thank goodness, a man of quality. He is Peter Hughes, the headmaster of St. Peter's, York, who does not like headmastering and wants to return to being a head of science as he was at Shrewsbury. I like him. He has plenty of energy left – at 52 – and the authority to get a grip on our science department. I ask him to return next week to meet people here and for me to make sure he really wants the job.

Wednesday 29 February

An unhappy mother. She and her husband have lost contact with and control over their 15-year-old son. She blames the school and puts me on the defensive by saying that they do things much better at St. Paul's. I should have been more constructive but spend too much time defending Westminster. We both seem to forget the interests of the boy.

Willie Booth comes and I share my frustration with him. He then tells me this story. He is talking about prayer to a form of 13-year-olds. After the lesson, a boy asks why his prayers are not answered. He has prayed for three weeks that his father will make contact with him but there is only silence. Father left home a month ago and has not written or telephoned.

Thursday 1 March

A young member of the English department has invited me out to dinner. He wants to tell me that he is depressed and feels isolated in the department. It is worth giving an evening to him and he is good company, despite his worries.

Sunday 4 March

On Sunday, with scholars to Abbey matins at which a canon preaches a monumentally dull sermon on the psalms. I have seldom felt so powerfully the nonsense of it all and I swim at the RAC this afternoon to wash away the memory of it.

Wednesday 7 March

This evening, I give whisky to six members of the common room who want to complain about the school's attitude to drama. They think I am unsympathetic and they have presented me with a short paper that begins, 'The official attitude of the school to drama is at best indifferent, at worst discouraging.' How I would have risen to that bait 10 years ago! But now I get out the hard stuff and we have a convivial and constructive discussion. I am all for drama out of school but not on the curriculum.

Monday 19 March

Two policemen to see. This is the story: a saxophone was stolen from our music centre last week. The director of music followed the matter up and rang all the likely shops. He struck lucky. The saxophone had been taken in for sale at a shop in Charing Cross Road. The young man who brought it in claimed to be called Haycraft and gave a telephone number. The man exists but he is neither a Westminster boy nor a parent. However, the saxophone was in a bag belonging to a Westminster boy; he had left his socks in the bag with his name on them. When I hear the name, I am amazed. The boy is innocence itself; he was confirmed in the Abbey the day before the saxophone disappeared.

The German play this evening but I understand little, so slip out and return to my desk.

Wednesday 21 March

I pursue the case of the stolen saxophone, questioning the owner of the bag in which the saxophone was taken to the shop. He is not altogether convincing, though I find it hard to believe he was the sole thief. I fear Westminster boys stole the instrument and intended to pocket a large sum of money. The saxophone is valued at £700. That is not a cry for help or adolescent rebellion nor is it a theft for kicks. Whoever did this was after the money.

Thursday 22 March

Up at 6am to run Daphne to Heathrow. She is off to India for five weeks to work in a leprosy village in north Bihar close to the Nepalese border.

This evening, a dinner in Jerusalem at which we ask our influential guests for advice on how to make our appeal for funds successful. I sit next to Lord Aldington who is warden (chairman of the governors) of Winchester and he asks my advice about finding a new headmaster as John Thorn is retiring in 1985. He says that men of the right calibre seem to be few and far between. He even seems to be saying, 'Have you thought of applying yourself?' When he asks what qualities are needed to be a successful headmaster, I reply, 'Stamina'.

After dinner, I change into rough clothes and join colleagues for the night watch but there is unlikely to be any trouble at this end of term. We spend an hour or so sitting in the common room drinking wine, eating Stilton cheese and talking in a relaxed way about the school. It is all worth it from that point of view and I doubt whether our occasional sorties around the school buildings are necessary. Bed by 2.30am.

Friday 23 March

The last day of the Lent Term follows its familiar low-key pattern. When all have left, I look forward to an early bed, but the term has one last farcical twist. At 10.30 in the evening, a housemaster rings to ask me to give a ruling. The football tour leaves tomorrow and the master in charge of the 1st XI is refusing to take a boy who has had 'a provocative'. Wearily, I go across to the boarding house where the boy's parents are arguing that the boy must be allowed to go. When I enter the room, I see at once that 'the provocative haircut' has been exaggerated out of all proportion by the end-of-term distorting mirror, so it is just a question of helping the football master to climb down with good grace and without feeling his authority has been undermined. It takes an hour. I return home and go to bed.

Easter Holidays

Friday 6 April
The parents of one of the suspects in the saxophone case telephones and asks to see me urgently. They come this evening. Their son has confessed. He stole the saxophone with another boy. It was a professional job, an open-and-shut case. I cannot give parents any comfort. Both boys will have to leave Westminster but I will try to call off the police. Expulsion is more serious than anything a juvenile court would impose.

Election Term 1984

Wednesday 25 April
Fine warm days to start the term instead of the usual raw winds and cricketers shivering on the boundary. We swing easily back

into the routine and for some reason I feel fresher and keener. Perhaps it is just the fine weather and the sense of life flowing back into the empty buildings.

Friday 27 April

The saxophone case ends at last. We know the name of the second boy but cannot prove his involvement, so I have asked the woman from the shop in the Charing Cross Road to come to the school to see if she can positively identify him. I take her into three classes in one of which the suspect is sitting. She has no hesitation in identifying him, but when I see him on his own, he continues to deny any involvement. He is cornered and tough. I am angry with him and sorry for him. I telephone his mother (father is in New York) and ask her to come in. In front of her, he still vigorously denies that he was involved. Later, mother telephones to say that on the way home her son had broken down and admitted that he was involved. I shall have to expel him, as I did the other boy. I am saddened because this boy has lied so convincingly to his mother, his housemaster, the police and myself. His mother says he is almost fanatically keen on school and could not bear to be expelled. I will do what I can to get another school to take him.

Monday 30 April

My article 'Why independent schools should be less secretive about exam results' appears in the *Times*. It is intended to be provocative but I believe parents should be able to compare one school's results with another – which is, of course, what most independent schools want to prevent.

At Latin prayers, I talk to the school about morality. I seldom do this because I doubt whether morality is a suitable subject on which to address half-listening pupils first thing in the morning, but the saxophone case prompts me to do so. What I try to get across is that stealing is morally wrong, not just something that may have serious consequences. Heaven knows whether any of this is heard, let alone taken in. It is a mistake to expect too much but it is still worth doing.

After teaching, I spend most of the day going round the school – visiting forms, watching games, going into boarders' supper in College Hall – in order to sense the pulse, in order to be seen, enjoying the company of the young.

Thursday 3 May

I receive a complaint from a parent that his son is not learning any maths because the young teacher cannot keep control. It is the sort of problem that must be dealt with quickly if the school's credibility is to be maintained, yet it is also a problem that is difficult to solve. Fortunately, there is in Eddie Smith a good head of department, and I ask him to tell the young teacher to use the sanctions that exist to curb the disruptive elements. The trouble with these new members of staff is that, despite all the good advice they are given, they will not punish boys until the situation is out of hand.

This evening, the bursar attends the housemasters' meeting. In the old days, with former housemasters and the former bursar, these joint meetings were a nightmare because some silly housemasters could not resist needling the bursar. 'I'm not quite clear, bursar, is anyone actually in charge of the school's finances?' And the bursar allowed himself to be provoked. Now it is a mature and professional discussion and even awkward issues are talked over in reasonable terms.

Wednesday 9 May

This evening, Daphne and I have all the school monitors to dinner together with Charles Douglas Home, the editor of the *Times*. After dinner, Charles Douglas Home speaks briefly about his job and answers questions. A number of Westminster boys and girls see journalism as the ideal career, as I think I might have done in their shoes.

Monday 14 May

An awkward moment in the common room in break. When I have made my announcements, the president, Ronald French, sounds off about what a waste of time it has been discussing the future of Saturday morning school when the headmaster has changed his mind about whether there should be two half-holidays in a five-day week. David Hepburne-Scott, his sidekick, then asks in all innocence whether Ronald has access to the governors on this matter. I am caught off guard and make a comment in a voice that must sound nervous. Angry with myself for allowing my critics to ambush me in this way, I return to my study reminding myself of the Golden Rule for headmasters – prevent at all costs an alliance against you of disaffected masters and interfering governors. If those two complain to the governing body, they may find one or two sympathetic ears.

This evening, to the Queen's Guard at St. James's Palace. A former pupil of mine, Giles Gittings, is the ensign of the guard. Unusually for a Westminster boy, he went to Sandhurst rather than university and was commissioned in the Coldstreams. A very agreeable evening: three other guests, red and black, candlelight and silver, easy, unpretentious conversation. Troubles fly away, but I can't help reflecting that if I was head of a boarding school in the depths of the country, I should have gone mad by now.

Saturday 19 May/Sunday 20 May

An annoying letter from the headmaster of the prep school that sent us one of the boys expelled for stealing the saxophone. Annoying because he puts all the blame on Westminster; he was such a good boy at prep school, butter wouldn't melt in his mouth, and we have turned him into a thief. We must accept some of the responsibility, of course, but this smug 'we produce angels and you corrupt them' line is infuriating. Decide not to reply for a few days to let my anger cool.

After attending Abbey matins with the scholars, I lunch at Farm Street with the Jesuits. The father provincial is a former Westminster boy. There can't be many schools that can produce at one time the head of the Society of Jesus in Britain and a general in the KGB.

Friday 1 June

A rain-soaked first of June. After a busy day, we dine with John and Patsy Grigg at Blackheath. Of all our friends, the Griggs are the ones whose hospitality is most likely to drive away any feeling of anxiety or weariness, and this evening is no exception. On the way home, when Daphne tells me that Patsy was told by a governor's wife that her husband thought it was essential 'to get rid of John Rae', I can only laugh. I have known for some time that this governor felt that way but I must make sure his feeling does not spread. I used to get disheartened by criticism from the governors but now I heed Burke Trend's advice and remember my fighting instinct.

Tuesday 5 June

Mother and son to see. He is 15 and on the edge of the cliff. Does he want to be expelled? Not in those simple terms but at that age – as I recall – a string of clashes with authority develops a momentum of its own; you go on kicking over the traces because you rather like the notoriety, the attention, the sense of destiny. I warn the boy that next time he defies authority it will be final.

Thursday 7 June

Talk to a special meeting of the common room to explain why I am opposed to the abolition of Saturday morning school. I have lost touch with the common room over this and have allowed my apparent neutrality to confuse my allies, so this is an important opportunity to reassert my authority and my credibility. I have prepared carefully and strike a positive note, acknowledging that there are arguments in favour of abolition, but leaving no room for doubt that while I am headmaster, Westminster will not become a five-day-a-week school. I am pleased with my performance; no hint of nervousness and questions handled well.

Wednesday 13 June

The House of Lords select committee on science and technology come to ask questions of sixth formers. Why are they not going to be engineers? Why are they not going into industry? The search for a cure for the English disease continues. It is all diagnosis and no answers. One lightweight Liberal peer suggests that the boys and girls should visit a factory or two. God! Doesn't he know the problem runs far deeper than that?

Saturday 16 June/Sunday 17 June

Very hot. Six hours of interviewing 104 common entrance candidates individually. Some good boys but I am worried that there are so many foreigners and so many who are described as 'no good at games'. Prep schools are sending us too many clever oddballs and we cannot have too many. I will speak to Alan Livingstone-Smith, who takes over as registrar in September.

Tuesday 19 June

It is still very hot and close. The boys and girls wilt in Yard. In the evening, they are draped over walls and wooden seats, just stirring, like the stunned survivors of some disaster.

I take an A level revision class on the causes of the French Revolution and then begin to come to terms with the consequences of the very large number of successful common entrance candidates. We have a record field, almost all of whom have easily passed our qualifying mark of 65 per cent. This means we shall have to admit six new boy forms instead of five with all the problems of space and manpower that will cause. I ring Eric Anderson at Eton. They have the same problem and we suspect that common entrance was easier than usual. Nevertheless, we must take the boys who have qualified, or risk jeopardising our relations with prep schools.

Friday 22 June

I have slept only an hour or two and cannot go back to sleep, so I have come downstairs to my study at 2am to work at my desk, clearing away routine matters that are building up in my in-tray. Cooler now with a breeze and a smell of rain. Why is my pattern of sleep increasingly disturbed? Is it anxiety about the struggle to hold off real and imaginary enemies on the governing body and in the common room or two glasses of port last thing at night?

This evening, a meeting of Westminster Cathedral Choir School governors. Basil Hume asked me to be acting chairman as he can seldom attend. I have to steer the governors and the headmaster through an awkward hour. The headmaster, Peter Hannigan, makes a statement attacking two governors for criticising his handling of the school's finances. Most of what he says is well chosen but he makes a tactical error in saying, 'the school is a thousand times better than when I came.' Hyperbole of that sort seldom wins friends.

Monday 2 July

Cooler. A lull before the end-of-term rush. An important meeting this afternoon of heads of department and housemasters to discuss the large number of boys and girls who want to apply for Oxford before A level. Oxford's intention to abolish the post-A level entrance exam has provoked this transitional problem. Colleagues are at their best, thoughtful, thorough and good humoured, despite it being the penultimate week of the school year.

Wednesday 4 July

The common-room dinner this evening. After the last one, I am not looking forward to it but it turns out to be an unusually happy occasion. In Ashburnham Garden after dinner, a curious incident. We are drinking Pimms and enjoying conversation on this soft, warm evening when David Hepburne-Scott appears before me like a disagreeable genie. We have hardly exchanged a word for some years now, though the cause of his coldness is lost on me and everyone else. But tonight, fortified by wine, he is all for reconciliation. He shakes my hand and talks in a rather incoherent way about putting our differences aside. I can only respond in a positive way and say that I shall be glad to do so. I am puzzled and a little embarrassed but if this puts an end to his childish behaviour in the common room, I shall be relieved.

Thursday 5 July

A blazing hot day. David Hepburne-Scott pokes his head round my study door. 'I haven't forgotten last night,' he says as though we had exchanged romantic promises under the moon. I say we must get together soon and talk but I do not relish the prospect. A rambling housemasters' meeting to finish the term and then Daphne and I go to the Festival Hall as guests of the Menuhins to hear Yehudi play the Bach violin concerto. Diana keeps referring to the orchestra, which Riccardo Muti conducts, as 'quite a good band', an odd sort of inverted snobbery like those Old Etonians who refer to their school as 'Slough Grammar'.

Saturday 7 July

Up early to start writing reports. After Abbey, the dean rings. It is not a crisis, Edward says, but could I go round to the deanery straight away? As it happens, the Dalai Lama is once again staying overnight, so I have to evade Tibetan bodyguards to reach Edward's study. Edward is clearly embarrassed and I wonder what on earth can be on his mind. It turns out to be the same thing as this time last year: some governors want to raise the question of discipline at next week's governing body meeting. Now what or who is behind this? I sip my coffee and watch Edward's flushed, unhappy expression. Does he know the antis are plotting? I ask who the governors are and I am not surprised to hear that David Carey is at the centre. I suspect that Ronald French has used his position as president of the common room to tell Carey that some senior members of the common room are worried about poor discipline. This sort of general slur is the most difficult to deal with because in any school at any time it is possible to find an example of poor discipline. Carey is an obsessive intriguer and there are a few others on the governing body who will enjoy a good moan about discipline and one or two who will use the occasion as an attempt to destabilise me.

Edward, as chairman, must let the critics have their say. This evening, I ring Burke Trend. He confirms that three or four governors are muttering about bad language, scruffy appearance and poor discipline in some of the houses. He suggests that we should propose an informal meeting in September at the beginning of the school year, between the critical governors and the housemasters. That, he says, should take the sting out of next Friday's discussion and ensure that we get through the governing body meeting without 'too much blood on the floor'.

Tuesday 10 July

David Hepburne-Scott invites me for a drink to talk over, as he puts it, how he can help. The whole business is odd but he is still an influential figure in the common room and I would rather have him on my side. He suggests we meet at nine this evening in the Charing Cross Hotel. The Charing Cross Hotel! He is a railway enthusiast – these odd cases often are. He is waiting for me in the first-floor lounge overlooking the station forecourt and has ordered a bottle of wine (which it turns out I have to pay for). It takes nearly two hours to sort out our differences, the conversation being hit and miss much of the time because I am not at all clear what he is after. He keeps saying 'I can help you' but in a way that implies he could be very awkward if he chose. Eventually, he says he wants a job, not necessarily an important one, but something to mark his return to the fold. That is something I can easily agree to – finding jobs for underemployed senior members of the common room is routine for a headmaster. But by this time, we have drunk two bottles of wine and I drive back down Whitehall hoping I won't be stopped by a policeman.

Thursday 12 July

A typical end-of-term storm in a teacup. I am told that the common room are angry about Huckleberry Harrod's hair. No satirical novelist would invent such a name or such a ludicrously trivial cause of conflict between the headmaster and the common room. Young Harrod is not the tidiest boy in the school but for some reason, his scruffiness has caught the eye of those in the common room who want to stir up trouble. They claim that the housemaster tried to insist that Huckleberry had a haircut and that when the boy refused, I failed to support the housemaster. It is all nonsense, of course, but it is annoying to have to spend time putting the record straight.

The whole thing may be a reaction to the letter I have sent to all members of the common room, reminding them that their contract of employment makes it clear that they are all responsible for seeing that the regulations, including those on dress, are enforced. I am trying to put pressure on those members of the common room who let a few colleagues carry the burden of seeing that pupils are well behaved, properly dressed and so on. It may sound petty but Westminster has for as long as I can remember suffered from masters who think it is beneath their dignity to tell a boy to tuck his shirt in. Of course, my letter has been prompted by the fact that the governors will raise the question of discipline at tomorrow's meeting.

This evening, an appeal dinner in Jerusalem. Kit Barclay, the master of the Sadlers, whose son was a school monitor a year or two back, tells me that when he was serving in the Western Desert, his mother sent him a fruit cake baked by his old nanny to supplement his rations. The cake had to take the long route round the Cape but it arrived safely and still fresh for him to consume with his friends outside Tobruk.

Friday 13 July
Grey morning that soon brightens so that the last day of term is fine and pleasantly warm. As I am saying goodbye at assembly to masters who are leaving, unknown to me, a scantily clad young woman is approaching the side door of the hall. A boy (or can it be a governor?) has ordered a Glamgram or Stripogram to come into assembly to embrace me in the middle of my farewells. As luck would have it, she was intercepted by a young master who was late for assembly, so that I am spared an incident that would not have strengthened my case at the governing body meeting.

The end-of-term ritual proceeds. I preach in Abbey, say goodbye individually to boys and girls who are leaving and then go to Jerusalem for lunch before the governing body meeting. But the room is empty. Then they all come in together as though from a special meeting upstairs in the deanery and I imagine they avoid looking at me like a jury that has decided on a guilty verdict. But I am being paranoid. When the meeting gets under way, it goes better than I had expected. Burke Trend's proposal for a meeting with housemasters at the beginning of the new school year to discuss discipline has, as he intended, taken the sting out of this afternoon's discussion. After the meeting, I give Burke a lift to his flat off Vincent Square and he tells me that for the moment the critics are quiet. He is a good friend without whom the politics of headmastering would be much more difficult to handle.

This evening, at the Election Dinner in College Hall, the critics are all smiles but I am not lulled into a false sense of security. The next school year should be interesting.

1984-1985
Play Term 1984

❧ ❧ ❧

Tuesday 4 September

I know the new term approaches because I receive a deliciously offensive letter from the grandfather of a boy who in our view is not good enough to try the pre-A level entry to Oxford. Grandfather is a fellow of his own Oxford college and his daughter has married into what he calls 'a family of high historical, social, academic and sporting distinction'.

Am I wrong to dislike this 'distinguished family' approach? According to grandfather, any Oxford college would be impressed by the member of a family that had displayed 'overwhelming talent since the days of Charles II in the church, in learning, in the Council Chamber, in test matches and cup finals...' 'Headmaster,' he continues 'you are famous for your charm but charm is not enough. For years you have treated my daughter and myself with nonchalance and contempt.'

I would enjoy replying in the same spirit but I ask my secretary to arrange a time for grandfather to come and see me.

Saturday 8 September

A portent of troubles to come. Rummaging in her son's room, a mother finds a letter from a girl and reads it. The girl warns her son to stay away from a boy who is selling drugs in the school. I am taken aback. The boy she accuses of being the seller of drugs is one of the brightest and best in the sixth form year. He is talented academically and musically with a literary gift that is free from the usual pseudo-intellectual overtones. He is the sort of boy no headmaster wants to lose. On the other hand, I am anxious about the return of the drug problem that caused us so much difficulty in the seventies.

We are still not free from drugs; no school is, despite the lies headmasters tell. So as a first step I shall see the mother who found the letter and get her permission to use its contents.

Monday 10 September

Tidy my desk to give the impression on this first day of term that I am as efficient and well organised as ever, despite the fact that this will be my 14th year as headmaster of Westminster.

See Damian Cope, the new captain of the school, to talk over the job. He does not have the maturity or the presence of his predecessor but he has a tough edge and he knows something of the problems I face, as his father, David Cope, is headmaster of Marlborough.

Friday 21 September

Sir Andrew Huxley comes to Latin prayers to beg a play on his appointment as master of Trinity, Cambridge. He is one of Westminster's most distinguished pupils – Nobel prize-winner, president of the Royal Society, master of Trinity. He is TH Huxley's grandson and Aldous Huxley's half-brother. I introduce him and he replies at just the right length and in just the right way. How few visitors faced with the school audience ever manage that.

As master of Trinity, Andrew Huxley becomes automatically a governor of Westminster. He is the sort of governor I would like to share problems with. For example, I have failed to persuade the mother who found the evidence of drug-selling to let me use the contents of the letter. Her son, she says, would never forgive her. But without the evidence of the letter, there is nothing I can do. I cannot accuse 'the brightest and the best' of selling drugs when I have no evidence that he has been doing so.

Monday 24 September

We have the school monitors to dinner, together with Peter Timms, a former prison governor. After dinner, Peter talks about his former job and provokes a lively discussion.

Tuesday 25 September

Three 15-year-olds to see before school. They have jointly written a pornographic 'novel'. It circulates among them and each adds his fantasy. I do not know at what level to pitch my disapproval. It is distasteful but just a characteristic adolescent creation. I do not think it would be fair to show their 'novel' to their parents but that is what I threaten to do if they produce a second edition. For now, I express my disapproval by taking the exercise book from them and attempting to tear it in half and throw it in the waste-paper basket, but the covers are tougher than I anticipated and I have to struggle. The boys watch patiently, controlling their mirth behind impassive faces.

Monday 1 October

An unusual problem. A 15-year-old boarder was caught lighting a fire in a metal waste-paper basket. He has a record at his previous school of odd behaviour, including lighting fires and playing with matches. He has recently seen a psychiatrist at Guy's and the report arrives on my desk this morning. The psychiatrist says the boy has a fascination with fire. I decide the boy must become a day boy – he lives close enough. Parents don't like it but I cannot take the risk of his setting fire to the house now that I know that possibility exists.

Wednesday 3 October

After school communion in Henry VII Chapel, I find a 16-year-old on my doorstep. He is at least 10 years out of date, an old-style freedom fighter who has, I guess, a poster of Che Guevara on his study wall. He has a list of those compulsions he wishes to see removed – compulsory attendance at Abbey, school uniform and so on. It is a long time since I had to defend any of these and I would have enjoyed defending them now if my antagonist had not been so serious.

He is a German boy whose parents work in this country and send their two sons to school here. We don't get very far, as I have to say that I have the last word on these matters and that if he does not like school uniform, he should have no difficulty finding a school that will allow him to wear what he likes. When I speak to his housemaster, I learn that the boy walks the streets at night, his parents being unable to persuade him to go to bed. He says he wants to be a doctor.

Wednesday 9 October

At the end of last term when a handful of governors were complaining about bad discipline, Burke Trend suggested that we should head them off with the promise of an informal meeting between those governors and housemasters at the beginning of this term. The meeting is held this evening in the deanery, but what could have been a constructive meeting goes wrong because Edward fails to give it the clear sense of direction it needs. Housemasters recognise that there are sometimes failures of discipline but they put this down to the impossibly large numbers in the houses. Busby's has 92 boys and girls, some boarding, some day; Liddell's has 89 and so on. At most schools, such large houses would be regarded as intolerable and unmanageable. Governors want to talk about failures of discipline and refuse to be sidetracked onto the size of houses. The meeting degenerates into an argument about what exactly the meeting is for.

Eventually, I lose my patience with Edward and take charge. If governors think discipline is bad, what exactly is their evidence? Is it anything more than hearsay – someone told you that Westminster boys were very bad-mannered and so on? That puts the governors on the spot because they have no direct evidence other than that some Westminster boys are, in their view, scruffy and behave badly the moment they walk out of Dean's Yard into the outside world.

The meeting ends on an agreement that the size of houses must be reduced and that any direct evidence of poor discipline should be reported to the headmaster, not raised at governing body meetings. That at least is constructive but the damage to housemasters' opinion of governors (which was low anyway) cannot be undone. As for the dean, his inability to take a grip on the meeting worries me. He is such a good friend and such a sane, civilised man, I should not welcome his retirement.

However, he is already 74 and so I think is obliged to retire in the next year or two.

Monday 15 October

I have made up my mind on the abolition of Saturday morning school and today hold a meeting to explain to the common room why I have come down against abolition. As the majority in the common room are in favour of abolition, it is bound to be a difficult meeting. Frankly, I am suspicious of the motives of some of my colleagues; they want a long weekend, not for the pupils, as they claim, but for themselves. This lobby is angry with me for not deciding in their favour long ago. Now I tell the meeting that the key to Westminster's future is that it retains its distinctive place in the market. Why send a boy to Westminster rather than to St. Paul's or Dulwich? The answer is that Westminster still runs as a boarding school; it still has, unlike St. Paul's and Dulwich, a significant number of boarders, currently 215 compared with just a handful at St. Paul's and Dulwich. If we abolish Saturday morning school, the number of boarders will fall, not least because parents will be reluctant to pay a full boarding fee for boarding four nights a week.

My argument is that to abolish Saturday morning school would mean Westminster will cease to have the distinctive character that gives it such a powerful pull in the market.

The abolitionists do not like it.

Wednesday 17 October

The governing body meets in Jerusalem. Two issues dominate the agenda. On the first I have a public disagreement with the dean, who chairs the meeting. On the question of the problems

330

housemasters face with such large houses, Edward opens the discussion by saying, 'There is general unease about discipline in the school.' I am furious. We agreed last night that we must keep the question of discipline separate from the size of houses and here he is running the two together. I interrupt him and say that I cannot accept his statement and that if the governing body believes there is a crisis over discipline, then the headmaster and the housemasters will be firmly opposed to them.

The dean flushes and is embarrassed. Governors come to the rescue by turning the discussion onto the reasons why houses are so big and what we can do about it.

The second issue that dominates the agenda is Saturday morning school but discussion here is easy and friendly because governors unanimously agree with me that it would be a mistake to abolish it. That is good news because it strengthens my position vis-à-vis the common room.

Wednesday 7 November
I have just joined the governing body of Arnold House Prep School in north London. It is one of our best suppliers of bright boys, so it is time well spent, but I find the first meeting bizarre to say the least. The chairman's style inhibits discussion; he ploughs through the agenda, brushing any interruption aside until one governor interrupts so forcefully he cannot be denied. This forceful governor turns out to be the former headmaster of the school, who should not be on the governing body anyway. But when he (the former head) gets going, he is impossible to interrupt too. What is more, he prefaces every statement with the disclaimer, 'I am not expressing an opinion but…' What a bore for the present headmaster. I shall ring him tomorrow and tell

him how I sympathise with his position and offer to help. That should get us one or two more bright boys!

Friday 16 November

It pours with rain all day. I have not written my address for Commemoration this evening. It gives me a small thrill to leave such things to the last moment. Or perhaps it is just the journalist in me, preferring to work to a deadline. The Commemoration service and the reception after go really well. There are 2,000 people in the Abbey: 600 pupils, 1,200 parents, Old Westminsters and staff. In bed soon after midnight.

Tuesday 20 November

Three Soviet educationists visit the school. I enjoy their company, though we have to communicate through an interpreter. They are astonished to find no corporal punishment and no prefects wielding canes. They have a picture of English public schools that is 50 years out of date. They tell me proudly that corporal punishment was abolished in Russian schools at the Revolution.

A long meeting to look over the results of our candidates in the common entrance exam. Since we dropped our own exam and switched to common entrance, it has been very difficult to find places for all the bright boys who want to come here.

This evening, a session with Willie Booth on pastoral matters. He is a joy to work with because he knows what I need to know and he knows that he can trust me to take no action if that is what he thinks is best. We talk about members of staff who are under stress and about boys and girls whose home background is making school life difficult for them. He is just the sort of parish priest the school community needs.

Wednesday 5 December

I have invited two striking miners from Yorkshire to talk to the John Locke Society. One is 51, the other 18. They put the case for the strike robustly and convincingly but their answers to questions about violence and intimidation are less convincing. The older man comes across as the quintessential Yorkshire man – tough, warm, unsophisticated and shrewd. What is the value of this session for the boys and girls? They are able to see the striking miners as individuals, not as a generalised ogre. And they can recognise that the miners are not foreigners from an alien land. These miners and their families have lived and mined in Yorkshire for generations. They are more truly British than many of those in the south-east, certainly more so than some of the pupils here.

This evening, Daphne and I are guests of the Raynes at the National Theatre, followed by dinner. It is a large party of between 30 and 40, made up of cabinet ministers, aristocracy, media personalities and so on. I enjoy it, while feeling faintly ill at ease because of the contrast with this morning's meeting with the striking miners. Do we all inhabit the same country?

Friday 7 December

Willie tells me that the Japanese boy who left in the summer, Takashi Funaki, is in the Royal Free Hospital with leukaemia and has lost his sight. The boy has fought a long, hard battle against the disease with astonishing calm and fortitude. Willie has a book for all to sign in which one master who knows the boy particularly well writes some lines from Hamlet:

'Remember thee!

'Ay, thou poor ghost, while memory holds a seat

In this distracted globe.'

This evening, Daphne and I stay with the Huxleys in the master's lodge at Trinity, Cambridge. Daphne is dining in the lodge with a number of wives while I am guest at the College's Audit Feast. My host is Mark Pepys, a former fellow of the college, now professor of immunology in London, whose son has just started at Westminster. Sitting opposite me is a boy I taught at Harrow who is now a research fellow in astro-physics. He spends much of the dinner telling me how unhappy he was at Harrow, though his memories are a mixture of nostalgia and revulsion.

Wednesday 12 December

While Willie Booth and I are talking, news comes that Takashi Funaki has died. Willie goes off to the hospital to be with the family. He has given so much time and trouble to the boy and his family and I tell him how much his care for the boy is appreciated by many members of the school community. Takashi had a place at Oxford to read chemistry and is the third Westminster teenager to die of leukaemia in recent years.

Saturday 15 December

I receive a letter from Loughborough University of Technology. It says that I have been suggested as a possible successor to the vice-chancellor who retires in the New Year. Am I interested?

A university of technology is not my milieu but if this is a question of exchanging one leadership role for another, then yes, I am interested. I write to say that I would be glad to come to Loughborough to talk about the job informally.

Just out of interest, I check in the universities year book and find that the chancellor of Loughborough University who would be responsible for overseeing the appointment of a new vice-chancellor is Burke Trend. So it is Burke who sends me a reminder, while at the same time offering me an outside chance of a worthwhile job. He is a good friend.

Christmas holidays 1984

This is the time for me to consider the future. I am in my 15th year at Westminster and the received wisdom in the independent school world is that 10 years are enough to achieve what you want to achieve. I have achieved a great deal at Westminster and I doubt whether I could achieve more, however long I stayed.

The key to my departure is the assisted places scheme. Boys on assisted places are already in the Under School and are due to come to Westminster in September 1985 or at the latest in September 1986. My well established opposition to the assisted places scheme means that I cannot possibly continue as headmaster after September 1986.

I have discussed this at length with Burke and Edward and they agree that I should resign in the New Year. Like all independent school headmasters, I have to give the governors three terms' notice of leaving. If I give notice early in the New Year, I shall leave either in December 1985 or at the end of the Lent Term in March 1986. The latter gives me plenty of time to find a new job and the governors plenty of time to find my successor.

Lent Term 1985

Wednesday 23 January

The bitter winter has given way to something like mild spring air. Welcome a speaker on interview techniques. He has been invited by the director of studies, who fears that Westminster boys (and Westminster girls?) are too often accused of arrogance by those who interview them at universities. I wonder. Bill Duncomb, the captain of the school this term, is anything but arrogant, though it is probably fair to say he is not a typical Westminster boy. Anyway, I attend the talk myself, thinking that I might need some tips on interview technique in the near future.

Apart from Daphne and a small circle of governors and the school solicitor, no one knows that I have set a date for leaving. Edward does not want it made public until after the governing body meeting on 29 January.

Tuesday 29 January

Teach my sixth form historians about Peter the Great this morning. Peter, the ruthless autocrat, is an excellent role model for headmasters, at least in their imagination. The governing body this afternoon raises no problem. I resign formally and governors who have been critical of me over the last year or so must be so relieved to hear me that they make no comment. After the meeting, I pick up a case and take a taxi to St. Pancras. At Loughborough, I am staying at the Quorn County Hotel. Dinner with five members of the selection committee. I do my best to impress them and certainly enjoy their company but I cannot make out whether they are genuinely interested in me or just going through the motions to please Burke Trend.

Wednesday 30 January

I look round the university with the recently retired development officer, who talks too much. I am glad to see the back of him and catch a train back to London. I come away from Loughborough pretty certain I do not want the job and that the university does not want me.

Tuesday 5 February

Tell the school at Latin prayers that I am leaving in just over a year's time. I had told the common room before Latin prayers and parents will receive letters tomorrow morning.

Lunch with Lucy Hodges of the *Times* at the Pelican Café in St. Martin's Lane, an engagement fixed some weeks ago but now useful for me so I can give Lucy the news of my departure before it reaches her colleagues on other papers. In return, would she do me a favour and write a piece for tomorrow's *Times,* making it clear that I am looking for a new challenge, in other words, for a new job.

Friday 8 February

Miss morning Abbey for the first time in 15 years, a sign, perhaps, of a shift in interest from Westminster to whatever the future holds. An interview with Linda Lee Potter of the *Daily Mail* followed by one with Sebastian Faulks of the *Sunday Telegraph*, spreading the news as far as possible that I am looking for a new job. Later this afternoon, I see two women from the *Mail on Sunday.* Would I write an article on public schools from the point of view of my departure? Can I do it in the next week or two? After that I shall cease to be news. A useful reminder of the reality of my position.

Wednesday 13 February

A few interesting letters in response to publicity about my departure. One offers me the job of setting up a British school in Copenhagen. This evening, Daphne and I go to the Lord Mayor of Westminster's dinner and dance at the Hilton Hotel on Park Lane. The leader of the Labour Group on the council greets me thus: 'Ah John Rae. The face of a saint and the mind of a s inner.' I did not think he knew me that well.

Saturday 23 February

A sad letter from a colleague who thinks that all he has done for the school has not been appreciated. 'Many people, some inside, some outside the school, have expressed to me the view that I have been poorly rewarded in terms of money, status and influence, for all that I have done for Westminster.'

I do not know how to reply, so I put the letter in a drawer and walk up to Trafalgar Square, where the miners are holding a rally. It is a fine afternoon, the soft sunshine almost warm enough to bask in. There is a note of defiant despair about the miners and their families that touches the heart and that is at odds with what Tony Benn is saying into the microphone about 'the means of production, distribution and exchange.' Some of the miners are already heading for Whitehall, which is barred by a double line of policemen. I walk down Pall Mall for a swim at the RAC. When I emerge, the sun is low and red over the far end of the street and the pale blue sky is feathered here and there with pink. I am bowled over by the beauty of it all.

Monday 25 February

I appoint Claude Evans housemaster of Ashburnham. After passing him over for boarding housemasterships, I am glad to have an opportunity to put him in a day house where I think he will do well. He is efficient and so much wants to be a housemaster that it is almost worth appointing him for that reason alone.

Monday 11 March

A 16-year-old to see after Latin prayers. He is in the first year of his A level course and it is going badly. Little work, some rudeness to staff, teachers and parents at the end of their tether. Only child, physically under-developed, alternatively childlike and shrewd (if those two really are alternatives). He sinks so deep into my sofa that his feet do not touch the floor. 'My parents do not like me,' he says. He has probably used that line before and it may be true. We talk about his changing A level courses and about leaving Westminster and going to a tutorial college. He says he wants to read law at Oxford. The gap between his ambition and achievement so far is huge. I suspect a good tutorial is the right answer as he has alienated too many people here. I will try to persuade parents.

Tuesday 12 March

There was a 'riot' in College Hall last night because supper — corn on the cob — was deep frozen and uneatable. Monitors, who meet this morning at 8.30, were unable to control a situation that got out of hand with frozen corn on the cob thrown about and boys refusing to move until a proper supper was provided. Eventually, the duty housemaster cleared the hall after assuring the rioters that their all-too-justifiable complaints would be brought to my notice.

The hostility towards the catering manager is exacerbated by rumours that he spends so much time and money on food for special occasions such as governing body meetings that he makes school meals a low priority. When all this is reported to me, I order a full report on the whole incident to be written, with a copy to the bursar as well as to housemasters and myself. I am determined to make the bursar take his responsibility and not to allow him to palm it off on housemasters as a purely disciplinary matter.

Friday 22 March

The end of term. In a year's time, it will be the end of my last Lent Term. Rain and grey skies. Boys and girls depart at lunchtime. This afternoon, when the skies have cleared, I walk across the parks, thanking God for a little fresh air and sunshine.

Easter Holidays 1985

Daphne takes me to the leprosy village in north India where she has been working. Halfway through our three-week stay, we spend a few days in Kathmandu. As we emerge from the airport bus that has brought us into the city, a voice hails us, 'Hello Sir!' It is Ben Hamilton, who left at Christmas and will go to Balliol in the autumn.

Election Term 1985

Friday 26 April

There are days when a headmaster's life is hectic and high-pressured; and there are days – like this – when I wonder what I am being paid for. I can deal with the business of the day in an hour or two. I can walk round the school, which I like doing, looking into this class or that, but it can all be done by late morning. What shall I do for the rest of the day? I am so easily bored. I need excitement and variety, but what other job will provide them? Being headmaster of Westminster has been just about the best job in the world for me, though it was beginning to lose its glamour and interest even before I resigned.

Monday 29 April

An hour with a woman maths teacher who is failing to keep order in any of her lower-school sets. I say she ought to be looking for another job. I am not giving her an ultimatum but advising her to look now before I am obliged to give her notice. She understands and agrees without hesitation. She cannot resist saying, however, that while she is here she feels she should point out that Westminster's attitude to women encourages boys to be aggressive and ill-mannered in their approach to women teachers. I point out that other women teachers have coped successfully at Westminster, but she says that her point is still valid and that as headmaster I would be unwise to ignore it.

Wednesday 1 May

A long talk with Christopher Morahan and John Cleese, who

want to pick my brains for a film they are making to be called *Clockwise*. In it a headmaster, obsessed with time, goes to pieces when he is diverted from his timetable, especially his visit as a guest at the annual general meeting of the Headmasters' Conference. I have great fun suggesting which schools' headmasters should play the most self-important roles at the AGM.

I have to expel a boy later this afternoon. For once, the argument that expulsion could not be avoided is beyond dispute. The story is this: he went out for the night last week to a night club, slipping out of the boarding house and sleeping with his girlfriend. That is an offence punishable by rustication and final warning. But in his absence, the housemaster looked in his room and found two wallets belonging to other boys. They had been stolen last week and the money taken. That is the expulsion offence. I know his father well – he has helped with our appeal – so we have a difficult interview. Mother says I should look more closely at the school I am running because stealing is so commonplace. I tell them both that I will help in any way I can to find their son a place at a good tutorial.

Wednesday 15 May
Four 16-year-olds come to explain an incident in College Hall. During a crowded supper, they banged on the table and called for silence. Then they announced the winner of the award of 'Miss Pretentious 1985'. They named a girl, who was presented with a mock crown to the cheers of the crowd. According to the boys, it was just a practical joke and they are surprised it was reported to me. But I have already heard from two school monitors that in their view it was a deliberate attempt to humiliate the girl. I have no doubt they are right. It is an unpleasant example

342

of bullying and I tell the boys how strongly I disapprove. But punishment is not easy to apply. The captain of the school, Bill Duncomb, advises me against sending the boys home because the school is angry at the common room's overreaction to the incident. So I settle for a rocket and ban them from College Hall for a week. The common room will think that hopelessly inadequate and so will some of the girls, but I fear that the girl in question will be the object of much casual hostility if I send the boys home as the common room wishes.

What is behind this incident? Resentment on the part of these four boys at the ease with which the clever girls in general, and this clever girl in particular, sail to the top of the class. Most boys are happy to compete but the few who can't, or won't, express their resentment in this boorish fashion.

Thursday 16 May
At Latin prayers, I refer to the incident in College Hall, explaining why I disapprove so strongly of what is in fact an unpleasant form of bullying.

Teach two periods on Louis XIV and then welcome Sir Richard Stone, Nobel Prize-winner in economics. I have invited him as a distinguished old Westminster to beg a play. When I have introduced him, I ask him to speak. He is 72 and slow in delivery, so that when he sets off on a journey through his schooldays, progressing slowly from one form to the next, I fear the school's patience will run out before he reaches the sixth form. But they listen politely until a pigeon appears. I have no idea how the bird got into the hall. Perhaps a boy kidnapped it in St. James's Park and smuggled it into the hall under his jacket. Anyway, the bird provides a distraction and a danger. If Sir Richard does not end soon, the pigeon will trigger bursts of laughter that may be difficult to control. Mercifully, he ends abruptly, either as he had intended or because he, too, sensed the danger. The applause drives the pigeon into a remote corner of the roof.

Friday 17 May

A chilling encounter this afternoon with a parent who is a multimillionaire. He asks about his son whom I teach. I reply that the boy is becoming more confident and prepared to stand up for himself in argument. Unwisely perhaps, I add that he might soon be able to stand up to his father. Father's expression loses what warmth it had. 'If he does that, he'll move out into digs,' he says.

Thursday 23 May

A boarding housemaster appears to be losing control of his house. This morning, he sent a 16-year-old to me because in the housemaster's note to me, 'he has stubbornly refused to wear the regulation shoes despite my giving him two warnings.' If a housemaster has to send a boy to me to get his shoes changed, the housemaster's days are numbered. There has been a lot of minor vandalism in the house. When I ask the housemaster what he is doing about it, he replies that he has assembled the whole house and asked the guilty to come forward. God help us. The man is a fool. I advise him as best I can but I fear the damage has been done.

The Challenge meeting his afternoon raises two interesting questions. Do we award scholarships on all-round ability or on extraordinary ability in one subject such as mathematics? Should we try to ensure that one preparatory school does not win too many scholarships with the result that others are discouraged? This last question has become more urgent since the expansion of the Under School. If the Under School wins too many scholarships each year, other prep schools may think twice before entering a candidate. With these thoughts in our minds, we elect candidates with more spark than competence, and with a little good sense on the part of my colleagues, we manage to elect nine scholars from nine different prep schools.

Friday 21 June

An unusual complaint from a parent. They draw my attention to what they see as political indoctrination. Their son has to choose a non-specialist subject to go alongside his A levels. The subject he chose was 'Culture and Ideology' and the explanatory notes on the subject read: 'No specialist knowledge is necessary. A sympathy to thinking on the Left, an advantage.'

The parents have a point. They are Russian and they left the Soviet Union when their son was three. When I ask the master responsible what the course is about, he rattles off the names of some contemporary left-wing French philosophers of whom I have never heard. I do not think the master is guilty of political indoctrination but I suggest to him that he should contact parents and explain to them the aims of the course.

Thursday 4 July

I am crossing Yard this morning when I meet a young teacher who is clearly very angry. 'I have lost my rag with X,' he says in quaintly old-fashioned jargon. Now X is the boy who sat on my sofa with feet not reaching the floor and told me that his parents did not like him. He has been rude to more than one master and now has incensed yet another of his teachers. When this young master handed back essays at the start of the lesson, the boy screwed his essay up, put it in his mouth and chewed it. Then he spat the remains onto the floor. Not much room for misunderstanding there. At the end of morning school, I summon the boy and send him home. It has already been decided that it would be better for him and us if he goes to a tutorial in September to finish his A level course.

Monday 8 July

Lunch at Lockets with Bernard Ashley[122]. I like Ashley; he is off-beat and self-made but not aggressive. We have been brought together by one of his senior management men, John Winter, who has a boy in the school. Bernard Ashley wants to set up an Ashley foundation and is interested in my being the first chief executive. Ashley's aims for his charitable foundation are still not worked out but will be in the medical and educational fields. I say I would be very interested and we agree to meet again soon.

Wednesday 10 July

At 6.30am, I am walking back from an early swim at the RAC in Pall Mall when I see three Westminster boys returning to school. They look tired and unshaven. They are all leavers and have probably been to an all-night party. They are almost on their last day. Why fuss? I walk past them and on into Dean's Yard.

Thursday 11 July

---

[122] Sir Bernard Ashley, chairman of Laura Ashley Ltd. 1954 to 1993.

Even early in the morning the sun is hot. A scholar to see. He refused to turn up for his German O level. When I ask him why, he gives a shrewd answer. He will be applying for Cambridge and wants to have straight As for O level on his application form. He knows he cannot get an A in German so he just fails to appear for the exam. No homily of mine about school policy makes any impression on him. He does not see why he should take an O level he does not wish to take and I cannot think of a convincing reply.

A night patrol for the last night of term. Good friends of mine mostly, drinking wine and eating Stilton cheese in the common room, occasional strolls round Little Dean's Yard on a soft, summer night. This is an occasion I shall miss. Bed by 3am.

Friday 12 July

The last day of my last Election Term. Abbey at 9am, an old sermon polished and updated. Goodbye to leavers in my study. Prize-giving. Assembly and goodbye to five members of the common room, then on to the governing body meeting in Jerusalem.

Between this meeting and the Election Dinner, I see Shirley Williams and Robert Maclennan, the leading SDP MP in Scotland. Robert doubts whether I could survive a by-election in this left-wing and nationalist seat. 'They'll cut the tyres on your car,' he tells me. I say I am prepared to fight the by-election all the same. Robert clearly thinks I am unsuitable – a posh speaking, English public school headmaster in a rough-tough Dundee constituency. What he doesn't know is that I thrive on the knockabout debate of public argument. Whether they will understand my accent is another matter. When Shirley Williams supports my case, Maclennan plays his trump card. The local constituency members are insisting on having a local candidate. I acknowledge that I am not a local candidate but my family have farmed at Laurencekirk, 40 miles north of Dundee, for over two hundred years and my cousins still farm the same land. I may not be local but my family is. Maclennan says he will think about it. I am not worried and ask Shirley Williams to let me know what is decided.

This evening, the Election Dinner is one of the best I can remember. When all the guests have gone, a few of us gather for a sing-song in Jim Cogan's drawing room: headmaster, under master, chaplain, one or two other members of staff, boys and girls who are leaving, one or two young Old Westminsters. It is a delightful occasion, rather Victorian in flavour, good fellowship and sentiment, ending at two in the morning with Auld Lang Syne.

1985-1986
Play Term 1985

~ ❧ ~

Sunday 8 September

Preparing to launch the school year for the last time. The A level results have been very good. I would love to publish results, but the Headmasters' Conference is firmly against.

To see Edward at the deanery this evening. We talk over some of the problems that will confront my successor David Summerscale, the headmaster of Haileybury. One is that some governors are already pressing David to introduce short-term contracts for masters. The pressure is coming from those governors who believe that discipline is poor because too many masters are unwilling to enforce it, and they think they can bring masters to heel with short-term contracts.

They are wrong, of course. Short-term contracts are strongly opposed by the Headmasters' Conference and by those teachers' unions to which our staff are likely to belong. They are wrong in another sense. The way to make masters insist on good discipline is to work through the headmaster. He is their leader. I believe that the great majority of Westminster masters are good disciplinarians; if they were not, I should have moved them on by now. No, the trouble is that the good masters and myself do not have the same idea about what constitutes good discipline as some of the governors. I will try to sort out this problem before I leave.

Tuesday 10 September

How much I have always enjoyed launching a new school year. It may be partly an ego trip but it is also enthusiasm for and pride in the school. September sunshine, a little hazy, floods Little Dean's Yard, where boys and girls greet one another with cautious hugs. How different from the atmosphere of Westminster 15 years ago. The girls, even in small numbers, really have made a difference.

The manuscript of a proposed new history of the school lands on my desk. It is by a former master, Charles Keeley, who left some years ago. I am amazed by what I read. It attacks every policy of mine he did not like. So he sneers at Westminster's 'gaderene pursuit of A levels'.

Wednesday 11 September

Housemastering. A new housemaster puts up a notice on the house notice-board and within minutes someone has put a match to it.

Monday 7 October

The parents of a 14-year-old come to see me. Boy is very disruptive and disorganised. A day boy, he sees a psychoanalyst five days a week. Parent and analyst think the long-term prospects are good but the school has to deal with the short-term disciplinary problems. We are not a home for the mildly disturbed. This boy's disruptive behaviour affects the learning of other boys, so either his behaviour improves or he goes.

Tuesday 8 October

Lunch at Lockets with Bernard and Laura Ashley's two sons, David and Nick. We seem to get on well and agree on what the immediate goals of an Ashley foundation should be. A pleasant lunch, no alcohol or cigar. A step towards an agreement on my becoming a director of the foundation? Probably, but they move slowly and I do not expect anything to be settled overnight.

Monday 14 October

To King's, Canterbury for a meeting of Eton Group headmasters. A level results are exchanged. Westminster is the best by a comfortable margin, leaving St. Paul's well behind, though London dinner tables insist on believing that St. Paul's has the better academic record. The loudest laugh of the evening comes when someone says that their school doctor is worried about AIDS being spread by the music department because musicians are prone to homosexuality. The disease could be passed on via the mouthpiece of the trumpet. Now why should this provoke such an explosion of laughter?

Wednesday 16 October

Dinner this evening in Jerusalem to say goodbye to the dean. Edward is retiring five months before me, so there will be an interregnum, which is sad. I would rather Edward had stayed to see me out but the Church of England has its rules.

Monday 28 October

Two school monitors, a boy and a girl, tell me that a boy in the senior school is selling drugs to younger boys. So the problem has not gone away. I ask for the evidence but as so often is the case, the evidence is in gossip and rumour. I tell them: 'We are agreed that this is wrong and that we want it stopped but I cannot act without evidence or at least a lead.'

'Couldn't you get the sixth form and the Remove together and warn them?'

'No, that will do nothing but drive the seller underground. Find me the evidence. I know it is difficult for you, but there is a lot at stake.'

Later, a chat with Willie. He does not have evidence but he guesses that the monitors are right.

Wednesday 30 October
Talk with Caspar Woolley, the scholar who is captain of the school this term, about drug rumours. He believes someone is selling drugs in the junior school but does not know who it is. John Harvey-Jones, the chairman of ICI, talks to the John Locke Society, the best session for quite a time; he is articulate, humorous, tough and realistic.

A senior boy comes to see me. I know he thinks he should be among the new school monitors I shall be appointing in the next few weeks. So he has come to say that he cannot name names but he is sure someone is selling drugs to junior boys. Even existing monitors, including the captain, are opposed to the suggestion that this boy should be made a monitor. They see him as too nakedly ambitious. I thank him for coming to see me. I do not mind ambition but I doubt whether this boy has anything more than ambition to offer.

Saturday 2 November
I take morning Abbey. The Philistines destroy the Israelites but in

commenting on the lesson I say 'Israelis' by mistake. No point in correcting myself; that would only confuse matters further. After Abbey, I walk out of the dark cloister into the dazzling autumn sunlight. A housemaster catches me to say that one of his boys who left five years ago has committed suicide. I remember him well. He was the star of his year: good-looking, school monitor and head of house, member of a successful 1st VIII, open scholarship to Balliol. During the day I pick up more information. He was doing a law conversion course in London. On Thursday, he went to his law tutorial and wrote an essay. On the way home, he went into a block of council flats and up onto the roof. Here he took off his jacket and folded it neatly on the ground. Then he jumped off. It is said that while he was at Oxford he found himself increasingly difficult to live with. But what does that mean?

Sunday 3 November
Daphne and I lunch with Bernard Ashley at the Grosvenor House. Bernard confirm that he would like me to be the director of the Laura Ashley foundation. So that is settled then.

Monday 4 November
A 14-year-old to see. I rusticated him for persistent disruptive behaviour. Now he returns to receive words of warning and encouragement from me. At the end, I say, 'Well, good luck.' And he replies, 'Good luck to you, sir, for your last term at Westminster.' What will happen to a boy like this, what will he do with his life?

Saturday 9 November
When I am interviewing sixth formers this morning, I suggest

353

to one boy that he should consult his father about Cambridge colleges, as his father was at Cambridge himself. But the boy tells me that his father is dead. It is an unforgivable mistake on my part. Why did I not know that his father was dead? There is no list of boys and girls with one or more deceased parents but there should be so that members of staff can check quickly.

Monday 11 November
At 6pm, to Poets' Corner for the unveiling of a memorial to First World War poets. The dean, who has the final say on whose names should go on the memorial, often talked late into the night with me about the merits of this poet or that. Edward was not all that keen on Julian Grenfell but I was and argued strongly for his inclusion. Michael Howard, who was my supervisor for my doctorate, gives an excellent address.

Wednesday 13 November
I attend Conrad Levy's champagne breakfast in Yard. It is cold but we sit huddled in our overcoats trying to be bright and breezy. A 15-year-old is sent to me, and when I have heard the whole story, I send him home for a week as a warning. He is an adopted son whose entire schooling until now has been in Newcastle. He is unhappy at Westminster and was found to be keeping a commando knife in his room. Housemaster confiscated the knife but could not prevent the boy attacking the house monitor who reported the knife. For once, I think the boy needs psychiatric help and parents agree to arrange this.

Thursday 14 November
To Oxford, where over dinner I meet the father of a Westmin-

ster girl and ask how she is getting on. He tells me she is a militant feminist lesbian working in Cambridge. Good heavens, is that what Westminster did to her?

Friday 6 December

A long discussion with the captain of the school, Caspar Wooley, about who should be his successor. There are two candidates. The more senior is a Queen's Scholar, honest, upright and out of touch. The other candidate is Lynda Stuart, a black girl from the Caribbean, who is able, much more in touch, quietly ambitious. Her father is medical officer to the Commonwealth. Lynda would be the first female captain in 425 years but why not? The fact that she is black will attract some comment but it will soon pass. The only thing that matters is who is the better candidate. Caspar and I are in no doubt that Lynda would be the better captain of the school.

Thursday 12 December

A 16-year-old who has a last warning hanging over him from the summer term is caught drinking by his housemaster on Monday. Instead of punishing him, the housemaster takes him for a walk round St. James's Park, a sort of mobile counselling session. Last night, he slipped away from a house outing and went heaven knows where. When the boy appears, he is argumentative and aggressive. That makes me angry but it is time someone was angry with him. He has had too much tea and sympathy. I tell him he is 'selfish and deceitful', at which he appears surprised, even hurt. No one has told him that before. I send him home even at this late stage in the term. I want to force the parents to face up to the fact that their son can be selfish and deceitful and is not the little boy lost in London of his mother's imagination.

See Lynda Stuart and tell her I want her to be captain of the school next term, filling a position held by such diverse Westminster figures as Charles Wesley and Warren Hastings.

Lent Term 1986

Monday 13 January

The *Times* carries a good item about Lynda's appointment, emphasising that she is the first girl captain of the school in 450 years – not that she is black. Other newspapers are more interested in the fact that she is black, but on the whole the coverage is sensible. One abusive phone call from a woman with a South African accent.

Friday 18 January

Feedback from Oxbridge interviews. One history don asked a boy candidate, 'What was the role of masturbation in the middle ages?' A girl candidate for medicine at Cambridge had not done physics, her A level subjects being mathematics, chemistry and biology. The two dons interviewing her spent most of the time asking her questions about physics, eventually dismissing her with the remark, 'Well, you don't seem to be very well qualified to read medicine.'

Wednesday 23 January

Monitors meet at 8.30am and talk about whether the scruffy appearance of a minority of boys and girls really does do harm to the school's reputation and, like the common room, the monitorial is divided but the majority take the liberal line that a few 'scruffs' do no real harm.

At 4.30pm, I go to Central Hall at the invitation of the All London Parents' Action Group. They have asked me to talk to a rally, which they assure me is non-political and is aimed at settling the long-running teachers' dispute with the government. I should have realised that this was the lion's den and far from being non-political and that a public school headmaster was bound to have a rough ride. So I do not attempt to please them. Teachers should not be paid a professional salary, I tell them, unless they act professionally in terms of accepting assessment and contracts. Cries of 'Rubbish!' I then add that the crisis in education is not the responsibility of the government but a long-term problem of government and teacher attitudes. More cries of 'Rubbish!', which I find stimulating.

Return across the Sanctuary to the housemasters' meeting and a discussion on this year's Oxbridge results. We have 72 firm places, a figure that would not have pleased my previous audience. It is the highest ever at Westminster but it is unusual in a different way. There are twice as many places at Cambridge as at Oxford. I cannot explain that.

Thursday 6 February
Pastoral. Willie tells me of a 15-year-old boarder whose parents have just told him they are splitting up. Boy is bitter, hates school, dislikes companions and so on. Willie says, 'All I can do is to go alongside. If he needs to talk, I am there.'

Friday 21 February

Katie Bassett[123], one of the editors of the *Elizabethan*, comes to see me. She protests about the headmaster having the right of veto over the material that goes in the magazine. How very strange. Of course the headmaster has the right of veto. She calls it dictatorship and I agree.

Lunch in Rigaud's. The housemaster, Cedric Harben, has asked me to sit at a table of disaffected 16-year-olds. They are pretty sour and inarticulate but not, I suppose, all that unusual. Some lines of conversation appear to be going well but they peter out in mutterings, glances and smirks. I couldn't do this every day and I am reminded how hard it must be for housemasters and house tutors who have to sit there several times a week.

Tuesday 25 February

The fact that I am leaving does nothing to relieve the flow of problems. the *Elizabethan* editors are continuing to argue against the headmaster's veto of material for the school magazine, and – much more serious – the senior members of the common room are demanding their right to see the school accounts and the governing body is totally opposed to the idea. These are only two of the unresolved problems that have landed on the headmaster's desk, but they are typical. One way or another, I shall have to try to deal with them before I leave.

Friday 28 February

The *Elizabethan* editors formally accept that the headmaster must

---

[123] Now a journalist with the *Independent*.

have the right of veto. My portrait painter comes for the last time. At my request, he has made my face less chocolate-boxey, so that I am closer to those Tudor portraits – wary rather than charming – than I am to those portraits of Victorian children.

Wednesday 5 March

Confirmation service in the Abbey this morning. Fewer boys and girls getting confirmed than usual. Why is this? Fewer committed Christians among parents. Westminster has an increasingly international intake but also an increasing number of British boys and girls whose parents are 'Church of England' only for the purpose of filling in forms. During the service, as the boys and girls line up to be confirmed by Bishop Launcelot Fleming, I recognise two boys I saw in Regent Street yesterday morning when they should have been in school. At the time, I did not know their names so they escaped detection. Now I hear their names called out as each one comes forward. Can I use the confirmation service as an identity parade? I think not. They will remain unidentified.

This evening, the governing body gives a dinner in Jerusalem in our honour. Sad that Edward has retired just too soon but Andrew Huxley, as master of Trinity, takes the chair. My portrait is much admired. A warm and friendly farewell occasion.

Thursday 6 March

A strange but interesting encounter with a 15-year-old who was caught stealing magazines from a newsagent in Victoria Street. Reported to police and given a caution. The boy sits on my sofa, head down, shoulders hunched, monosyllabic in his answers. I warn him about the school's reaction if he should be caught stealing again. When I ask him why he stole the magazines, he says, 'I've been feeling low for the past few weeks.' He was a bed-wetter when he arrived as a 13-year-old but I gather from housemaster that is cured. He is still quick, even violent-tempered and has on one or two occasions had to be stopped from going for another boy. A loner who spends time and money on fruit machines. The prospects are not good but I will ask Willie to help.

Saturday 8 March

A beautiful spring day. The father of the boy caught stealing magazines in Victoria Street flies from Paris to see me. A powerfully intelligent and articulate man. Are parents too brilliant for their son to cope with? I find father sympathetic and understanding of his son's difficulties and that is a good sign.

Wednesday 12 March

This evening the school community puts on a farewell dinner in College Hall for Daphne and myself. If we had imagined an ideal send-off, it would have been like this. College Hall filled, good food and wine, a most warm and friendly atmosphere, a good speech by Jim Cogan, and a number of friends from the past such as Martin and Jane Rogers. Bed by 1am, happy that it all went so well.

Wednesday 19 March

See Graham Turner from the *Daily Telegraph*, who is writing a long article on public schools along the lines of 'who's in fashion and who's not'. Eton, Westminster and Radley form what he calls a 'super league'. Rugby is down after a number of bad headmasterships, Harrow is coming up under Ian Beer, Winchester is in a trough, Marlborough has serious discipline problems, Charterhouse is 'anaemic' and so on.

Thursday 20 March
It is my 55th birthday and my last full day as headmaster, indeed, my last full day as a schoolmaster, a profession I embarked on at Harrow in 1955, 31 years ago. Westminster has been good to me, despite anxious times and I have been good to Westminster, despite the occasional clash with governors and I leave the school with its reputation high. I have critics inside and outside the school and admirers too, so that it seems impossible to find anyone who is neutral about my headmastership.

At 5.30pm, the school monitors come round with bottles of champagne to toast our health and wish us well. A bouquet of flowers for Daphne and an expensive book on the cinema for me. How well they know me. In addition, a bottle of port for us both that should not be drunk until 2001.

Friday 21 March
Term ends today. No frog in the throat. I have been so long leaving, in my own mind I have already left. Last sermon in Abbey, short and low key; last assembly, teetering on the edge of anarchy, I just manage to say goodbye before I know it is time to head for the exit. As I leave the hall, I hear three cheers loudly given.

Outside in Yard, some boys and girls come up to say goodbye; others hurry past heading for the holidays. Then as the school empties, I come upstairs, tired and happy to fall asleep on my sofa. This evening, Daphne and I go to the RAC for a swim and stay on to have dinner together. On this pleasant note, my career in education comes to an end.

John Malcolm Rae was headmaster at Westminster School between 1970-86. He is author of *The Custard Boys* (1960). He has also written books on education, including the best-selling *Letters from School* (1987) and five books for children. He died in December 2006.

In case of difficulty in purchasing any Short Books
title through normal channels, please contact
BOOKPOST Tel: 01624 836000
Fax: 01624 837033
email: bookshop@enterprise.net
www.bookpost.co.uk
Please quote ref. 'Short Books